Beckett's Art of Mismaking

Beckett's Art of
Mismaking

Leland de la Durantaye

Harvard University Press

Cambridge, Massachusetts · London, England

2016

Copyright © 2016 by Leland de la Durantaye
All rights reserved
Printed in the United States of America

First printing

Library of Congress Cataloging-in-Publication Data

De la Durantaye, Leland.
Beckett's art of mismaking / Leland de la Durantaye.
pages   cm
Includes bibliographical references and index.
ISBN 978-0-674-50485-1 (cloth : alk. paper)
1. Beckett, Samuel, 1906–1989—Criticism and interpretation.
2. Beckett, Samuel, 1906–1989—Technique.
3. Beckett, Samuel, 1906–1989—Literary style.
4. Errors and blunders, Literary.   I. Title.
PR6003.E282Z624755   2016
842'.914—dc23   2015011242

To H., for the fire

Let each considerate person have his way, and see what it will lead to. For not this man and that man, but all men make up mankind, and their united tasks the task of mankind. How often have we seen some such adventurous, and perhaps much-censured wanderer light on some out-lying, neglected, yet vitally momentous province; the hidden treasures of which he first discovered, and kept proclaiming till the general eye and effort were directed thither, and the conquest was completed;—thereby, in these his seemingly so aimless rambles, planting new standards, found-ing new habitable colonies, in the immeasurable circumambient realm of Nothingness and Night! Wise man was he who counselled that Specula-tion should have free course, and look fearlessly towards all the thirty-two points of the compass, whithersoever and howsoever it listed.

—Thomas Carlyle, *Sartor Resartus*

Contents

Note on Sources and Abbreviations

All citations from Beckett's principal works are from the *Grove Centenary Edition of the Works of Samuel Beckett* (2006) (identical in pagination to the 2011 paperback edition: *Selected Works of Samuel Beckett*), the first edition to bring together (almost) all of Beckett's creative and critical writing. The exception to this rule is *Waiting for Godot,* which is cited from the Grove bilingual edition of the play.

Writings not included in that edition—Beckett's first novel, *Dream of Fair to Middling Women;* his first play, *Eleutheria;* his abandoned short story "Echo's Bones"; his extensive correspondence, theatrical notebooks, and *Disjecta*—are cited separately.

In cases where a work by Beckett was first written in French, the page number from the French edition follows the English.

Unless otherwise indicated, all translations are my own.

Abbreviations

GC   *The Grove Centenary Edition of the Works of Samuel Beckett / Selected Writings of Samuel Beckett.* 4 vols. Edited by Paul Auster. New York: Grove, 2006/2011.

LSB   *The Letters of Samuel Beckett.* 3 vols. Edited by George Craig, Martha Dow Fehsenfeld, Dan Gunn, and Lois More Overbeck. Cambridge: Cambridge University Press, 2009-2014.

Beckett's Art of
Mismaking

Introduction

The Art of Mismaking

SAMUEL BECKETT'S WORKS feature figures in jars, garbage cans, crawling along forest floors, rolling in mud, babbling all the while. There are blind, lame, maimed creatures cracking whips and wielding can openers who are funny when they should be chilling, cruel when they should be tender, warm when most wounded. There is no wine-dark sea, no singing of arms and the man, no *In mezzo del cammin di nostra vita la diritta via era smarrita.* There isn't a *diritta via,* there isn't even a *via.* There isn't a proper beginning, ending, anything. And so Beckett's audience quite naturally asks what it all might mean.

They are, however, not the first. *Happy Days* (1961) revolves around a woman buried to her midriff in hardened mud. The question as to what this woman in her mound is meant to mean is given voice by a character, albeit one who never appears on stage. Winnie recalls for the audience, and her rampant husband, how a Mr. Shower, or Mr. Cooker (she isn't sure, though she is sure that he was "a coarse fellow"), asked at the sight of her, "What does it mean?" "What's it meant to mean?" (GC 3.294).[1] Aptly enough, the coarse fellow in question has a companion who turns the tables on him, "And you, she says, what's the idea of you, she says, what are you meant to mean?" (GC 3.294). None of us knows what we are meant to mean, and perhaps none of us truly knows what we mean. But there are differences of degree, and one does not have to be particularly curious or particularly coarse to see a woman up to her midriff in a mound of earth, buried to the waist, in the waste, to ask what she is meant to mean.

All answers to the question presuppose doing something which Beckett's works make phenomenally difficult: relating work to world, meaning to making. The making in question, of course, is not just any making, and not conceived in just any fashion. Beckett, for his part, called it *"la malfaçon créatrice voulue"*: "willed creative mismaking" (Beckett 1984, 122). *Mismaking*, like *malfaçon*, is a strange word, which is as it should be, for it is a strange thing. The history of art is the history of artists, and is thus as diverse as are people themselves, but across that millennial history there are common elements, chief among which is expressively artful making. Whether painted on the walls of a cave thirty-five thousand years ago or published on handmade paper in 1922; whether an ornamental dagger from the Malaysian highlands or a cathedral in northern France; whether singing of the wrath of Achilles or justifying the ways of God to man, the aim of art has been fine making. And then along came an Irishman named Samuel Beckett who ended the whole thing, closed the proceedings, put art to rest, at last, for it was very tired.

Such a fable, for that is all it is, tells of what distinguishes our art from the art of the past. It is one thing for an artist to lack talent or vision and thus to make mistakes or make poorly through lack of skill, talent, or time. But it is another thing entirely to do what Beckett did: to mismake *on purpose,* to mismake *by design*—and to do so not to denigrate oneself, or one's audience, nor even to reconnect with a child or a savage within, but from the belief that such mismaking is in the interest of art, and will shape its future.

Artistic Character

"Willed creative mismaking" sounds simply anarchic so long as it is not heard as a response to something more sweeping: a changed status of the work of art. Those who write about the art of the last century find themselves confronted with a phenomenon they can everywhere

see and nowhere explain. The first words of *Aesthetic Theory,* the unfinished late work Theodor W. Adorno planned to dedicate to Beckett,
are: "It has become self-evident that nothing concerning art is self-
evident any more: not its relation to itself, not its relation to what is
around it—not even its right to exist" (Adorno GS 7.9). A more fundamental uncertainty would be hard to envision, as would be one more
broadly shared. It led Adorno to diagnose an *Entkunstung der Kunst,* an
alienation or "de-arting" of art that is progressive, pernicious, and best
visible in Beckett's writing (Adorno GS 7.32). One need not, however,
accept those terms to see that the ideas which have shaped the experience of art for centuries—and in some cases, millennia—no longer serve
for its understanding, beginning with *work* and *art.* The question *what
is art?* has become so difficult to answer as to invite summary dismissal.[2]
Things stand no better for the idea of the *work.* In 1924 Virginia Woolf
wrote:

> On or about December 1910, human character changed. I am not
> saying that one went out, as one might into a garden, and there saw
> that a rose had flowered, or that a hen had laid an egg. The change
> was not sudden and definite like that. But a change there was,
> nevertheless; and, since one must be arbitrary, let us date it about the
> year 1910.

Woolf aligned this change in human character with the First Post-
Impressionist Exhibition (which introduced the English public to the
works of Cézanne, Gauguin, Van Gogh, and others). A no less fundamental change took place during these same years to *artistic* character.
One did not walk outside one day and see that the self-evidence of the
work of art had disappeared like a rose from a bush or a thief in the
night. The change was not, of course, perceptible as an event that
occurred on or about a certain day. Another modern master, Ernest
Hemingway, has a character respond to the question of how he went
bankrupt: "Two ways. Gradually, then suddenly" (Hemingway 2006, 141).
The same can be said for the massive loss of the capital of clarity concerning *art* and *work* during the first half of the twentieth century. And
while no event or exhibition simply and straightforwardly caused this
change in artistic character, the exclusion of a work from an exhibition

seven years after the Post-Impressionist one shows it in particularly stark relief.

By No Definition

On a spring day in 1917, the twenty-nine-year-old French artist, and future chess partner of Samuel Beckett, Marcel Duchamp left his studio on West 67th Street in New York City on a peculiar errand. He went to the J. L. Mott Iron Works at 118 Fifth Avenue, made a few polite inquiries, and then asked for a single white porcelain urinal. Duchamp then took his new purchase back to his studio and begin work.

There was nothing strange in an artist personally selecting his raw materials. Michelangelo was famous for spending long hours in the marble quarries of Carrara, and it was often said that he could feel a tremor of future form in the rough-hewn blocks. Once the marble was quarried and carted back to his studio in Florence, Rome, or wherever else he happened to be working, he would spend still more time examining the stone, watching and waiting before at last taking up hammer and chisel. Once begun, his work was long, hard, and physically exhausting—one of the reasons that Leonardo da Vinci looked down upon it, dismissing sculptors as workmen, and rating their manual labor considerably lower than the more intellectual *cosa mentale* that was, for him, painting. Michelangelo cared nothing for such distinctions, and over the course of thousands of hours of arduous work, covered from head to foot in marble dust, he feverishly sought to liberate his vision from the rough stone until what remained before him was a work such as his *Pietà*, the Redeemer and the Mother who immaculately conceived him, who loved him and lost him, the world's sorrows concentrated into a crushing burden which she held with sunken head and outstretched arms—and which a vandal would one day attack with a hammer in St. Peter's.

Half a world and half a millennium away, the young Duchamp proceeded differently. He may have looked long and hard at the matter before him, may have listened with passionate intensity to the white porcelain, wondering how to make it tell the truth of its times, but whatever the nature and extent of Duchamp's deliberations, his physical activity was minimal. The urinal that emerged from his studio was much the same as the one that entered it. The slight but crucial difference lay in its signature: "R. Mutt 1917." The rough pseudonym Duchamp chose was a suggestive one: Mutt was only a letter away from the name of the initial producer of the object. It being a work with a less-than-exalted artistic pedigree, Duchamp also found appealing the name's mongrel associations, ones particularly alive to him through his reading of "Mutt and Jeff" comic strips, as well as from one of dogs' favorite activities: urinating (to mark territory). These low-cultural notes were, however, accompanied by a high-culture critique. When heard with ears trained in the language with the most lofty tradition of aesthetic reflection—German—"R. Mutt" sounds less like a name and more like an indictment. When spoken aloud, it sounds just like *Armut*, German for "poverty." Perhaps Duchamp's "R. Mutt" wanted to remind spectators of the poverty that surrounds us, and alongside of which art might seem like a craven escape. Or perhaps the poverty was of a less literal sort: a poverty of imagination and invention, a poverty of possibility for today's artists with the Leonardos and Michelangelos of the past crowding the horizon, filling minds and museums, and leaving all later work to pale by their light. When asked later, Duchamp replied that R. stood for "Richard," which could have meant a great deal—*richard* is French slang for a wealthy man—or nothing at all.

Duchamp's urinal was destined for the 1917 Independents art show to be held in the Grand Central Palace and funded by a host of wealthy New York patrons. It was to be the largest exhibition ever held in America and would present 2,125 works by 1,200 artists. It was to stretch over nearly two miles and thus double the size of the legendary 1913 Armory show where Duchamp had attracted so much interest with his *Nude Descending a Staircase*. It was announced that every artist was welcome to exhibit at the Independents show so long as the entrance fee ($6) was paid. Two days before the scheduled opening, R. Mutt's urinal was quietly delivered to the Grand Central Palace with the required membership fee and a title: *Fountain*. Put to this extreme test, the Independents' board of directors refused it. The ground given was that it was, in the words of the president of the board, "by no definition, a work of art."

This was, of course, only the beginning. R. Mutt's real identity was discovered. A gallerist took up its cause, and Duchamp's *Fountain* assumed its sphinx-like position in debates on art, posing the riddle of what defines the work of art in the age of mechanical reproduction (the answer is the same as for Sophocles: "man"). At the time of his death in 1968 Duchamp's urinal was the century's most famous piece of free-standing art in the world (appropriately enough, the original had disappeared, and the austere Duchamp had authorized copies). Whereas the president of the Independent's board of directors could claim that *Fountain* was "by no definition a work of art," by literally every definition in today's world of art exhibition and collection it has become one, raising the question of what, if anything, has changed.

The reader might well wonder what this illustrates about a crisis in the idea of the work or a change in artistic character. It speaks, to begin with, of things to come, from the "reciprocal readymades" suggested by Duchamp (such as "using a Rembrandt as an ironing board") to the amateur artist and seed merchant Pierre Pinoncelli, who was to enter a museum and urinate in one of the authorized Duchamp *Fountains,* to Damien Hirst's pile of artful garbage (half-full coffee cups, ashtrays full of butts, strewn newspaper, empty beer bottles, an easel, etc.) disposed of by the janitor of a Mayfair gallery at a loss of hundreds of thousands of dollars. Duchamp took the viewer out of the traditional museum space and led him next door (to the restroom). He stood, as would Beckett a few years later, at a crossroads of artifice. Something begun in the previous century when the subtle mastery of Ingres and the salon artists gave way to the works Woolf saw at the First Post-Impressionist Exhibition was taking its course.

What allows a janitor to mistake the garbage he is paid to clear away from garbage being sold for over a hundred thousand dollars? What allows critics to see signing a urinal as one of the most radical artistic acts of its century? The answer is that the idea of the work—of what makes a work of art one—has not only become mysterious, this mystery has become one of art's central subjects. It is impossible to isolate a Patient Zero for this crisis, to designate what event or work first fully revealed this loss of self-evidence or first ushered in this era of uncertainty, whose most iconic representative was to become Samuel Beckett. The reason no such patient can be found is that it is not that sort of a change. It was gradual, and then it was sudden, and, by the time Duchamp put brush to urinal and, a decade later, Samuel Beckett put pen to paper, it was no more possible to reverse than bankruptcy.

Is It Difficult?, or On Riddles

This book is addressed to those who find Samuel Beckett engaging, delighting, and delightful, as well as to those who find him mysterious, befuddling, and exasperating. It aspires to treat of the essential difficulty of his art, and so an initial word on difficulty is in order. If the question is whether Samuel Beckett is a difficult writer, the answer is: of course he is! He is hugely difficult. He was a walking, talking, writing, writhing riddle. Wrapped in a mystery. Inside an enigma. The first essay he published is on the most difficult work which our culture possesses—*Finnegans Wake*—and its central argument is that *Finnegans Wake* is not difficult. His first published poem is a wild, whirling excursus on the astrological and dietary habits of Descartes difficult enough that its publisher demanded footnotes. His first novel has as self-directed directive "continuity bitched to hell" (*Dream*, 139). And that is just the beginning. The author who wrote Beckett's early works was difficult, the one who wrote his mature works was difficult, and the author who wrote his last works, with the darkness descending, cooling and contracting until all was away and away was all, he was difficult too.

This difficulty did not, of course, go unnoticed. The single most famous essay on Beckett, Adorno's "Understanding *Endgame*," has as its bluntly subtle argument that what *Endgame* gives us to understand is that there is nothing to understand. Another of Beckett's first great critics, Stanley Cavell, after a long bit of close reasoning pauses to concede: "Perhaps I hallucinate," and will stop more than once to say such things as: "This can't, I think, be the right track" (Cavell 2002, 121, 148). The first book-length study of Beckett's work, Niklaus Gessner's *Die Unzulänglichkeit der Sprache: Eine Untersuchung über Formzerfall und Beziehungslosigkeit bei Samuel Beckett*,[3] published in Zurich in 1957, noted that while such a work as *Waiting for Godot* had already attained great popularity, instances of "normal people"—whom Gessner nicely defines as "those who are not literary critics"—having read from beginning to end the last volume in the trilogy,[4] or even the first volume, "must be quite rare" (Gessner 1957, 35). It is easy to make light of what normal people had in store for them in Beckett's later works, but of more interest is how the remark highlights the degree to which Beckett's are exceptionally taxing works, and exceptionally taxing in a new way.

Identifying difficulty is not of much assistance unless, of course, you circumscribe what is difficult, and why. Samuel Johnson is said to have once listened as a musician struggled through a challenging passage. On being told that the piece was difficult, he retorted: "Difficult do you call it, Sir? I wish it were impossible" (Seward 1797, 267). We do not say this of Beckett, although Beckett said it of himself. Asked by a radio journalist in 1952 for his ideas on the theater, Beckett replied, "I have no ideas about theater. I know nothing about it. I do not go to it" (LSB 2.316). This was a typical response. A few years later he told a director of his plays: "My work is a matter of fundamental sounds (no joke intended),[5] made as fully as possible, and I accept responsibility for nothing else" (Harmon 1998, 24). Of his first famous play Beckett said, "I do not know in what spirit I wrote it . . . I do not know who Godot is. I do not even know if he exists. And I do not know if they believe he does, these two who are waiting for him" (LSB 2.316). When asked about the isolated mouth of *Not I* (1972) he replied, "I no more know where she is or why thus than she does" (Schneider 1986, 246). Beckett's stance on the questions his works raised seems simple: "If I knew, I would have said so in the play."[6]

Beckett's remarks on his art and its difficulty are as little immediately clarifying as were those of the Joyce who gleefully noted that he had put enough riddles in *Ulysses* to "keep the critics busy for three hundred years" (Ellmann 1982, 703). Beckett is not difficult, however, because he put in so many riddles, but because he left so many out. Ten years after the premiere of *Endgame*, the severely retiring Beckett gave a brief interview he allowed to be included in the program for a German production of his play. His questioner noted how *Endgame*'s first audiences experienced *ein Gefühl der Ratlosigkeit*, "a feeling of helpless uncertainty," upon seeing the play, and that this feeling was intensified by the sense they were being posed riddles whose answers the author himself did not know (Beckett 1984, 114). Beckett's reply was in German: "Endspiel *wird blosses Spiel sein. Nichts weniger. Von Rätseln und Lösungen also kein Gedanke. Es gibt für solches ernstes Zeug Universitäten, Kirchen, Cafés de Commerce usw.*" (Beckett 1984, 114). Many years later, in a volume entitled *Disjecta*, Beckett republished the interview, still untranslated—with reason. "Endspiel *wird blosses Spiel sein*" can with equal justice be translated as "*Endgame* is merely a play" and "*Endgame* is mere play." The rest of Beckett's remark is easier to render: "Nothing less. Thus no riddles and no solutions. For such ponderous matters you can always go to universities, churches, *cafés de commerce*, etc."

There is a complexity, and felicity, in the first part of Beckett's phrase, as *blosses Spiel* not only echoes the German title of what is about to begin *(Endspiel)*, it also tells the audience what is about to begin. *Bloss* means both *mere* and *bared*, and so in a single word Beckett contrived to say all he had to say about his work. There is no solution because there is no riddle, no answer because no question. The play is only a play, nothing but a play, nothing but playing about. And while there are those addicted to earnest inquiry—the layabouts in universities, cafés, churches, and the like—and while they will doubtless come up with questions so as to come up with answers, Beckett insisted that all that could not be more foreign to the world of his works. In an early French essay (about an invented French poet) Beckett wrote of "an art that is perfectly intelligible and perfectly inexplicable," and this is an ideal toward which he strove, and which leads to his unique difficulty (Beckett 1984, 42).[7]

Beckett is thus saying several things, all of which he can say with special intensity, and concision, thanks to the foreign language in which he is saying them. Because the German, like the English, word for the general activity *(play)* is the same as that for the specific event *(a play)*, Beckett can say in a single breath that *Endgame* is mere playing about and that it is merely a play. During these same years Beckett entitled one of his plays, simply, *Play* (1963). When an actor plied him with questions about *Waiting for Godot*, he replied, "It's so simple. It's just a play" (Knowlson 2006, 180). It is as silly to ascribe a serious meaning to the play as it would be to ascribe a serious meaning to the play of children. It may remain important, it may remain amusing, it may remain essential—as is the play of children—but that does not make it something it is not. Beckett indicates that the literary level is the only one in play and that symbolic systems—be they religious, philosophical, psychological, sociological, or other—should keep their distance.

If we then take Beckett at his word, his works have neither riddles nor solutions, are not about moral reasoning or Auschwitz, late capitalism or the unconscious, Hiroshima or metaphysics, because they are not *about* anything. Declaring that *Endspiel* is *"blosses Spiel"* is not only an elegant way of echoing a title, it is an eloquent way of presenting an idea about meaning, which is that there is none. Early and late, Beckett said there was in his works no mystery, no difficulty, nothing esoteric, nothing to find because nothing hidden, nothing difficult but the despair depicted. This does not, of course, mean that he is not diffi-cult, merely that he is not difficult for any of the customary reasons—not because of the weight of erudition, the range of reference, the com-plexity of syntax, scene, or setting. Like any great artist, he is uniquely difficult. Perhaps an example is in order.

Watt?

Beckett's last English novel, the wonderfully wearying *Watt* (1953)—a book so strange that when Beckett arrived in England in April 1945 the manuscript was confiscated on the suspicion that it might be a German code[8]—is constellated with question marks, centered and set apart from the text. Like this:

?

They do not follow questions—at least not stated ones. At points they seem to do nothing other than light up the night sky of the story. At others they seem to represent the author, or his envoy, throwing up his hands, asking himself whether he can go on, whether he must.

In Beckett's preceding novel, Murphy is not fond of the material world, but he nevertheless seeks solace in nature—or, at least, in the peace of certain gardened parts of it. Watt, however, has no such luke-warm feelings. "If there were two things that Watt loathed," we are told, "one was the earth, and the other was the sky" (GC 1.196). There was no love lost between Watt and his world because there was no love to begin with. Like a knight (very) errant crusading against naturalism, vitalism, animism, and all the other *-isms* in their bright train, he wanders a countryside supremely alienated from the natural world. More to the point of Beckett's works, Watt's alienation from nature finds its complement in an alienation from anything *symbolic,* an alienation from anything that might guide our understanding of the relation of work to world, a separation from every and any sense that man is the measure of anything but his own shambling self.

His best efforts to the contrary, Watt is, however, not able to keep signs and symbols forever at bay. Soon after his installation in mysterious Mr. Knott's house a pair come knocking at the door. The specter of symbolic significance first raises its head at this moment, as the Galls, *père et fils,* piano tuners by trade, arrive. Upon being let in they do nothing other than their job: they tune Mr. Knott's piano. And yet, Watt, "who had not seen a symbol, nor executed an interpretation, since the age of fourteen, or fifteen," finds himself seeking some significance in excess of the "face value" of the event (GC 1.226). The reader is in no position to divine why this event and not another seems both to carry and conceal some symbolic sense from Watt, though the narrator is careful to note its "bad effect" on him (GC 1.226). One suggestion, however, is offered: the "fragility of the outer meaning" (GC 1.226). It is not Arsene's long speech—full of dark and light import—that fills Watt with this strange symbolic feeling, but, instead, this most everyday of occurrences. By virtue of seeming to be nothing but itself—an event perfectly without symbolic import—it awakens Watt's long dormant symbolic sensitivities. It appears that even an impoverished nature like Watt's abhors a symbolic vacuum.

One reason this episode seems so strange to both Watt and his readers is that this "fragility of the outer meaning" is ubiquitous in his world. And yet at this point in the story it poses a problem for Watt—a character, it is to be kept in mind, specially crafted for his limited interest (subjective and genitive). Beckett's narrator has been careful to stress how up until this point "the first look . . . had always been enough for Watt, more than enough for Watt" (GC 1.226). *Watt's* story indeed involves precious few turns of plot, but this is one of them: the introduction of a point which curiously incurious Watt wonders whether to endow with meaning. *Watt* has often been compared to Kafka's *Castle.* Both works depict a strange supremacy over an extensive estate, but the resemblance between the books lies less in their hidden masters than in the manner in which the most incidental of events can be made to suddenly loom large as a problem of insoluble import.

After the departure of the piano tuners their suggestion of symbolic significance spreads like wildfire through Watt's world. "For the incident of the Galls father and son was followed by others of a similar kind," we are told, "incidents that is to say of great formal brilliance and indeterminable purport" (GC 1.227). It would be difficult to find a more fitting description of Beckett's aesthetic effect than that it is rich in formal brilliance of indeterminable purport. The visit of the Galls does not prove the end of Watt's wrestling with the gray angel of meaning. Its question is, however, next raised in response to a work of art. After much difficulty Watt gains illicit entry into Erskine's room, where he finds a painting. It depicts "a circle, obviously described by a compass, and broken at its lowest point," accompanied "in the eastern background" by "a point, or dot" (GC 1.272).[9] "The circumference was black. The point was blue, but blue! The rest was white" (GC 1.272). Confronted with this abstract painting, Watt cannot resist humanizing it; faced with its flat surface he cannot keep his mind from lending it a natural depth and imagining it in human terms. Of the circle and point we are told that Watt "wondered if they would eventually pause and converse, and perhaps even mingle, or keep steadfast on their ways, like ships in the night, prior to the invention of wireless telegraphy" (GC 1.272).

Watt's difficulty is, in one respect, the same as that of any viewer of abstract art, and the same as any reader of Beckett's mature writing. It is not hard to see a broken circle and a point as a broken circle and a point, but as soon as one sees them as the creation of an individual— however inscrutable that individual may be judged—a mode and manner of divining intention and understanding meaning begins which is impossible to check. As soon as such an object is hung on a wall to be contemplated at leisure, as soon as it is secreted away from the common gaze (it is no easy matter to get into Erskine's room), the human element tiptoes in. We are told that Watt "wondered what the artist had intended to represent (Watt knew nothing about painting)" (GC 1.272). Knowing something about painting may temper an impatient grasping after a human tale (such as one of ships in the night) or symbolic significance (such as one of ships in the night), but it will not eliminate such searching. Eyes this austere may exist, but they are rare, and they do not come naturally even to those in Watt's world. Beckett's protagonist may know nothing about painting, but even those who know a great deal trace an intention, and read a message, therein—including in cases where that message is like the one Beckett describes in his letters on painting: one of a refusal to symbolize and an inability to express.

Word-Storming, or Logoclasm

In flight from a promising career as a literature professor at Trinity College, Dublin, Beckett undertook in late 1936 and early 1937 a six-month trip through Nazi Germany. Its goal was to study art and German. Beckett had an exceptional interest in foreign languages, and often found himself, linguistically speaking, more at home abroad. He was far from seriously considering switching languages at this point, and far from being capable of doing so (his French letters of the period are those of a relatively fluent foreigner, but still worlds away from the range and intensity of his French writing a decade later). Alongside of French Beckett found German during these early years an almost equally intriguing medium through which to consider whatever it was he was considering. His first theatrical attempt dates from this period and is in German. *Mittelalterliches Dreieck,* "Medieval Triangle," presents a love triangle formed by a Saracen giant named Ferrau, a Carolingian knight named Rinaldo, and King Galafron's daughter Angelica (all characters from Ariosto's *Orlando furioso*).[10] Both in that first theatrical try and elsewhere Beckett writes in a highly idiosyncratic and hugely expressive German where he often seemed to feel almost free to make his artistic aims clear. Once home from his trip Beckett wrote a long letter in German in which he comes as close as he ever will to outlining the enterprise which has made him so famously difficult. The letter contains incomparably direct (as well as incomparably gnomic) statements about Beckett's ideas of language and literature, literature's relation to the other arts, the relation of English to other languages, and Beckett's own relation to the modern masters nearest him, Proust and Joyce. Aptly enough, the letter may never have been sent; equally apt is that it was written to a man Beckett barely knew.[11] Among its topics are "energetic misuse," "literature of the unword," and "nominalist irony." But none is more evocative, emblematic, or enigmatic than what Beckett declares therein as the thing which will be his literary intention: *Wörterstürmerei im Namen der Schönheit* (LSB 1.515).

This phrase was rendered by the letter's first translator as "assault on words in the name of beauty." More recently it was retranslated as "word-storming in the name of beauty."[12] Both translations make it seem like a merry allegory of a phrase, as though the artist were a knight of the mind storming the castle of language to liberate the damsel of beauty. It may be in part this that Beckett had in mind, but it was far from all that he did. He begins with a word that does not exist in German—or, at least, did not exist before he coined it. To English eyes *Wörterstürmerei* looks like the ringing and resounding *word-storming,* but to German ones like those of the man to whom Beckett was writing, a different register would have been foremost. Beckett is not only making a new word, he is crafting a clever pun, for his new word, *Wörterstürmerei,* is modeled on an old one, *Bilderstürmerei* (German for *iconoclasm*).[13] The most accurate, if not most elegant, translation of *Wörterstürmerei* is thus *logoclasm.* Were this not enough to clarify what Beckett had in mind, in a letter written in English a few days after the one in which he announced this *Wörterstürmerei* Beckett informed a correspondent, "I am starting a *Logoclasts' League* . . . I am the only member at present. The idea is ruptured writing" (LSB 1.521; Beckett's emphasis).

This translational matter would be of little importance if it did not offer such a succinct expression of Beckett's artistic aim and the difficulty to which it would give rise. *Iconoclasm* is easy enough to effect. You take down an icon and dash it against the flagstones, or walk into a museum and slash a canvas, or urinate on a work. The difficulty is moral and logistical, but not conceptual. *Logoclasm* is different in this regard. You cannot take a word from the wall, or pluck one from the air, and break it. Words do not admit of such treatment. "I hammer and hammer," wrote Beckett, "hard as iron, the words. I'd like them reduced to dust" (LSB 3.334).

The same year as his trip through Nazi Germany Beckett wrote a poem called "Cascando" (1936). The falling motion named in the title is that of language and concerns love:

the churn of stale words in the heart again
love love love thud of the old plunger
pestling the unalterable
whey of words. (GC 4.34)

Even when speaking of the most living thing—love—language remains inert, and no matter how hard our hearts pound it remains unaltered. Elsewhere in that same poem language is called the "occasion / of word-shed," being, as it is for Beckett, something between waste and harm (GC 4.34).

This idea of a ruptured writing, of word-storming logoclasm, is one Beckett explored for the remaining sixty years of his writing life, from the Unnamable's "wordy-gurdy" to the "worsening words" of *Worstward Ho* (1983) (GC 2.392; 187; GC 4.478). There was no goal, but there was an enemy: the reason (or *logos*) for language's being. Whether called *logoclasm* or *word-storming*, whether in poetry or prose, on page or stage, in German, French, or English, Beckett's writing took stumbling, staggering, stunning aim at words and their concerted use. It should perhaps come as no great surprise, given the undertaking, that the name Beckett gave to the four-year period during which he wrote nearly all the works for which he is best known is "the siege in the room."[14] Beckett's logoclasm—or his dream of it—thus presents two faces. It is a calm and clear-sighted experiment in the name of language, literature, art, and beauty: an analytical adventure, an attempt to illuminate art's infrastructure, an exploration of uncharted territories, a study in logoclasm. And it is also a ravening, raving, raging vengeance to be wrought on something the speaker knows not to name.

Hic sunt leones

When Roman cartographers didn't know what a region held they wrote *hic sunt leones,* "here are lions," just to be on the safe (and exciting) side.

Critics are not so different, and beyond our limits we may say that nothing exists, or nothing of interest, or lions. One question raised by Beckett's art of mismaking is *how* he mismakes. Another is *why*. Given the state of his art it should come as no surprise that some have seen signs of a personal disorder, just as it should come as no surprise that a recent issue of *Beckett Studies* was dedicated to questions of neuroscience and psychology. It is not outlandish to feel that Beckett writes of damaged persons and places because he was damaged in his person and by his places. It has, however, no place in this study. For even if there is some normatively true sense in which Beckett was clinically depressed, or the victim of some more delicately named pathology, those are truly lions that lie beyond our limits, and as little explain or exhaust our interest in his works as would ascertaining that Vladimir Nabokov harbored pedophile desires end all discussion of *Lolita*. Beckett wrote Pamela Mitchell in 1954, "Yes, I'm gloomy, but I always am. That's one of the numerous reasons you shouldn't have anything to do with me. More than gloomy, melancholy mad" (LSB 2.444). If we merely see Beckett's works as the anatomy of his melancholy then we see something compelling, but only narrowly—and focus on the life rather than the art.

• • •

A word on languages: the reader will find more foreign words and phrases in the following than ease of reading would counsel. Not only did Beckett read widely in four living languages (English, French, German, and Italian) and one dead one (Latin), he did more than half his writing in French, and the majority of the works that made his fame were first written in French. I have endeavored, nevertheless, to keep foreign language references to what Beckett once called a "most mere minimum" (GC 4.472).

First Forms to Accommodate the Mess

A Brief Bit of Biography

Samuel Barclay Beckett was born, aptly enough, on a Good Friday that was also Friday the thirteenth.[1] He was about to turn twenty-three when he began his sixty-year publishing career in 1929. Although reputed to be retiring, sullen, and misanthropic (even, and especially, by himself), the many letters and reminiscences from these years paint a portrait of the artist as a young man who is none of these things. The Beckett on display is kind, congenial, wry, and ribald. While he hasn't quite followed the advice offered to him by Lucia Joyce—"to accept the world and go to parties"—he has made inroads. These early years are far from uneventful, from writing a prize-winning poem (overnight, for money) entitled "Whoroscope," to being stabbed on Twelfth Night by a deranged pimp named Prudent, with car wrecks, intrauterine memories,[2] and literary longings, the whole interspersed and enlivened by what Beckett called "the usual drink & futility" (LSB 1.1.24).

Early and late Beckett was a remarkable reader, and the work which he found most fascinating, which he most read and reread, from his student days to his deathbed, was Dante's *Divine Comedy*. Therein, Virgil explains to the poet that, following the supernatural laws of purgatory, the higher they climb the easier climbing will become. Overhearing this explanation, a voice calls out from behind a boulder: "Perhaps you will be obliged to sit before then" (*Purgatorio* 4.98–99; 40–41). Dante turns to find a figure slumped forward with his head between his knees, looking "lazier than if sloth were his sister" (*Purgatorio* 4.110–111; 40–41). When the figure asks, "Why go up?," Dante at last recognizes his friend Belacqua's tone of voice and turn of mind (*Purgatorio* 4.114; 42–43). While casting about for a name to give the ideally listless protagonist of his first two fictions—*Dream of Fair to Middling Women* (1932)[3] and *More Pricks Than Kicks* (1934)—Beckett chose Belacqua, for, "say what you will, you can't keep a dead mind down" (GC 4.184).

The world notwithstanding, plans for the future were made, amended, and, as a rule, abandoned. Beyond translational projects, such as an English edition of the Marquis de Sade's *120 Days of Sodom,* and clerical ones, such as correcting galleys of *Finnegans Wake* ("stupefying work"), Beckett explored the possibility of becoming a commercial pilot, a composer of advertising slogans, and a cinematographer, going so far as to write Sergei Eisenstein to request assistance with the last of these dreams (LSB 1.565). During these early years Beckett held his first (and last) regular job—lecturer in Romance Languages at Trinity College, Dublin. He was exceptionally good or exceptionally poor at this depending on whom you ask. (If you asked him, he was exceptionally poor.) What is certain is that he was exceptionally unhappy—"a tall thin streak of misery," a former student recalled. One of her classmates noted: "We had a saying that 'he despised us with the utmost despision.'"[4] The problems with life in Dublin did not, however, stop at the College gates. These are clearly expressed to fellow Dubliner Thomas McGreevy, then in Paris: "How can one write here, when every day *vulgarises* one's hostility . . . ?" (LSB 1.49; Beckett's emphasis). With his hostility debased, and its creative possibilities neutralized, Beckett found himself with nothing to write to, from, for, or with but a "tired abstract anger" (LSB 1.55). It was difficult to stay and difficult to go, with all the while the lurking fear: "I'll be here until I die, creeping along genteel roads on a stranger's bike" (LSB 1.125). Ultimately, Beckett mustered the funds and energy to make the first of several escapes. On the eve of a departure in 1931, he wrote McGreevy, "And as usual I'm not burning any boats! I'm hoping to be able to spit fire at them from a distance"

(LSB 1.100). A student recalls asking after he had left, "Where's our Sam?" and someone offhandedly replying, "Gone to Paris to commit suicide" (Knowlson 2006, 53).

Beckett was not, in fact, off to Paris (nor did he attempt suicide), but this does not mean that he was to have an easy time of it. In *More Pricks Than Kicks,* Beckett's narrator tells us that Belacqua "enlivened the last phase of his solipsism . . . with the belief that the best thing he had to do was to move constantly from place to place" (GC 4.99). In this he follows the movements of his maker. Beckett displayed a restlessness in his departures from city to city, from Dublin to Paris to London, as though he had adopted as his own the slogan he invented for his imaginary French poet, Jean du Chas: *"va t'embêter ailleurs"* (Beckett 1984, 38). (A conventional rendering of this motto would be "Bore yourself elsewhere," although Beckett chose instead the more concise translation: "Feck off.")[5] Beckett returned to Dublin again and again, each time with as much misgiving as the last. In 1938 he wrote to McGreevy that "all the old people & the old places, they make me feel like an amphibian detained forcibly on dry land, very very dry land" (LSB 1.637). In darker moments he seemed to anticipate, and apply to himself, the remark in *Watt:* "for all the good that frequent departures out of Ireland had done him, he might just as well have stayed there" (GC 1.374).

As a rule, however, Paris seemed a better place than others, with one arrival there from Dublin described as being "like coming out of gaol in April" (LSB 1.567). This is not to say that the city served as a constantly safe haven to the young Beckett, who wrote to McGreevy in 1931, "Paris (as such) gives me the chinks at the moment and it's about the last place in the world I want to go. Too many Frenchmen in the wrong streets" (LSB 1.88). There are reasons to avoid Paris, but none better than finding "too many Frenchmen in the wrong streets"—in addition to the notable fact that Beckett came within a literal inch of losing his life to a Frenchman encountered in the wrong street (the deranged pimp who would stab him six years later). After the *Wanderjahre* that were his twenties, with long stays in Dublin and London, Beckett took up residence in Paris, where he would reside for the remaining fifty-two years of his long life.

Settling where to live was, however, only the beginning. Before spitting fire on the professorial path, Beckett had begun to express uncertainty as concerned his calling, declaring, "I don't want to be a professor," and adding that it is "almost a pleasure to contemplate the mess of this job" (LSB 1.72). Although the mess is waded through as quickly as possible, its resumption in another locale is contemplated, with a long list of proposed teaching destinations coming up for review, from Paris to Cape Town, London to Rhodesia, the University of Milan to Harvard. Most of the time, however, Beckett tried to make a go of it as a writer. Consequently, he often writes of the pain of writing and the difficulty of crafting works that were not merely "*facultatif*" (LSB 1.130). Though there was no love lost between the young Beckett and Rilke, the former shared the latter's concern with poetry that comes unbidden and thus looked with disdain at those products of his pen which were merely *facultatif,* repeatedly using the French word (for optional) when writing in English because of the stress it allowed him to lay on the idea of writing being a faculty which one may exercise at will, whereby what Beckett longs for is literature that comes unbidden (LSB 1.133). Beckett wondered whether this was "a very hairless way of thinking of poetry," but stuck to it (LSB 1.133). He deplored works he found "a statement and not a description of heat," the reason that he did not like Mallarmé, who was for him too "Jesuitical" (the "Jesuitical poem," he said, is "an end in itself and justifies all the means" which, he notes, "disgusts" him, though he also notes he does not understand why it "disgusts me so much") (LSB 1.134). This fear of the *facultatif* is the reason that years later Beckett would cryptically observe in the painting of André Masson "the scars of a competence that must be most painful to him," linking facility, capacity, and competence to a sense of suffering that was all his own (GC 4.557). The problem of writing something that didn't merely exercise his (remarkable) faculties was a great one, but it did not mean that his early years were poor in literary projects, from ones that found their way quickly into print, like "Dante . . . Bruno. Vico . . . Joyce" (1929), "Whoroscope" (1930), and *Proust* (1931), to the more purgatorial paths of *More Pricks Than Kicks, Echo's Bones and Other Precipitates* (1935), and *Murphy* (1938), to those writings that remained in the inferno of a desk drawer, such as a good deal of verse, the novel *Dream of Fair to Middling Women,* and the draft notes for a play about the love life of Samuel Johnson (LSB 1.397). Beckett's extensive correspondence, as well as the three major biographies in English, can give the reader a fuller sense of these years before Beckett was, by his own account, "damned to fame," but this summary might suffice to set the scene against which Beckett's first— highly autobiographical—works were written.

Balzac, Bathos, Chloroform, Clockwork

Aptly enough, Samuel Beckett's first published story, "Assumption" (1929), is the tale of a man who, after a period of painful containment, screams himself to death. The narrative arc of Beckett's first novel, *Dream of Fair to Middling Women,* is a good deal less taut, though no less full of throttled energy—much of it directed at upsetting the conventions of storytelling. The "chest into which I threw my wild thoughts," as Beckett referred to his first novel, is largely autobiographical, drawn from his experiences during the years 1928–1930. For the purposes of fiction, Beckett renamed the Austrian town of Mödling Mödelberg and its Schule-Hellerau was rechristened Schule Dunkelbrau (making the German word "light" [*hell*] "dark" [*dunkel*]—and adding a *b* for beer). It is not only an ostensibly real world, it is an ostensibly autobiographical one. Even minor items and incidents such as Belacqua's merciless boots and his ill-fated climbing expedition had clear corollaries in Beckett's life.[6] Despite the fact that the names of people underwent far more radical reconfigurations than those of place, they too are clearly drawn from life. Peggy Sinclair, Beckett's first love (and first cousin), is easily recognizable as the jiggling, jostling Smeraldina. (So openly was the character based on the letters and person of Peggy Sinclair that Beckett's recycling of passages from this novel in *More Pricks Than Kicks* hurt members of his family.)[7] Lucia Joyce becomes the Syra-Cusa; Ethna MacCarthy, Alba; Beckett's brother Frank, John; his Trinity College professor and erstwhile mentor Thomas Rudmose-Brown, the Polar Bear; Beckett's Aunt Cissie and Uncle "Boss" Sinclair, Mammy and the Mandarin; Jean Beaufret, Lucien—and so on. Richard Ellmann recounted how, a decade earlier, "when Dubliners asked each other in trepidation after *Ulysses* appeared, 'Are you in it?' or 'Am I in it?' the answer was hard to give" (Ellmann 1982, 364). Had Beckett found the publisher he sought for his first novel, curious Dubliners would have had no similar difficulty (although they may have been tempted to deem it what Lucia's uncle Stanislaus called his brother's writing: "lying autobiography").

It may come as no surprise that the Beckett of these years liked Keats, but the terms of his endearment are worth noting, as he praised the poet's "crouching brooding quality," which leads Beckett to envision him "squatting on the moss, crushing a petal, licking his lips & rubbing his hands"—an image he will like enough to embed in his *Proust*, written that same year, where Keats is "crouched in a mossy thicket, annulled, like a bee, in sweetness" (LSB 1.21; GC 4.553). "I like [Keats] the best of them all," Beckett said during these years, "because he doesn't beat his fists on the table" (LSB 1.21). Self-aggrandizing fist-beaters come in for special abuse during these early years—whether in the form of insufferable "Balzac gush" or, closer to Beckett's day, Gabriele d'Annunzio (e.g., "I was reading d'Annunzio on Giorgione again and I think it is all balls and mean nasty balls") or the wooden-worded ("I bought the Origin of Species yesterday for 6d and never read such badly written catlap") (LSB 1.41; LSB 1.111). Not beating his fists on the table, not gushing, not being content with catlap, but crouching, brooding, and managing not to get drunk on the past are what Beckett hopes in these early years for his art.

As its title would suggest, Beckett's first novel is about—or, more precisely, structured around—a series of women. Its minimally moving center is the beguilingly indolent Belacqua, the author's slumped, slovenly, overweight, and undermotivated double. The sexual appetites of the women Belacqua attracts distress him to no end. Although he allows Smeraldina to "rape" him, her desires are subsequently treated with a distaste verging on disgust, and the carnal longings of the Syra-Cusa are presented at less length, but with equal misgiving (*Dream*, 50). These middling fair women are succeeded by the beautiful Alba, who invites Belacqua in on the novel's last, rainy, night—having "a fire and a bottle" and the young miscreant's heart (*Dream*, 238).

Beckett has the Belacqua of this book declare: "If ever I do drop a book, which God forbid, trade being what it is, it will be a ramshackle, tumbledown, a bone-shaker, held together with bits of twine" (*Dream*,

139). This metafictional metacommentary is a rough description of the dropped book that was *Dream of Fair to Middling Women,* just as it is a precise one of fiction Beckett would write one war, one language, and twenty years later. "To find a form that accommodates the mess," Beckett was to remark, "that is the task of the artist now" (Driver 1961, 23). In *Dream of Fair to Middling Women* and its successor *More Pricks Than Kicks* (a number of scenes, incidents, and descriptions are taken directly from the former into the latter) Beckett did not so much find a solution to the riddle of form as turn his back on it, throwing open his doors and calling for the mess to come in and take whatever place it liked. Only later would Beckett find that it does not simply come when you call.

More Pricks Than Kicks is not a mere collection of short stories, it is a series of them, in that the individual tales are ordered chronologically and connected to one another by the continuous presence (alive and dead) of a single figure. Fair and middling women are drawn to him, wed him, and die mysteriously. Then he dies. That said, the individual tales are not stitched together tightly. The first story ends with Dante's *Paradiso* and a lobster plunged live into boiling water and the last one with Dantean Belacqua put dead in the ground, and while other thematic arcs may be traced, none shines brightly.[8]

Dream of Fair to Middling Women and *More Pricks Than Kicks* express a wide variety of anxieties, but none so intense as that concerning *form.* Midway through the novel there is a connecting (or, perhaps, disconnecting) inter-chapter entitled "UND" (German for "AND") wherein the narrator discusses the difficulties his disorderly tale creates. In mock dismay he exclaims: "And we with not a single Chesnel in our whole bag of tricks! (You know Chesnel, one of Balzac's Old Curiosities)" (*Dream,* 118). The figure in question is from Balzac's *The Collection of Antiquities* (*Le cabinet des antiques,* 1822)—a text Beckett had studied at Trinity College and whose stereotypical mirror held up to a stereotypical nature the young Beckett also finds in the hands of Dickens (author of the other half of Beckett's portmanteau title—*The Old Curiosity Shop,* 1841). This is not the only occasion on which Beckett will fire "parthian shafts" at great writers in the realist tradition (GC 1.46). Beckett noted to a friend during these same years, "Am reading Cousine Bette. The bathos of style & thought is so enormous that I wonder is [Balzac] writing seriously or in parody" (LSB 1.245).[9]

In *Dream of Fair to Middling Women* not having a Chesnel means not having stock figures at one's disposal. As his temperature mounts, the novel's narrator declares that Balzac's tales "take place in a spellbound backwash," and that "to read Balzac is to receive the impression of a chloroformed world" (*Dream,* 120). After a wild, whirling reflection on form, Beckett's narrator states with relative clarity what bothers him about the realist writing of the previous century: "The procédé that seems all falsity, that of Balzac, for example, and the divine Jane and many others, consists in dealing with the vicissitudes, or absence of vicissitudes, of character in this backwash, as though that were the whole story" (*Dream,* 119). A few years later, Beckett told readers "*The Amaranthers*[10] is art, not horology. Ariosto to Miss—*absit nomen*" (Beckett 1984, 89). For more than alliterative reasons it is clear that the "missing name" is Miss *Austen* (as well as being a pun on *absit omen,* "barring omen"). The reason for the sideswipe at "the divine Jane" is the same as for those made at Balzac: a tick-tocking "horology" that results in preformed deformations of life, and thus art. The issue that Beckett is confronting is, in short, how to view "the chartered recountants," as he called them, of the past, for he imagines a very different relation between teller and told (Beckett 1984, 89).[11] "To have been a dupe, wishing I wasn't, thinking I wasn't, knowing I was, not being a dupe of not being a dupe," is how one of Belacqua's descendents—the Unnamable—will put it (GC 2.308; 46). For the moment, however, verbally abusing "realistic" writers is made to suffice.

The "clockwork" constancy of character in Balzac, Austen, Dickens, and others is, for the young Beckett, a consequence of *character*: of their characters having been chloroformed from the start. As his reflection winds to a close he readily concedes that enjoying Balzac is possible, but asks, "Why call a distillation of Euclid and Perrault *Scenes from Life?* Why *human* comedy?" (*Dream,* 120; Beckett's emphasis). The problem is not in finding Balzac—or Austen or Dickens—worth one's while. It lies in treating their works as anything approaching true to life. In Beckett's eyes, Balzac, for instance, is part fairy-tale ("Perrault") and part geometry ("Euclid"). While this may be an interesting enough combination, calling it true to life could hardly be more wrong-headed, as is, for Beckett, anything subjected to "the grotesque fallacy of a realistic art" (GC 4.545).

The premises of Beckett's argument, deemed important enough by the young writer to be placed into the plot of his first novel, are concealed, although just barely. Beckett rejects realism not because it aspires to reflect the world around it, but because it so abjectly fails at the task. Taking up the cause of contemporary painting, Beckett concedes that "the 'realist,' sweating next to a stream and swearing at the clouds, has not ceased to enchant us," but adds: "He should stop bothering us [*nous emmerder*] with his talk of objectivity" (Beckett 1984, 126). Beckett will have his narrator declare of such objective portraitists, "We are neither Deus enough nor ex machina enough to go in for that class of hyperbolical exornation, as devoid of valour as it would be of value" (*Dream*, 117). Beckett sees something at once dishonest and cowardly in choosing a god-modeled narration, and as for "exornation" (a rare term for *embellishment*), we are told what to do with that. As the reviewer for the *Irish Times* remarked when the novel was at last published, posthumously, in 1992, "to cope with this book you will need some French and German, a resident exegete of Dante, a good encyclopedia, the OED, the patience of Job and your wits about you."[12]

The Artifice of Artificiality

The winter before writing *Dream of Fair to Middling Women,* Beckett sent the editor of *Dublin Magazine* a poem entitled "Eneug" (Provençal for "complaint") that ends with a startlingly direct borrowing from the pen of another young poet: "the silk of the seas and the arctic flowers! / (they do not exist)" (LSB 1.97–99).[13] The borrowed line is from Rimbaud's prose poem *"Barbare"*: *"la soie des mers et des fleurs arctiques; (elles n'existent pas.)"* (Rimbaud 1972, 144). The lines are important enough to Beckett that when he quotes them in a letter twenty years later he is careful to underline their importance to him (LSB 2.83). Poem and poet are, moreover, on prominent display in Beckett's first novel (written the same year as Beckett's translation of Rimbaud's *Le bateau ivre*). The core of Beckett's first novel is what he calls "the incoherent continuum as expressed by, say, Rimbaud and Beethoven," and two of the things that so clearly appealed to Beckett about Rimbaud were the rejection of unity and the display of artificiality—the preferred image for which was his inexistent arctic flowers (*Dream*, 102).

"The fact of the matter," we read in the novel's opening pages, "is we do not quite know where are in this story" (*Dream*, 9). This note is struck early and often. Things have not improved later when a string of shoe-related anecdotes is concluded with the announcement, by way of explanation and apology: "The only unity in this story is, please God, an involuntary unity" (*Dream*, 133). The content of such statements may sound like a modern innovation, but need not. This newest of narrative gestures is, of course, also a relatively old one—at least as concerns the novel—and the confiding whimsicality of Beckett's first narrators recalls as much eighteenth-century models as it anticipates the metafictional experiments of the latter half of his century.[14] If at such moments Beckett is far from the Flaubert who declared that "an author in his book must be like God in the universe, present everywhere and visible nowhere," he is close to Fielding, whom Beckett was reading with great interest while writing *Dream of Fair to Middling Women* (cf. LSB I.129). Of all he found there what most enchanted Beckett was what he called Fielding's "giving away of the show pari passu with the show" (LSB I.129).

This is precisely what Beckett attempts to do at many points in *Dream of Fair to Middling Women,* and which he will do, as never before, in his mature French writing. The inter-chapter "UND" resembles, in fun-house mirror fashion, Fielding's inter-chapters. George Eliot noted how Fielding "seems to bring his arm-chair to the proscenium and chat with us in all the lusty ease of his fine English" (George Eliot 1985, 170). Lusty or not, Beckett's early narrators attempt to content themselves with this compromise. But in Beckett's great writing the chair is there from the beginning. By the second volume of the trilogy it has become a bed, and by the third we seem to have ventured so far backstage that we have stumbled upon the writer himself, in a sorry state. In 1959 Maurice Blanchot asked: "Who is speaking in Samuel Beckett's books?" He found no single satisfying answer because of what he called "that still deeper deception" Beckett practiced, "which is to show his hand [*cette plus profonde ruse qui est de divulger son jeu*]" (Blanchot 1959, 286).[15] Many rules can be changed in the fictional universe, but none make it real, and so pointing to the artificiality of a work does not, of course, make the artificiality disappear: it either redoubles it, or reduces it to triviality.

In *Dream of Fair to Middling Women* the effect is often trivial, the reason why it is abandoned in Beckett's next novel, *Murphy*. But then, just as Beckett's reader might begin to assume it to have been no more than a youthful enthusiasm, it returns with a force and on a scale which, it is safe to say, surpassed all expectation.

Beckett is drawn to the "giving away of the show pari passu with the show" because he is "neither Deus enough nor ex machina enough" for the sort of supreme narrative control exercised in the past (*Dream*, 117). *Dream*'s narrator scoffs at how Balzac has "turned all his creatures into clockwork cabbages and can rely on their staying put wherever needed or staying going at whatever speed in whatever direction he chooses" (*Dream*, 120). And yet Belacqua is, for all his wild leaps and starts, not any the less his author's creation—nor, for that matter, will be the Unnamable. Balzac's characters are their author's pawns, but one might ask what else they should be. Is it any less a contrivance or a conceit to present them as uncontrollable than to present them as obedient? Beckett is silent on this question, for a time.

The frank artificiality—whether on the avuncular model of Fielding or the more jarring one of Rimbaud—only answers one of the aesthetic problems Beckett sees. The fact that Beckett is unsure how to proceed is nowhere so clear as in his pausing midway through his first book to offer a vituperative apologia for what he finds himself doing. The extremity of his views on the matter, and of the situation in which he has placed himself, can be seen clearly in the fact that he equates novelistic development of character and story—the placing and the clearing of obstacles, an interpersonally intelligible world, and so on—to what is usually dismissed as the most facile of dramatic designs. *All* traditional novelistic movement and *all* continuity seem to Beckett like what Aristotle deplored in *Medea:* a facile contrivance, deus ex machina.

Seen from a narrative perspective, Beckett's problem here is simply stated: freedom. Playing a God without machina is no easy matter. If all traditional narrative movement sounds to his sensitive ears like the ticking of a factory clock, if all unity seems to his sharp senses cooked, all stable characters chloroformed, all movements preprogrammed, and all traditional storytelling so facile and *facultatif* as to be without value or valor, the question of what remains becomes a difficult one. Elsewhere in his first book Beckett's narrator finds a name for the clockworking and chloroforming he denounced in Dickens, Austen, and Balzac: "the gehenna of narratio recta" (*Dream*, 168). With this same freedom and facility in mind, Raymond Queneau would remark five years later how "anyone can drive along before him, like a gaggle of geese, an indeterminate number of apparently real characters, across the field of an indeterminate number of pages or chapters" (Queneau 1950, 12). Queneau sought strict formal responses to this state of affairs—culminating in the activities of the collective he was to found twenty-five years later, OuLiPo. In a register more familiar to the young Beckett, Keats declared in "On the Sonnet": "Let us find, if we must be constrain'd, / Sandals more interwoven & complete / To fit the naked foot of Poesy" (Keats 1977, 340). Beckett found the arbitrary ease with which figures were moved about the traditional storyboard distressing. The solution, however, was not to be found in formal constraint, whether in new stanza forms or the radical reductions of Queneau's fellow Oulipians Georges Perec and Italo Calvino—just as little as it was to be sought in the mythical templates employed by the modernist masters Beckett was reading during these years, such as Joyce and Thomas Mann. In response to his dilemma the young Beckett adopts two principles which will guide all of his subsequent writing: the embrace of artificiality and the rejection of unity. In *Dream of Fair to Middling Women* Beckett's narrator declares, "There is no real Belacqua, it is to be hoped not indeed, there is no such person" (*Dream*, 121). Thirty years later, in *How It Is* (1961), we read: "all these calculations yes explanations yes the whole story from one end to the other yes completely false" (GC 2.519; 224).

Excessive Freedom, or Drama

This problem of telling stories, of finding forms to correspond to the mess, is not confined, of course, to the page. It is a notable—and heartening—fact that the most celebrated dramatic career of the twentieth century, and one of the most celebrated in all of Western literature, began with three failures in three languages. In order of failure they are *Mittelalterliches Dreieck* (German), *Human Wishes* (English), and *Eleutheria* (French). German language and chivalric setting notwithstanding, *Mittelalterliches Dreieck* feels like many a later scene from Beckett's drama, with Ferrau's helmet clownishly falling in the river, Angela defending a "rationalist virginity," and a combat between Saracen and Christian in which "neither can procure the slightest advantage" (Beckett 2006b, 123, 124). Even the clash of swords and civilizations is reduced to a dramatic minimum. Once back from Germany Beckett began in greater earnest another unlikely literary-historical drama, this one based on the love life of Samuel Johnson, with Johnson in the role of "Platonic gigolo" (LSB 1.397). Tentatively titled "Human Wishes," but called by Beckett in his letters an array of things, such as "the Johnson fantasy" and "the Johnson blasphemy," the play was never to be completed. When Beckett could not go on, he didn't, although he would consent to publish a fragment of it almost fifty years later, as the fourth and final part of his *Disjecta* in 1984 (LSB 1.522; Beckett 1984, 153-165). Next came French, with Beckett's first full drama, *Eleutheria* (ancient Greek for freedom). It too fails, in part because it presents the problem of freedom in a place where it has a hard time existing: the stage.

Eleutheria's protagonist's father asks of a (mad) doctor: "I wonder what use you'll be in this comedy [*Je me demande à quoi vous allez servir dans cette comédie*]," and it is possible to envision this as an ironic statement made from within the world of the play, just as it is possible to imagine one actor asking another the same (39). In this it is like a rehearsal for some of the finer lines in *Endgame*, as where Clov turns his spyglass on the audience and says, "I see . . . a multitude . . . in transports . . . of joy [*une foule en délire*]," after which he asks: "Don't we laugh? [*On ne rit pas?*]" (GC 3.112; 43). *Eleutheria*, however, does not walk this fine line between work and world: it hops back and forth over it. After father and doctor we are presented with a glazier (cf. reflection) who antagonizes the protagonist, enjoining him to start acting less like a person and more like a character. "No one can believe in you," he laments (84–85). A Chinese torturer arrives, the Prompter tosses the text on stage, and organized heckling begins, as a member of the audience, or, rather, an actor pretending to be one, leaps onstage and starts berating all present, with matters descending from there. As had been the case in *Murphy*, and as, in very a different manner, will be the case in *The Unnamable*, what drives the drama is the refusal of the protagonist to participate.

Playing God, or *L'inemmerdable*

When asked by his Parisian students in 1929 to translate the lyrics of African American spirituals for them, Beckett complied, "accompanying his impromptu translations with skeptical remarks about the trust the negro slaves put in religion to save them" (Knowlson 1996, 95). Eight years later in Dublin's High Court, Beckett was called as a witness in the libel trial filed by his uncle against Oliver St. John Gogarty (better known to literary history as Buck Mulligan—stately, plump, and anti-Semitic). A defense attorney seeking to discredit Beckett asked him whether he was a Christian, a Jew, or an atheist, to which Beckett replied: "None of the three" (Knowlson 1996, 279). This is a nondenomination common in Beckett's books (and elsewhere, as in an interview from 1961 where he remarks, "I have no religious feeling. Once I had a religious emotion. It was at my first Communion. No more") (Driver 1961, 23).

In *Watt* we learn that "God is a witness that cannot be sworn," and in the work to follow "the unwitnessed witness of witnesses" is, instead, sworn at (GC 1.172; GC 4.336). Frustrated beyond the limits of endurance by a malfunctioning umbrella, Mercier looks to the sky, in Beckett's first French novel, and cries out *"Charogne"* and *"Enculé"* (*Mercier et Camier,* 38). Neither epithet is translated in Beckett's English version of the novel (beyond "Mercier used a nasty expression . . . He used another nasty expression"), but his next address to the heavens is: "As for thee, Fuck thee [*Quant à toi, je t'emmerde*]" (GC 1.399; 38). This leads to an exchange on the nature of the divinity, ending with the epithets "Omni-omni" and *"l'inemmerdable"* (translated as the "the all-unfuckable") (GC 1.399; 39). Later in the tale, as though warming up for the theater, Mercier asks Camier, "What have we done to God?" (GC 1.439; 125). Camier replies, "Denied him [*Nous l'avons renié*]," to which Mercier exclaims, "You're not about to tell me he's that vindictive [*Tu ne me feras pas croire qu'il est rancunier à ce point*]" (GC 1.439; 125).[16]

"Yes, I believe all their blather about the life to come," the narrator of *From an Abandoned Work* (1957) announces, "it cheers me up, and unhappiness like mine, there's no annihilating that" (GC 4.345). The strange vein in which remarks about the "Omni-omni" are made is seen most clearly in prayer. In *Molloy* Moran composes his own Paternoster, "Our Father who art no more in heaven than on earth or in hell, I neither want nor desire that thy name be hallowed, thou knowest best what suits thee. Etc." (GC 2.161; 227). In *Endgame* Nagg intones the same Lord's Prayer—or tries to. As he begins, "Our Father which art—" Hamm cries him down, "Silence! Silence! Where are your manners?" When Nagg then lets fall, or finishes, his silent prayer, remarking, "Nothing doing," Hamm suddenly exclaims, "The bastard!! He doesn't exist" (GC 3.132; 76). Although Beckett was often telling directors things such as "the less I speak about my work the better," he made an exception to stress that "the bastard he does not exist is most important" (Harmon 1998, 16, 29, 30). Under prolonged pressure to satisfy English censors, Beckett staunchly resisted any change to this passage, deeming it "indispensable" (Harmon 1998, 16, 29, 30).

The Unnamable will ask the same question that Mercier asks Camier: "what have I done to God," before adding, "what have they done to God, what has God done to us," and then offering as answer, "nothing, and we've done nothing to him, you can't do anything to him, he can't do anything to us, we're innocent, he's innocent, it's nobody's fault, this state of affairs," which would be the end of the story were it not for his immediately asking, "what state of affairs" (GC 2.379; 165). Back on stage, in *Happy Days* Winnie's mere murmuring "God" is enough to lead her and her husband to laugh together for the only time in the play (GC 3.287). In *All That Fall* (1957) Maddy quotes the scriptural, "The Lord upholdeth all that fall and raiseth up all those that be bowed down," and thereby provokes "wild laughter" both in herself and her husband (GC 3.186). The dominant position on the question of how much the Lord upholdeth is expressed, however, in a different play, *Play,* where "all is falling, all fallen, from the beginning"—either because He's a bastard, or because He doesn't exist (GC 3.363). In Beckett's most famous monologue, Lucky's learning turns on precisely this still point:

> Given the existence as uttered forth in the public works of Puncher and Wattmann of a personal God quaquaquaqua with white beard quaquaquaqua outside time without extension who from the heights of divine apathia divine athambia divine aphasia loves us dearly with some exceptions for reasons unknown but time will tell . . . [17]

The white-bearded *Inemmerdable* at whom, for whom, and to whom we quaqua seems to show—and not only to Lucky's eyes—exceptions for which reasons are lacking and we are wanting.[18]

Divine proximity is, in short, no easy matter in Beckett's works, a fact which will set his creations very progressively adrift. In his first novel Beckett stressed how he had been "neither Deus enough nor ex machina enough" for playing God as others did. *Watt*'s narrator describes sitting down by a stream and being overrun by rats which would "glide up our trouserlegs, hang on our breasts" (GC 1.295). This inverted idyll intensified by the feeding of the rats—first with morsels of cheese, then with "bird's eggs, and frogs, and fledglings," and then with worse:

> And then we would sit down in the midst of them, and give them to eat, out of our hands, of a nice fat frog, or a baby thrush. Or seizing suddenly a plump young rat, resting in our bosom after its repast, we would feed it to its mother, or its father, or its brother, or its sister, or to some less fortunate relative.
>
> It was on these occasions, we agreed, after an exchange of views, that we came nearest to God. (GC 1.295)

Artificiality, or The Hatchet Is Mightier Than the Pencil

If the game is not to play God, it can only be to play man. *Molloy*'s Moran begins his account: "It is midnight. The rain is beating on the windows" (GC 2.89; 125). In the book's last lines we read: "Then I went back to the house and wrote, It is midnight. The rain is beating on the windows. It was not midnight. It was not raining" (GC 2.170; 239). This last line reverberates like a thunderclap through all that preceded it. We might not have particularly cared whether it was raining or midnight beforehand, but now we do, for we have to wonder if it was just the weather and the time of day that was altered, or every single line. An unreliable narrator is always, of course, a partially reliable narrator. (A totally unreliable narrator, one who said only invented things, would, of course, in fiction, be indistinguishable from a totally reliable one.) It is when a narrator gets some things right, like the weather, and some things wrong, like who Molloy is, or what happened to him, that our comfort is compromised. As the life in Malone fades he prepares to drown his book, dying into it. There is a nautical outing of the mentally ill, a visit to an island, a male nurse goes mad (or madder) and murders many with a hatchet (there is "a Saxon" along for the ride who cheers him on). Back in the boat, we read of Lambert's hatchet still wet with the blood of innocents—blood that is "never to dry, but not to hit anyone, he will not hit anyone, he will not hit anyone any more," for he will never again harm anyone, not with the hatchet

> or with his hammer or with his stick
>
> or with his fist or in thought in dream I mean
>
> never he will never
>
> or with his pencil or with his stick or
> (GC 2.28–281; 190–191; Beckett's spacing)

In the list of things with which he will not harm is almost hidden the only active one in the tale: the pencil. Malone has made no secret of the fact that his are stories he is inventing—that not only are they fictions in our world, they are fictions in his. He tells them, so he says, to calm his dying moments, and the artificiality is not only nothing he attempts to mitigate, it is something he does everything to underline—with pencil, stick, and hatchet. This makes his stories the indirect means for the telling of his own story, and whose message is that he finds he has nothing to say that seems worth saying of his world, or to it, and yet on he goes, driven by a force he can as little understand as control. By the time we reach *How It Is* the narrator will say of a still more minimal character that he will "never be but for me anything but a dumb limp lump flat for ever in the mud but I'll quicken him you wait and see and how I can efface myself behind my creature when the fit takes me" (GC 2.446; 82).

"What I need now is stories," observes Molloy, "it took me a long time to know that, and I'm not sure of it" (GC 2.9; 15). The first book-length study of Beckett's work concludes that "Beckett's stories tell of and treat the end of stories [*Seine Geschichten handeln vom Ende der Geschichten*]" (Gessner 1957, 113). Two years later Blanchot would write of *The Unnamable* that "it is no longer a question of a story" because the book "begins there where it is impossible to continue, at the point beyond which there is nowhere to go" (Blanchot 1959, 286; 290). What continued for him in its place were pure pulses of language, pure pulses of being. Kenner found in 1973 that "by the time we arrive on the scene, as readers or spectators, the story is over" and that what we have is "the wreckage the story has left" (Kenner 1973, 9). That same year, in the notes for a lecture to be entitled "To Begin and to End," which he did not live to complete, Italo Calvino said of Beckett that "perhaps for the first time ever we have an author who tells of the exhaustion of all stories [*che racconta l'esaurirsi di tutte le storie*]" (Calvino 1995, 753).[19] Still more recently Martha Nussbaum has heard the voices in Beckett's trilogy "make increasingly radical attempts to put an end to the entire project of storytelling and to the forms of life that this practice supports" (Nussbaum 1990, 287). More than a half-century of Beckett's best readers have heard him telling, again and again, the end of stories. The figures within Beckett's worlds, however, will not hear of such an idea. What could ever come at the end of something that claimed never to have started, and vowed never to stop? Their goal is to find what stories transport, and defile it. *What sort of creature has such a craving for stories?* they ask. *Surely one with a problem,* they answer.

Baudelaire recounts an anecdote about Balzac being shown a painting of a wintry scene with peasants and their poor habitations, upon which he exclaimed, "How beautiful! But what are they doing in those cabins? What are they thinking of? What are their sorrows? Was the harvest good? *They must have bills to pay!*" (Baudelaire 1975–1976, 2.147; Baudelaire's emphasis). It is little wonder that Beckett was so impatient with Balzac. Balzac was in many respects a careless writer, albeit one of genius, and what made him careless was his unbelievable belief in characters. He needed only to be shown a representation to feel its reality, to wonder and worry his way into its world. No novelist has a more fitting death, in his sending away doctor after doctor, all the while demanding the attentions of one who could not come, the Dr. Bianchon who worked such wonders in his fiction. "Perhaps I shall be obliged," the Unnamable remarks, "to invent another fairy-tale, yet another, with heads, trunks, arms, legs and all that follows, let loose in the changeless round of imperfect shadow and dubious light"

(GC 2.301; 35). For him even having heads and trunks is too obvious. The Unnamable will not willingly suspend disbelief in anything, including himself (not for nothing does he begin: "I, say I. Unbelieving" GC 2.285; 7). No one in his world has bills to pay, no harvest will be good, and no belief in such real states of affairs is encouraged.

> So long as one does not know what one is saying and can't stop to enquire, in tranquility, fortunately, fortunately, one would like to stop, but unconditionally, I resume, so long as, so long as, let me see, so long as one, so long as he, ah fuck all that, so long as this, then that, agreed, that's good enough, I nearly got stuck. (GC 2.392; 187)

Storytelling can be complicated, with things falling 32 feet per second (per second), just as it can tell the story of saying, "ah fuck all that." Provided there is "this, then that," you have all you need.

In his first short story Beckett's narrator spoke of "casting an effect in the teeth of his audience," prescient terms for an art that would one day mismake itself through such a cast (GC 4.58). In the thirteenth (and last) of the *Texts for Nothing* Beckett writes:

> Whose voice, no one's, there is no one, there's a voice without a mouth, and somewhere a kind of hearing, something compelled to hear, and somewhere a hand, it calls that a hand, it wants to make a hand, or if not a hand something somewhere that can leave a trace, of what is made, of what is said, you can't do with less [*c'est vraiment le minimum*], no, that's romancing, more romancing [*c'est du roman, encore du roman*]. (GC 4.337; 216)

Wrestling with similar concerns, the Unnamable reassures himself, noting, "I've plenty of time to blow it all sky-high, this circus" (GC 2.317; 60). And yet, as we are told in *First Love*, "I sometimes wonder if that is not all invention, if in reality things did not take a quite different course, one I had no choice but to forget" (GC 4.234; 22). The mood, however, passes, and he soon tells his audience that the rest of the story will be withheld for "other reasons better not wasted on cunts like you" (GC 4.236; 26).

CHAPTER TWO

The Will to Mismake, or Fish and Chips

THE PREFERRED ACTIVITY of Beckett's Murphy is to strip naked and bind himself with seven scarves to a rocking chair. In this state he can take refuge from the pressures surrounding him by rocking himself into "will-lessness." In bound motion he wants nothing, not even not to want, wills nothing, not even not to will. Murphy's successor, Watt, has a similar aspiration, and receives counsel on the matter. As his predecessor in the House of Knott informs him:

> it is useless not to seek, not to want, for when you cease to seek you start to find, and when you cease to want, then life begins to ram her fish and chips down your gullet until you puke, and then the puke down your gullet until you puke the puke, and then the puked puke until you begin to like it. (GC 1.203)

From *Watt* to *Stirrings Still* (1989) the word on the will is that it is nauseating, through to Beckett's last instructions on the matter: "Throw up and go" (GC 4.471). The will, creative or otherwise, is one of Beckett's main concerns, as evidenced by the fact his creations find nothing so strange as that they have one. In the early poem "Malacoda" (1935) we read: "must it be it must be it must be" (GC 4.29).[1] In his later works the route from question ("must it be") to resignation ("it must be") is a good deal longer, but without change in direction.

M Is for . . .

Although after *More Pricks Than Kicks* Beckett had been considering "a new series of yarns: *Less Kicks than Pricks* or *More More Pricks*," his next book, *Murphy,* moved in a different direction (LSB 1.313). Murphy resembles Belacqua in being a bending reed of laziness, but is nevertheless a character of a very different sort, more austere (he does not drink, as his narrator discloses with horror), and on better, albeit strange, terms with himself. Murphy is the first of Beckett's protagonists not to be named Belacqua and the first whose initial initial is the thirteenth letter of the alphabet (to be followed by Mercier, Molloy, Moran, Malone, Macmann, Mahood, and others).[2] At the book's opening, we learn the capital fact about Murphy: "life in his mind gave him pleasure, such that pleasure was not the word" (GC 1.4). In a subsequent chapter dedicated to the metaphysics of Murphy's mind, we are told that the more confused and unconnected things appear to him, the happier he is. Despite this personal preference, and despite Beckett's earlier lamentations, there is a great deal of *recta* in *Murphy*'s *narratio.* For not only is Murphy on better terms with himself than his predecessor Belacqua, his narrator is on better terms with him. Gone are the complaints about the protagonist's unpredictability or intractability, gone the difficulty of forcing his ungainly person into a Procrustean plot, gone the complaints about having to play deus ex machina, and in their place is a novel with unity of character, concern, and intrigue. We might well wonder why.

Although *Murphy* is one of the best known of Beckett's works (Joyce, for instance, knew passages by heart), some summary is in order so as to understand the problem of mind it poses. The outer life and outward plot, that of what is called the "big world" in the novel, is a great chain of desire. Like Belacqua before him and Watt after him, Murphy is not a particularly agonistic protagonist. "To die fighting," we are told, "was the perfect antithesis of his whole practice, faith and intention"

(GC 1.26). Nevertheless, the movements of his desire for others and those of others for him move the plot at a steady clip.

"The sun shone, having no alternative, on the nothing new," we read in the book's opening lines, and that compelled star shines on London (GC 1.3).[3] Murphy has taken up residence there, supported, though just barely, by a "well-to-do n'er-do-well" Dutch uncle, after having interrupted his studies at a Pythagorean school in Cork run by a sage (of sorts) named Neary, whose principal attraction, and attainment, is his ability to stop his own heart (GC 1.13). Neary does this in "situations irksome beyond endurance, as when he wanted a drink and could not get one, or fell among Gaels and could not escape, or felt the pangs of hopeless sexual inclination" (GC 1.4). Though Murphy has left Cork behind, the mark he left there in the heart of one Miss Counihan puts the story's "big world" plot in motion. While all the principal parties were still in Ireland, Neary loved "Miss Dwyer, who loved a Flight-Lieutenant Elliman, who loved a Miss Farren of Ringsakiddy, who loved a Father Fitt of Ballinclashet, who in all sincerity was bound to acknowledge a certain vocation for a Mrs. West of Passage, who loved Neary" (GC 1.5). This circle is soon to be broken, however, as no sooner has Miss Dwyer "made Neary as happy as a man could desire," then he loses interest in her, and soon thereafter falls under the charms of Miss Counihan, still pining for the departed Murphy she believes is preparing a new life for them in London (GC 1.32). Murphy is doing nothing of the sort, never having intended to and, on top of that, having fallen in love with a former prostitute named Celia. Miss Counihan, unable to contact him, nevertheless has faith in faithless Murphy. To Neary's intense chagrin, he cannot stop his heart from loving Miss Counihan, and she will not consider a transfer of her affections before having word from Murphy, whose precise location is unknown to her.

Though Miss Counihan is beginning to despair of the return of Murphy, she is holding out hope, for which reason Neary undertakes to give her what she requires to displace or to cement her affections—proof either that Murphy is in England earning money for their new life, or has forgotten her. Neary is prevented from doing this in propria persona because he is persona non grata in London, where his estranged wife, Ariadne, pulls too many strings for Neary to move about freely in search of Murphy. Neary thus sends his agent, Cooper, given to drink and possessing numerous physical peculiarities (such as an inability to sit or remove the bowler he will hand down to a host of figures in Beckett's later writing). Despairing of Cooper succeeding in his English quest, Neary follows Miss Counihan to Dublin, is pulled out of a pinch by a former pupil, Wylie, known to Murphy and, like Neary, also in love with the desirable Miss Counihan. Additional intrigues and minor betrayals follow the Irish subplot while Celia and Murphy defy their stars in England.

As will Krapp, Murphy has ambitious "plans for a less . . . engrossing sexual life" (GC 3.224; Beckett's ellipsis). This is an ambition that had long preoccupied Beckett. In his first published story an unnamed "artist" is repeatedly interrupted for erotic, and more than erotic, interludes with an unnamed female visitor. She does not pull him more into the big world, more into life, but out of it, and out of everything. "When at last she went away," after one such visit, "he felt that something had gone out from him, something he could not spare, but still less could grudge, something of the desire to live, something of the unreasonable tenacity with which he shrank from dissolution" (GC 4.60). This has all of the counterintuitive compression of Beckett's early prose, for it is presumed that not simply giving way to "dissolution" is "unreasonable." And yet it is not only erotic connection which presents the problem of dissolution.

The Issue, or Fellowship

Murphy's intrigue is, in a certain sense, simple and serial, following the force of desire, whose various combinations are run through and whose changes turn the plot. Unlike the other Irish parties, Murphy and Celia enjoy reciprocal affection, but there are problems of faith and funds. Murphy loves Celia (inasmuch as he is capable of overcoming his intellectual love of himself for his bodily love of her) and Celia loves Murphy (without restriction). This keeps them together for a time, and might have done so longer were it not required of him that he find a job—which, improbably enough, he does, "washing the bottles and emptying the slops of the better-class mentally deranged" (GC 1.56). In this place Murphy's dualism comes to a head. The battle between the life his body wants to lead in Celia's arms and the one his mind wants to lead in its own is intense, and significantly complicated by his employment in the Magdalen Mental Mercyseat (based in part on Beckett's own observations at the Bethlehem Royal Hospital in Beckenham where his friend Geoffrey Thompson worked and where Beckett was allowed access to the wards).[4] For in this place he finds someone so removed from the world—a certain chess-loving Mr. Endon—that Murphy entertains hopes of fellowship.

The chapter of *Murphy* that introduces us to the Magdalen Mental Mercyseat has something rare in that work, and in Beckett's writing: an epigraph: *Il est difficile à celui qui vit hors du monde de ne pas rechercher les siens* (GC 1.95). Beckett gives the author but neither a translation nor the name of the work from which it is drawn, André Malraux's *The Human Condition* (1933). "It is difficult for one living out of this world not to seek his own" is what Murphy finds in his madhouse. Malone will recount of his own attempts at fellowship with a certain Jackson:

> I could have put up with him as a friend, but unfortunately he found me disgusting, as did Johnson, Wilson, Nicholson and Watson, all whore-sons. I then tried, for a space, to lay hold of a kindred spirit among the inferior races, red, yellow, chocolate, and so on. And if the plague-stricken had been less difficult of access I would have intruded on them too, ogling, sidling, leering, ineffing and conating, my heart palpitating. With the insane too I failed, by a hair's-breadth. (GC 2.212; 72)

Murphy's failure is a similarly close call, but it is far more drawn out. Murphy sees through, or around, the suffering of the patients under his care to an ideal state where the conflict between the little world of one's own mind is given primacy over the big world where other minds commingle, also called in that novel (borrowing a phrase from William James) the "big blooming buzzing confusion" (GC 1.5; 1.21). As if reaching the same conclusion as Freud during these same years about the discontent to which civilization consigns each individual, Murphy seeks a special exemption from the dictates of desire, which he dreams might be found in more resolutely residing in the "little world" of his mind. And yet he cannot help wondering if there is not another like him, and cannot check his desire to find out. Struck by the same notion, the Unnamable exclaims:

> that would be lovely, my first like [*mon premier semblable*], that would be epoch-making, to know I had a like, a congener, he wouldn't have to be like me, he couldn't but be like me, he need only relax, he might believe what he pleased, at the outset, that he was in hell, or that the place was charming. (GC 2.371; 152)

The Belacqua of Beckett's first book invokes what he calls his "precarious ipsissimosity" (*Dream*, 113). In *More Pricks Than Kicks* the phrase becomes "*precious* ipsissimosity," and thereby presents the problem that will dominate the minds of all Belacqua's successors—for as long as they believe they have one (GC 4.164; my emphasis). The patients in the Magdalen Mental Mercyseat seem to Murphy champions of the "little world," proud possessors of an ipsissimity that has ceased to be precarious. So intense is its power that it dwarfs any and all "big world" considerations and holds out to Murphy the promise of peace. It is impossible for Murphy then not to seek his own amongst them, to want to share a human condition in which he is free from desire. His search ends with a game of chess. Murphy plays the king of the mad: the most retiring, the most distant, the most sovereignly indifferent patient, the mysterious Mr. Endon. Taking the measure of Mr. Endon's indifference to the big world, the big blooming buzzing confusion in which Murphy is just one more mote, Murphy discovers in himself a desire for contact. After their final game of chess (whose every move is noted in the book, along with wry annotations), Murphy lowers his head in defeat. He has lost the game (a very strange one), but more significantly he has lost to a big world consideration he had not been fully aware that he had, and which his will cannot master. He wants a like, a congener, a fellow and friend, and he cannot find it in Mr. Endon. The complicity he thought they had subtly, silently achieved proves to be no complicity at all. What Murphy saw as a strange sort of communication was, for Mr. Endon, chess. Mr. Endon does not—or, perhaps, cannot—even deign to reject Murphy's offer of idiosyncratic friendship. He allows Murphy to take his head into his hands and fix his eyes upon his own, but what he offers to Murphy's gaze is nothing but Murphy's own reflection. Murphy sees that "the relation between Mr. Murphy and Mr. Endon could not have been better summed up than by the former's sorrow at seeing himself in the latter's immunity from seeing anything but himself" (GC 1.150). "The issue," we learn, "as lovingly simplified and perverted by Murphy, lay between nothing less fundamental than the big world and the little world, decided by the patients in favour of the latter, revived by the psychiatrists on behalf of the former, in his own case unresolved" (GC 1.107). Murphy discovers that he is sad to find no fellowship in those who have cast their vote for "the little world." And it is in this final sense that Murphy has lovingly simplified and perverted "the issue."

This issue of isolation will stay with Beckett to the end, in increasingly acute form. In *Ill Seen Ill Said* (1981), the protagonist "shows herself only to her own [*aux siens*]. But she has no own" (GC 4.453; 15). A more elaborate search shapes Beckett's fantastical *The Lost Ones* (1970). That work begins with a strange setting: *"Séjour où des corps vont cherchant chacun son dépeupleur* [Abode where lost bodies roam each searching for its lost one]" (GC 4.381; 7). What, a French reader of 1970 might wonder, is a *dépeupleur*? The term is strange, but it has a like in French literature: a poem by Lamartine's entitled—aptly enough—"Isolation," where we read:

> *Que me font ces vallons, ces palais, ces chaumières,*
> *Vains objets dont pour moi le charme est envolé?*
> *Fleuves, rochers, forêts, solitudes si chères,*
> *Un seul être vous manque, et tout est dépeuplé!*

> What are they to me, these glens, these palaces, these cottages,
> Vain objects the charm of which has flown.
> Rivers, rocks, forests, beloved solitudes,
> You lack a single being, and all is unpeopled! (Lamartine 1963, 3)

In the state Lamartine describes, the loss of a single person leads to the loss of everything: the world is depopulated by the loss of the loved one. The narrator of *The Lost Ones,* like all in that abode, searches for his like. The special cruelty of the work lies in that he is suffered to find her, only to find her lost to him. With the same gesture as Murphy's with

Mr. Endon, he will gaze into "the calm wastes" of her eyes, inaccessible and forever lost (GC 4.399; 55). Finding his lost one does not repopulate his world any more than Murphy finds fellowship in the Magdalen Mental Mercyseat. "What mattered to me most in my depeopled kingdom," says the narrator of Beckett's first French fiction, *First Love*, "that in regard to which the disposition of my carcass was the merest and most futile of accidents, was supineness in the mind [*la supination cérébrale*], the dulling of the self and of that residue of execrable frippery known as the non-self and even the world, for short" (GC 4.234; 21).

The Life of the Mind

In chapter 6—given the Spinozian heading *"Amor intellectualis quo Murphy se ipsum amat"* ("the intellectual love through which Murphy loves himself")—the narrator declares, "It is most unfortunate, but the point of this story has been reached where a justification of the expression 'Murphy's mind' has to be attempted" (GC 1.67). For Murphy, "life in his mind gave him pleasure, such that pleasure was not the word," but not just any life, and not just any mind, would do when dealing, in the words of one of Murphy's successors, with "a mind like the one I always had, always on the alert against itself" (GC 1.70). In *Dream of Fair to Middling Women* Belacqua asked, "Could anything be better, in this world or next," than "the mind, dim and hushed like a sick-room, like a chapelle ardente, thronged with shades; the mind at last its own asylum" (*Dream*, 44). Murphy finds the answer to this question in an actual asylum. For Belacqua, the conscious, willing mind casts a glaring light that obscures the seen and the seer, and for this reason Beckett has him dream of "the mind suddenly reprieved, ceasing to be an annex of the restless body, the glare of understanding switched off" (*Dream*, 44). This "starless inscrutable hour," as Beckett called it in "Whorosocope," is the one for which Belacqua, and all that fall after him, pine (GC 4.6). Belacqua had called this mental no-man's-land "the tunnel," and his experience of it made up what he deemed the most "real" element of his existence—"in the umbra, the tunnel, when the mind went wombtomb, then it was real thought and real living, living thought . . . live cerebration that drew no wages and emptied no slops" (*Dream*, 45). For this reason

Belacqua rejects Alba's term for his mental activity. "'I do not brood' he said resentfully. 'My mind goes blank. It is no brooding, it is no reflecting. It is the abdication of the daily mind, it is the hush and gloom ousting the workaday glare'" (*Dream*, 191).[5] Whereas for Belacqua "it was impossible to switch off the inward glare, willfully to suppress the bureaucratic mind," Murphy has refined a technique (chair, scarves) allowing him to outwit his will and its attachment to the world (*Dream*, 123).

What does Murphy then find there, in the dark of his mind? In *Dream of Fair to Middling Women* there is a point when du Chas accosts Belacqua, who finds himself thereby "violated in the quiet of his mind" (*Dream*, 203). In *More Pricks Than Kicks* the same scenario is repeated, this time leaving Belacqua "violated in the *murmur* of his mind" (GC 4.110; my emphasis). By *Watt* this murmur is already loud enough to start drowning out the outside world, as when Watt hears next to nothing of Mr. Spiro's tale in the train "because of other voices, singing, crying, stating, murmuring, things unintelligible, in his ear" (GC 1.190). Beckett does not often grant his reader a glimpse into the innermost reaches of Watt's mind, but when he does the unintelligible litany reemerges, as at the end of the book we read, "In [Watt's] skull the voices whispering their canon were like a patter of mice, a flurry of little grey paws in the dust" (GC 1.359). In the works that follow, these voices rise in pitch. Belacqua's initial quietude becomes increasingly rare in Beckett's work, replaced by a murmur that Murphy will try to rock away and that his successors will hear ringing in their ears to their dying day (*Dream*, 44, 113; GC 4.164).

As the narrator carefully explains, Murphy's mind is divided into multiple regions which it is capable of reaching on the condition that it is freed from Murphy's body. "There were three zones," we are told, "light, half light, dark, each with its specialty" (GC 1.69). The first, "a radiant abstract of a dog's life," is wish fulfillment—or, as Beckett's narrator more simply calls it, "reprisal" (GC 1.69). In such a fantasy-formed state Murphy recasts past experience. "Here," we are told, "the whole physical fiasco became a howling success" (GC 1.69). The second circle of Murphy's mind, that of "half light," has less contour. In it are "forms without parallel" where "the pleasure is contemplation"—though *what* is contemplated cannot be defined (GC 1.69). "Here," the narrator continues, "was the Belacqua bliss and others scarcely less precise" (GC 1.69). Whatever it is, this contemplation clearly involves some sort of organized, albeit abstract, thought. In this it differs from the third and essentially spaceless space, the night of Murphy's mind in which all dogs are gray. "The third, the dark," we read, "was a flux of forms, a perpetual coming together and falling asunder of forms" (GC 1.70). In the dark of his mind Murphy loses all sense of self and any conscious control of the movements of his mind: "Here he was not free, but a mote in the absolute freedom" (GC 1.70). This proves, however, short-lived.

In Beckett's early fiction the dominant dream is less of fair to middling women than of sovereign isolation in the mind. The terrible turn this takes in Beckett's great works is that his mature creations live only in the little world, and find no relief from it. *Murphy* could dedicate an entire chapter to Murphy's mind. By the time we reach the trilogy doubt will be cast as to whether such a thing exists. The Unnamable will refer to a finding that "shocked me profoundly, to such a degree that my mind (Mahood dixit) was assailed by insuperable doubts" (GC 2.315). As concerns questions he will say, "perhaps before long, who knows, I shall light on the happy combination which will prevent them from ever arising again in my—let us not be over-nice—mind" (GC 2.305). The Unnamable may have a mind, but it is nothing to dwell upon. In *Not I*, the voice says, "like maddened . . . all that together . . . straining to hear . . . piece it together . . . and the brain . . . raving away on its own . . . trying to make sense of it . . . or make it stop" (GC 3.410; Beckett's ellipses). The brain in Beckett's later work raves away all on its own because it cannot make sense of its surroundings and cannot stop trying, resulting in voices like that of *Eh Joe* (1965), denouncing "that penny farthing hell you call your mind" (GC 3.393).

How Not to Read Philosophy, or Reading Schopenhauer

In the 1970s a much marked-up first edition of Beckett's first book, *Proust*, was discovered in a Dublin bookstore. On its title page was the note: "I have written my book in cheap flashy philosophical jargon." The handwriting proved to be Beckett's own (Bair 1990, 109). Beckett was rarely happy with his work, and juvenilia is never easy to revisit (as Krapp is made to hear), but aside from the matter of self-castigation we might ask what philosophical jargon Beckett saw himself employing—all the more as *Proust* seems quite free of philosophical jargon. What there is, however, is from a single source: Arthur Schopenhauer.

In 1961 Beckett was asked whether "contemporary philosophers had any influence on your thought," to which he replied: "I never read philosophers." When asked why not, he said, "I never understand anything they write" (D'Aubarède 1961, 1). More than thirty years earlier, as Beckett was preparing his book on Proust, he wrote to McGreevy from the *École Normale* in Paris, "I am reading Schopenhauer. Everyone laughs at that" (LSB 1.32-33). The "everyone" in question are the *normaliens* McGreevy knew well (having preceded Beckett at the post), such as the young Jean Beaufret, who was to become the tip of France's Heideggerian spear, and who presumably found Schopenhauer's considerations on willing in the world less than riveting. Beckett adds in his letter, "but I am not reading philosophy, nor caring whether [Schopenhauer] is right or wrong or a good or worthless metaphysician" (LSB 1.33). The statement "I am not reading philosophy" is one that Beckett trusts McGreevy to understand in several senses. He is underlining the fact that, unlike Beaufret and the other *normaliens,* he is not reading philosophy so as to pass an examination and is thus under no obligation to read systematically, or even sensibly. But Beckett is also saying something more to his literary purposes: that he reads philosophy for literature. "It is a pleasure," as Beckett said elsewhere of Schopenhauer, "to find a philosopher that can be read like a poet" (LSB 1.550). While laid up with gastric influenza in 1937 Beckett "found the only thing I could read was Schopenhauer" (LSB 1.550). "I always knew he was one of the ones that mattered most to me," he added, "and it is a pleasure more real than any pleasure for a long time to begin to understand now why it is so" (LSB 1.550). Schopenhauer's "intellectual justification of unhappiness—the greatest that has ever been attempted"—was, it appeared, reason enough (LSB 1.33).

Schopenhauer was a pessimist in almost every sense of the term. He deems the world and its societies formed by "chance and error," and finds that excellence in any domain of human thought or action is "as rare as a meteorite" (Schopenhauer 1986, 1.444). Looking at the woe which is our world, Schopenhauer thinks of the literary figure most dear to Beckett, asking his reader, "Where else than in our real world did Dante find that from which he made his *Inferno?*" (Schopenhauer 1986, 1.445). *Jede Lebensgeschichte ist eine Leidensgeschichte,* "the story of every life is a story of suffering," is the clearest formula it is given in *The World as Will and Representation* (Schopenhauer 1986, 1.444). The reason for this dreadful state of affairs is not something Schopenhauer has a hard time naming: it is the *will.* For Schopenhauer, the problem with life is nothing historical and nothing contingent: the problem with life is life. The only way to lessen the pain is to loosen our ties to its source: the world in which we live.

In *Molloy* Moran hears a story in which a certain Gaber tells of how a certain Youdi (their employer, and perhaps a lunatic) had told him that "life is a thing of beauty," and, what is more, "a joy for ever." Moran has seen something of the world and interrupts him: "Do you think he meant human life?" (GC 2.158–159; 164). It is difficult to surpass in pessimism Beckett's early work, except in his middle and late work, from the tailor in *Endgame* who compares the world (very unfavorably) to his pants, to the figure in *Ill Seen Ill Said* who "rails at the principle of all life" (GC 4.451; 7). It is one thing to call the world names, another to advance an intellectual justification of unhappiness in it, the reason Schopenhauer was deemed by the young Beckett such fine company. Beckett called Schopenhauer's "an *intellectual* justification of unhappiness" because, for Schopenhauer, life is not accidentally painful, it is essentially painful, and it is even knowable as such. Schopenhauer describes this pain with all the sensitivity and subtlety of a poet, but he also traces it as would a philosopher: to a source. The source of suffering is the source of life, and to this thing he gives the slightly confusing name *will.* We suffer because we want, or will, things. We suffer if we do not get what we want, just as we suffer when we do get what we want, for no sooner gotten than the spark leaps, the fire spreads, and away our will goes blazing anew. This is a vicious circle that all Beckett's early protagonists are given to see, resulting first in measures such as Murphy's, then in those which move right out of the world, in the trilogy.

This first part of Schopenhauer's philosophy is intuitive enough. What set it apart for Beckett—as it had for so many before him, from Nietzsche to Tolstoy to Thomas Mann—is the assertion that this *will* was not peculiar to individuals. *Will* was the name Schopenhauer gave to the generative principle in life itself. Not only do we strive for certain things, all life manifests this same striving. Nonhuman animals obviously want things, even if they want them in different ways, and obviously strive to obtain them. They impose their wills. Even plants, Schopenhauer found, show this striving principle in their growth. By *will,* then, as the young Beckett read, Schopenhauer means a force pervading, animating, and, in a sense, constituting all life. For Augustine the will accounts for the presence of evil in the world;[6] for Schopenhauer it accounts for the world itself. The meaning of Schopenhauer's title *The World as Will and Representation* was to be found in the fact that, for him, in its core and essence, the world *is* will—not as the sum of individual wills, plant and animal, but as a single force of which individual wills partake and from which they only *appear* to be distinct (which is where *representation* enters the picture).

As Beckett well knew, Schopenhauer found a relief and release from the ever-turning will in art, as through art "Ixion's wheel comes to a stop" (Schopenhauer 1986, 1.283). For Schopenhauer, art represented a respite from willing, and it was the great virtue of art that it allowed us to achieve an aesthetic remove where Ixion's wheel of willing stood still, where the movements of the individual will cease and we can hear in the silence the sound of another will, a will greater than ours, a will of which ours is but the echo. This latter, transcendental, aspect of Schopenhauer's philosophy Beckett ignores entirely, and it leaves no trace in the philosophical terminology, jargon or not, of his first book.

In *Rough for Theatre II* (1976), as the inspectors A and B discuss the case of C, perched on a windowsill ready to leap, they rifle through his papers and find among the "bits and scraps" reasons to refrain from killing oneself. These include concrete matters such as "the good graces of an heirless aunt" and an "unfinished game of chess with a correspondent in Tasmania," intermixed with more metaphysical ones such as the "hope not dead of living to see the extermination of the species"— followed by "literary aspirations incompletely stifled . . . bottom of a dairy-woman in Waterloo Lane . . . you see that kind of thing" (GC 3.248; Beckett's ellipses). It is of course the essence of that play's wit, and world, that the pleasure of witnessing the extermination of the human species is set alongside that of watching the bottom of a dairy-woman in Waterloo Lane, as well as the greatly-to-be-wished extinction of literary striving.

The Artist's View

Schopenhauer's discussion of art is conducted from the side of the spectator, and involves a detailed analysis of forms. Beckett's view of art differs in that it is seen from the side of the artist—or of the character in the work who is creating, who is trying to create and trying to stop, all the while powerless to still his individual will. What most captivated Beckett was not the transcendental element of Schopenhauer's philosophy, but the problem it is made to solve: that the individual will is the source of universal woe. From this Schopenhauer forms his highest aspiration—found in the experience of great works of art—which is freedom (or respite) from the will. The wheel is still there and we are still as tightly fixed to it as Murphy is to his chair, but it stops its torturous turning for a moment. It is this idea that Beckett will develop, turning the tables of art, turning from the freed state of the spectator to the bound one of the creator. The reason that Beckett does not care whether Schopenhauer is a "worthless metaphysician" or not is that he does not care about the metaphysical postulate of Schopenhauer's pessimism. For he never even entertains the central element of Schopenhauer's philosophy: the transcendent will of which all wills are but a part. With it goes all durable respite—even, and especially, in art. It is in this respect that Beckett's view of art, and life, is far more bleak than Schopenhauer's.

The best study of *Watt* begins by noting, "*Watt*, an improbable novel, was written under impossible conditions. Or vice versa" (Ackerley 2010b, 5). The finest critic of Beckett's early writing calls *Watt* "manically intransigent" and "the oddest of all Beckett's works" (the reader may recall how stiff the competition is in this category), adding that "so peculiar is [*Watt*] that one may find oneself imagining a personal crisis," despite the notable fact that "the biographical evidence is at best ambiguous in this connection, and in fact offers some proofs to the contrary" (Pilling 1994a, 37, 35). Marjorie Perloff suggests that the reason

Watt is so strange is that it mimics the espionage code the author had employed in the French Resistance (it is unlikely that she had in mind the fact—little known when she wrote her essay—that Beckett's novel was actually mistaken for code by British authorities). In short, even the most astute and informed of Beckett's critics find *Watt* to present a mystery that is difficult to explain without recourse to an unknown event or obscure key. We might even include Beckett himself in this uncertain group, as he wrote as early as 1951, "I re-read almost all of that odd work and was able to establish, to my satisfaction, that I no longer understand anything of it" (LSB 2.276; 277; translation modified).

One reason for *Watt*'s difficulty is the will to resist, and the means taken to try and tax the will. For this reason *Watt* reads at points like a variation on the theme of variations, from frog-croaking to Mr. Knoll's mealtimes to Arsene's generations:

> And the poor old lousy old earth, my earth and my father's and my mother's and my father's father's and my mother's mother's and my father's mother's and my mother's father's and my father's mother's father's and my mother's father's mother's and my father's mother's mother's and my mother's father's father's and my father's father's mother's and my mother's mother's father's and my father's father's father's and my mother's mother's mother's and other people's fathers' and mothers' and fathers' fathers' and mothers' mothers' and fathers' mothers' and mothers' fathers' and fathers' mother's fathers' and mothers' fathers' mothers' and fathers' mothers' mothers' and mothers' fathers' fathers' and fathers' fathers' mothers' fathers' fathers' and fathers' fathers' mothers' and mothers' mothers' fathers' and fathers' fathers' fathers' and mothers' mothers' mothers'.
> An excrement. (GC 1.205)

The world is an excrement—or, as the epigraph to *Proust,* taken from another great pessimist, Leopardi, puts it: "And the world is mud." *Watt* lists variations as *The Iliad* lists warriors, with the exception that the lists are meant to be mind-numbing. Tom Stoppard has a character in *If You're Glad I'll Be Frank* remark: "I used to say ad nauseam but it goes on long after you feel sick" (Stoppard 1978, 12). *Watt*'s variations do not stop once the initial point is made that things might have been otherwise. This is then the mystery of Beckett's variations, and what sets them apart from such serial experiments as those of Gertrude Stein. Her "Picasso" (1912), for instance, begins, "One whom some were certainly following was one who was completely charming," and its first paragraphs consist of variations on this phrase, displacing now one term, now another, without the permutations ever becoming wholly predictable (Stein 2008, 104). Beckett, however, goes through his serial variations one by one, making them painstakingly predictable, and is so careful in doing this that while writing *Watt* he made grids in which he then meticulously checked them off, despite the fact that any reasonable reader is able to fill in the blanks without the slightest difficulty. This is indeed odd—so much so that it is not odd that Pilling, Perloff, and others have searched for biographical reasons, for a crisis or pathology, to explain them—as if to say, *Murphy* was so much fun, albeit strange fun, so why this negation of fun, why this deliberate unpleasantness, why this pointless punctiliousness? Beckett's "maddeningly prolix pseudo-logic," as Northrop Frye once called it, is pleasing for some but trying for all (Frye, 1960, 444). The reason for these mind-numbing variations is, however, precisely that they numb the mind and still the will—the very message the young Beckett read between the poetic lines of Rimbaud and the philosophical ones of Schopenhauer.

What is common to Beckett's philosophical reasoning—to his readings of Democritus, Descartes, Leibniz, Geulincx, Schopenhauer, Sartre, Heidegger, Wittgenstein, and many others—was his vehement rejection of any transcendent term, from the Will of Schopenhauer to the God of Geulincx, to the being that all beings share in Heidegger and essential existence in Sartre. The striking commonality to be found in Beckett's use of philosophical ideas and doctrines is in how he hollowed them out, how he excised the transcendental element.

Schopenhauer's most admiring, insightful, and demanding reader, Nietzsche, found that Schopenhauer's work fell short because "like everyone else he *believed* in the simplicity and immediacy of all willing—whereas willing is actually such a well-practiced mechanism that it almost escapes the observing eye" (Nietzsche 1999, 3.483; Nietzsche's emphasis). When Beckett's speakers begin to realize this, they experience a natural frustration and respond with unnatural ferocity. In

Dante's *Inferno* the damned will in death as they did in life. Dante sees the lustful wanting, and therefore willing, the storm of passion in which they are blown about; the vengeful wanting, and thereby willing, retribution in a river of blood. In Beckett's "willed creative mismaking" we find something similar: a will over which his creations have literally no control, and which becomes not just *a* theme in Beckett's greatest works, but the central one.

CHAPTER THREE

Nature Painting

As HAD WATT, *Endgame* presents a picture concealed from sight. When the stage lights come up it is turned against the wall. Perhaps what it depicts has fallen into disgrace, perhaps depicting has. Later in the play it will be replaced by an alarm clock. In the meantime, Hamm, not much for stories, tells one on this theme:

> I once knew a madman who thought the end of the world had come.
> He was a painter—and engraver. I had a great fondness for him. I used
> to go and see him, in the asylum. I'd take him by the hand and drag
> him to the window. Look! There! All that rising corn! And there!
> Look! The sails of the herring fleet! All that loveliness!
>   [*Pause.*]
> He'd snatch away his hand and go back into his corner. Appalled. All
> he had seen was ashes.
>   [*Pause.*]
> He alone had been spared. (GC 3.122; 62)

Hamm admires the prescient gaze of the painter—and engraver. And this choice of calling is unsurprising from someone such as Beckett, who thought seriously about becoming an art historian, who would go on to collaborate with contemporary artists such as Giacometti and

Avigdor Arikha, and who would remain his whole life long fascinated by the visual arts. In his first books Beckett's interest in painting and its prophetic gazes is almost embarrassingly present. *More Pricks Than Kicks* plays, for instance, a game borrowed from Proust: having a character see his love through the eyes of Renaissance painting. Just as Odette's charm in Swann's eyes was enhanced by her resemblance to Botticelli's daughter of Jethro, the Ruby Belacqua follows is made more appealing by her resemblance to the Magdalene of Perugino's *Pietà*. Beckett's letters of the 1930s, 1940s, and 1950s are full of paintings as, for instance, when the Irish National Gallery acquired a Perugino (*The Lamentation over the Dead Christ*, 1495) about which Beckett wrote to Mc-Greevy (then little more than a student, but who would go on to direct the National Gallery) to praise its virtues, irreverently delighted as he was by the "lovely cheery Xist full of sperm & and the woman touching his thighs and mourning his jewels" (LSB 1.100). Beckett will be equally inspired in later years by other paintings, although he will be careful to keep them out of sight. To intimates, however, he repeatedly noted such things as that the inspiration for *Waiting for Godot* came from Caspar David Friedrich, and that *Not I* was conceived while gazing at Caravaggio's *Beheading of John the Baptist* (Gussow 1996, 34). Though such direct reference as Belacqua's will grow rare in Beckett's later works, it will never disappear, as where a much-diminished Malone recalls "Tiepolo's ceiling at Würzburg" (GC 2.228; 101). In 1936 Beckett wrote, "I used never to be happy with a picture till it was literature, but now that need is gone" (LSB 1.388). The process of learning to look at paintings in and for themselves involved a long period of apprenticeship during which Beckett looked to painting for an aesthetic he could understand in the terms of his own art.[1] Of particular importance for understanding Beckett's art is, however, a genre with which he is not often associated: landscape painting.

Landscape Painting and the Forest of Symbols

Exasperated by codependence, Estragon turns to Vladimir and exclaims: "You and your landscapes! Tell me about the worms!" (In the original he is still harsher: *"Alors fous-moi la paix avec tes paysages!"*: "Fuck off with your landscapes!" *Godot*, 206; 207). A decade earlier, however, no such impatience was to be heard, and the focus was still solidly above ground. Beckett found that Cézanne "seems to have been the first to see landscape & state it as material of a strictly peculiar order, incommensurable with all human expressions whatsoever" (LSB 1.222). Beckett loved the landscapes of Old Masters, but saw Cézanne surpassing them in terms that were epistemological as much as aesthetic. Cézanne's artistic achievement was based, for Beckett, on an insight into the relation of man to nature, which is no intelligible relation at all. Through his "atomistic landscape with no velleities of vitalism" Cézanne effected, in the young Beckett's eyes, a revolution of representation (LSB 1.222). For Beckett, Cézanne went so much farther than "Manet & Co." by venturing toward a point where "he could understand the dynamic intrusion to be himself & so landscape to be something by definition unapproachably alien, unintelligible arrangement of atoms, not so much as ruffled by the kind attentions of the Reliability Joneses" (LSB 1.223). In the art which most moved Beckett, man is emphatically not the measure of all things, so much so that Beckett will include in a list of those things "capable of ruining for us poetry, music, painting and philosophy for the next fifty years" "the philosopher who says: Protagoras was right" (Beckett 1984, 132).

Cézanne, however, does more than put man in his place. Beckett will also praise how he expresses "the sense of his incommensurability not only with life of such a different order as landscape but even with life of his own order, even with the life . . . operative in himself" (LSB 1.227). It is not only the outside which is "incommensurable" with the inside, the inside is incommensurable with itself. With such achievement in mind the narrator of Beckett's first novel will remark, "we were once upon a time inclined to fancy ourself as the Cézanne, shall we say, of the printed page" (*Dream*, 178). What Beckett scrutinizes so closely, admires so intensely, and writes of so passionately in Cézanne's paintings is an estranged image of the natural world. Beckett finds a fellow traveler down this artistic road in Jack Yeats (the poet's brother). "What I feel he gets so well," Beckett remarked, is "the heterogeneity of nature & the human denizens, the unalterable alienness of the 2 phenomena" (LSB 1.540). During his trip through Nazi Germany, Beckett praised how

Karl Ballmer's painting presented "not nature convention, but its source, fountain of Erscheinung [appearance]. Fully a posteriori painting. Object not exploited to illustrate an idea" (Beckett 2011, 156). Reflecting on "the dramatic predicament" facing Masson—that of "an artist who seems literally skewered on the ferocious dilemma of expression"—Beckett cryptically commented, *"The stars are undoubtedly superb,* as Freud remarked on reading Kant's cosmological proof of the existence of God" (GC 4.558; Beckett's emphasis). Freud's remark wryly distinguishes the starry skies above from the moral law within, and it is just this sort of separation Beckett himself would prize, whether in the canvases of Cézanne or Freud's critique of pure reason. In a talk given at the National Gallery of Ireland (where Perugino's *Lamentation* still hangs), John Banville declared, "my contention is that Beckett is an old-style landscape artist, certainly in his novels anyway" (Banville 2006, 91). Banville went on to note that "few support my view, and Beckett is thought of as a man who deprecated nature" (Banville 2006, 91). Beckett indeed did not deprecate nature, but he did deprecate with rare vehemence the domesticated image of it made by man, and from which he felt that artists must free themselves.

Elsewhere in Beckett's German letter to Kaun there is something of an epigram: "For in the forest of symbols (that aren't ones) the tiny birds of interpretation (which isn't) are never silent [*Denn im Walde der Symbole, die keine sind, schweigen die Vöglein der Deutung, die keine ist, nie*]" (LSB 1.514). Beckett makes several claims here, all of which are confusing. If the symbols in the forest of symbols are not symbols, why call them thus? If the interpretation of the tiny birds of interpretation is not interpretation, why call it thus? An initial answer to these questions is to be found in the image Beckett has in mind, and hopes his reader will summon up.

In his first book, six years earlier, Beckett had told readers that Proust "admires the frescoes of the Paduan Arena because their symbolism is handled as a reality, special, literal and concrete, and is not merely the pictorial transmission of a notion" (GC 4.547). The frescoes in question are the Vices and Virtues of Padua decorating the small Scrovegni Chapel (also known as the Arena Chapel) painted by Giotto at the beginning of the fourteenth century. Proust's treatment of them had interested Beckett enough for him to weave them into an early poem.[2] The cycle they form is among the most famous allegorical works of the Renaissance, which might lead us to forget for what Giotto was famous when he completed them: his mastery of *realistic* representation. Boccaccio, for his influential part, saw Giotto's "extraordinary genius" in the fact that "there was nothing of all that Nature, mother and mover of all things . . . that [Giotto] could not render with pencil and pen and brush—and so closely that it was not just similar, but seemed to be the thing itself" (Boccaccio 2013, VI.5, 550). Vasari's description of the young Giotto follows the same lines as he recounts how Cimabue happened upon the young Giotto in the act of drawing, perfectly, on a rock, the sheep he was meant to guard (Vasari 1906, 370-71). Like the great painters of classical antiquity, such as the Zeuxis whose work was so realistic that it was said to attract birds who would try to peck at its painted grapes, or the Apelles whose depictions of horses were rumored to make real ones neigh, Giotto's art was seen by his contemporaries as so great that it seemed to transcend art and trick nature. It was for this reason that he enjoyed, in the words of his friend Dante, *il grido* ("great acclaim").[3]

Beckett reminds his reader that Proust found Giotto's Vices and Virtues so special because they fused particular and general, presenting *Caritas* and *Invidia* not as abstract allegories, but as "reality, special, literal and concrete." To this reminder Beckett appends an appraisal, the most gnomic one in the book: "for Proust the object may be a living symbol, but a symbol of itself. The symbolism of Baudelaire has become the *autosymbolism* of Proust" (GC 4.547; Beckett's emphasis). It is one thing for a great artist to depict an object with such skill and inspiration that it seems alive. But this is not what Beckett is saying—or not all that he is saying. The object depicted is not only living, it is a living *symbol*, so much so that it is able to do that which should be impossible: symbolize itself. The "symbolism of Baudelaire" to which Beckett here opposes Proust's "autosymbolism" is another reference he expects his readers to recognize, finding expression as it does in one of the most famous poems in French literature, Baudelaire's "Correspondances." That poem's first stanza reads:

La Nature est un temple où de vivants piliers
Laissent parfois sortir de confuses paroles;
L'homme y passe à travers des forêts de symboles
Qui l'observent avec des regards familiers.

Nature is a temple, where the living
Columns sometimes breathe confusing speech;
Man walks within these groves of symbols, each
Of which regards him as a kindred thing.
(Baudelaire 1975–1976, 1.11; Baudelaire 1993, 19)

Beckett sets Proust's manner of describing the world around him as opposing Baudelaire's evocation of a Nature in which the poet is addressed by his surroundings.[4] For Beckett, nature is not "like a temple," because it is not *like* anything man-made. (This is, at the very least, an exaggerated image of Baudelaire's poem, but one which Beckett felt strongly enough about to repeat on several occasions.) Elsewhere Beckett wrote of a "promeneur solitaire, micturating without fear or favor in a décor that does not demand to be entertained," and it is precisely such a stroller he missed in Baudelaire and found in Proust (LSB 1.228).

In the wilds of *Watt,* well before we are given the last word on symbols and intention, we read: "Through the grass the little mosspaths, bony with old roots, and the trees sticking up, and the flowers sticking up, and the fruit hanging down, and the white exhausted butterflies, and the birds never the same darting all day into hiding. And all the sounds meaning nothing" (GC 1.199). This could hardly be farther from the forest of Baudelairean concordance Beckett denounced. In *Watt,* "nature is so exceedingly accommodating, on the one hand, and man, on the other," only for those willing to live the lie of it (GC 1.200). Beckett's version of pastoral thus involves unexpected elements, as where we find "the crocuses and the larch turning green every year a week before the others and the pastures red with uneaten sheep's placentas and the long summer days and the newmown hay and the woodpigeon in the morning" (GC 1.205). The minute observation of nature's lovely rhythms is interlaced with the unlovely gore (strewn sheep placentas, blood-clotted grass, and images of sheep feasting on afterbirth not being part of the traditional pastoral repertoire). In the forest of Arden we hear that "this our life, exempt from public haunt, / Finds tongues in trees, books in the running brooks, / Sermons in stones, and good in every thing" (*As You Like It*, 2.1). Beckett's characters find no tongues in trees, see no parallel between books and brooks, sense no sermons in stones, and, as for the good, the less said the better.

Autosymbolism demands an autonomy for the work of art so great that it is out of range of human projections. As Molloy surveys things from his room—the movement of the boughs without, the shifting of the light within—he is confused. "But that there were natural causes to all these things," he says, "I am willing to concede, for the resources of nature are infinite apparently. It was I who was not natural enough to enter into that order of things, and appreciate its niceties" (GC 2.39). Beckett's first step in mismaking is to nullify the natural order. In *Molloy* the natural world with copses, bogs, hills, and dales is on its way out of Beckett's writing, and by the end of the trilogy the Unnamable will find himself in no need of such niceties. Beckett wrote of Jacob van Ruysdael's *Entrance to the Forest* that "there is no entrance anymore nor any commerce with the forest, its dimensions are its secret and it has no communications to make" (LSB 1.222). In the same spirit Beckett will dismiss "reasonable" painting where "every brushstroke is a symbol [*chaque trait symbole*]" (Beckett 1984, 127). Beckett favored a very different image of nature, from the flagging tree of *Waiting for Godot* to the clear-cut worlds of *All Strange Away* (1964) and *The Lost Ones*. It is this space that Beckett will champion, defending "all that painting offers of the unreasoned, the naive, the not-a-trick, the botched [*de l'irraisonné, d'ingénu, de non-combine, de mal-léché*]" (Beckett 1984, 127). As work was underway on the set for *Waiting for Godot* Beckett repeatedly lost patience with what he called "Wagnerism," and by which he meant all that would make for a mellifluent merger of man and nature. "In *Godot*," Beckett declared, "it is a sky that is sky only in name, a tree that makes them wonder whether it is one, tiny and shriveled. I should like to see it thrown up any old way [*foutu n'importe comment*], sordidly abstract as nature is [*sordidement abstrait comme la nature l'est*]" (LSB 2.218). All the -isms Beckett opposes—"realism," "vitalism," "animism," "rationalism," and "naturalism"—are, for him, versions of the same deceptive impulse: to fool an audience into thinking what is on stage is real, alive, reasonable, and natural. Divining what Beckett's works might say to, for, or about the world in which they were made is so difficult because Beckett has set his depth charges deeper than historical significance or cultural connection: they are set at the level of natural relation. By the time we get to *How It Is* this is programmatically laid before us: "mix it all up change the natural order play about with that" (GC 2.489; 166). Beckett's art, *foutu n'importe comment,* presents an idea of natural connection which is *no* connection. With it goes all sense that man is the measure of anything but his own shifting, shambling, shivering self. In *Godot*'s successor we find a more succinct statement of the matter. After Hamm laments, "Nature has forgotten us," Clov reminds him, "There's no more nature" (GC 3.99; 23).

CHAPTER FOUR

The Alibi of a Foreign Language

THE SUBJECT of Beckett's first book, Proust, once wrote that "beautiful books are always written in a sort of foreign language [*les beaux livres sont toujours écrits dans une sorte de langue étrangère*]," a paradoxical position that Beckett was to show every sign of having taken to heart—and then literally (Proust 1971, 299). Before changing literary languages Beckett routinely expressed artistic anxieties in foreign tongues. When these were letters it was not, as a rule, because the situation demanded it. A number of Beckett's most artistically revealing letters from the 1930s are written in French or German, but with a few (important) exceptions, they are addressed to individuals who not only speak English, but whose native language is English. During the same period, and in the same city, Walter Benjamin occasionally sent letters to German friends such as Gershom Scholem or Max Horkheimer in French. He began a letter to the former in January 1930, *"tu vas me trouver fou sans doute,"* "you will no doubt find me mad," excusing his change of language by explaining that the difficulty he was experiencing in writing in their native language was so great that he could only overcome it through what he called, in an elegant solecism, *"cette façon d'alibi qu'est pour moi le français"*— "that aspect of an alibi which French is for me" (Benjamin 1966, 505). Beckett does not go to the trouble of speculating on whether his correspondent will think him mad or not, but he makes clear that he is often able to write more freely in a foreign language. In his first novel Beckett refers to a "nonsens unique," a pun combining the French term for one-way street, *sens unique,* with nonsense, *nonsens,* producing both "unique nonsense" and the suggestion that this is best done by moving the wrong way—e.g., out of English (*Dream,* 66).

Beckett's most revealing early expression of literary intent, and discontent, is, however, to a foreign correspondent—the German one mentioned earlier. This was the most famous letter Beckett would ever write, in any language, and the closest thing to a literary manifesto he would ever offer. Aptly enough, the letter may never have been sent; equally apt is that it was written to a man Beckett barely knew.[1] Had Jacques Lacan known of its existence, it could only have reinforced his certainty that a letter always reaches its addressee. This was done during Beckett's lifetime, as the letter was included in the miscellany *Disjecta* that Ruby Cohn persuaded Beckett to publish, where it appeared in the original German (with some minor corrections of Beckett's highly idiosyncratic German) together with an excellent translation by Martin Esslin. In the first volume of Beckett's letters it appears again, shorn of the silent corrections Esslin made to Beckett's German and in a new translation by Victoria Westbrook.[2] In the context of Beckett's (relatively numerous) German letters of these years it displays a startling leap in language proficiency, so much so that it is clear that writing it must have entailed either a great deal of work on Beckett's part, a helping hand, or both.[3]

Although Beckett had no formal training in German, he had worked hard at it over the years, occasionally trying his hand in letters—most often, as noted, to Anglophone friends. These are frolicsome and, from a grammatical point of view, richly flawed. But Beckett's interest in German was not confined to private communication. As noted, Beckett's first short story ends with a man screaming himself to death. His second one, "Sedendo et Quiescendo" (1932), ends with a more articulate expression of discontent: "Beschissenes Dasein beschissenes Dasein Augenblick bitte beschissenes Dasein Augenblickchen bitte beschissenes" (GC 4.68; see also *Dream,* 73). Beckett offers no translation, but a literal one would read: "Shitty existence shitty existence a moment please shitty existence the tiniest of moments please shitty." Sections of his first novel, *Dream of Fair to Middling Women,* take place in German-speaking locales, and even when the scene is Dublin, bits of German are common (as in the Polar Bear's spicing of his speech with German terms of appraisal and opprobrium). An entire story in that first work's successor, *More Pricks Than Kicks,* is written in the broken English of a broken-hearted Germanophone. Of the letter's recipient, Belacqua, we are told that "scraps of German played in his mind in the silence that ensued; grand, old, plastic words" (*Dream,* 191). *More Pricks Than Kicks, Murphy,* and *Watt* bear continued witness to an interest in the German language's resources, profane and other. One of the entries from *Watt's* "Addenda" is "die Merde hat mich wieder," taking Goethe's dramatic *"die Erde hat mich wieder"* ("the earth reclaims me"), from *Faust,* and defiling it with a French M (*merde* is French for *shit*) (GC 1.376). Moran will adopt another line from *Faust* as pedagogical and paternal axiom, *"Sollst entbehren"* ("you should do without"), something Beckett himself often found easier in a foreign tongue (GC 2.105; 149).

When Beckett left Hamburg for Berlin in late 1936 an acquaintance put him in touch with Axel Kaun, a man who knew much about painting and literature, and who was friendly. The two met for a drink, and got along so well they decided to spend the evening together. As Beckett noted in his journal, they spoke of many matters, such as Thomas Mann's recent denationalization, and made a late night of it.[4] Three days later, despite Beckett's lamentable physical state (a painful swelling "between wind and water" which left him unable to sit), he went to Kaun's for dinner, bringing a copy of *Echo's Bones* as gift (and reclined as much as possible) (LSB 1.422; Tophoven 2005, 123).[5] This was the last time the two men would see one another. In 1958 Kaun immigrated to America, working as, among other things, the translator of George Steiner's *Language and Silence* (1967), in which Beckett is often invoked for precisely the sorts of language and silence he wrote about in his letter to Kaun. When Beckett tried to track Kaun down nearly a half century after their meeting, he received as reply a postcard from San Francisco informing him that Kaun had died two years earlier (Tophoven 2005, 126).

The encounter with Kaun led to one of a great many aborted projects from these years—that of Beckett translating a selection of Joachim

Ringelnatz's poems into English. This project—or, more precisely, its cancellation—is the occasion for Beckett's letter, the writing of which had been on his mind for months, as witnessed by a laconic notebook entry from March of that year: "Try to write Kaun. Give it up."[6] Three months later Beckett returned to the task. His letter begins with an amusing allusion to the matter at hand, as Beckett thanks Kaun for his latest letter and apologizes for the overdue reply, saying that he had been on the point of writing when he was forced to travel, "rather like Ringelnatz's male postage stamp, albeit under less passionate circumstances" (Ringelnatz had written a poem in which a male postage stamp is kissed by a princess and is unable to return her kiss because he must take a trip, and because he is a postage stamp) (LSB 1.512).[7] Beckett moves quickly from this *incipit* to the business before him, bluntly stating that upon further consideration he does not think Ringelnatz worth translating, although conceding that "as an individual Ringelnatz was of quite extraordinary interest"—having, presumably, in mind, the other occupations the poet exercised: sailor, window-dresser, librarian, painter, minesweeper, and cabaret comedian (LSB 1.512).[8]

In his brisk dismissal of Ringelnatz, Beckett calls him, bizarrely enough, a "rhyme roller" (LSB 1.512). This expression, *Reimkuli,* introduces all that is difficult in rendering Beckett's imaginative and highly idiosyncratic German. Esslin had mistranslated the strange expression Beckett invents as the (offensive) "rhyme coolie" (Beckett 1984, 171). Westbrook turns *Reimkuli* into the innocuous "rhymester" (LSB 1.512; LSB 1.517). But what Beckett is thinking of is quite specific—a (somewhat outmoded) word for ballpoint pen—*Tintenkuli*—a German term Beckett carefully noted in his journal after the rather laborious selection process of a new pen in Hamburg.[9] What Beckett finds so off-putting in Ringelnatz is not that he is enslaved to his rhyme schemes, but the pat facility and smooth superficiality with which they roll off his pen. As Beckett tells Kaun, reading Ringelnatz put him in mind of Goethe's dictum, *"Lieber NICHTS zu schreiben, als nicht zu schreiben,"* "better to write NOTHING than not to write anything."[10] Beckett indicates that there is more he might say on the matter, but limits himself to the above, offering, however, to expand upon the "disgust" excited in him by Ringelnatz's writing on another occasion, should his correspondent wish it.

From the business of translating, Beckett then turns to the pleasure, or, perhaps, displeasure of writing. Alluding to Kaun's request that Beckett write to him often and abundantly in English, he replies (in German) that it is "becoming continually more difficult, indeed, more senseless, for me to write official English [*offizielles Englisch*]" (LSB 1.513). Though *Murphy* was not to be published for another year, Beckett had completed the book and felt that there was something perfunctory to it. His feelings were no warmer toward its predecessors—the still-unpublished *Dream of Fair to Middling Women* and the "fiasco" of *More Pricks Than Kicks*. In addition to being an allusion to his own difficulty in shaping a creative prose to his purposes, Beckett's "official English" points to the type of writing of which he has been speaking, and which he found so insufferable in Ringelnatz and Goethe. Beckett made no secret of the fact that he found the official rank and recognition, the lofty propriety of such figures as Goethe distasteful, and his letter to Kaun takes him from the stiff and somnolent correctness of such literary exemplars to his own plight in his own language.[11] In a number of letters from these years, Beckett asks his addressees to "please pardon the rant"—frequently using the French term *dégueulade*, at least in part for its latent vulgarity.[12] After this introduction of sorts, with its rejection of official poets and official English, the letter to Kaun becomes a combination of literary manifesto, theoretical excursus, and rant, with Beckett setting his sights on a "disgust" far more intense and complex than any felt for German poets such as Ringelnatz and Goethe.

"More and more," Beckett writes, "my own language seems to me like a veil that must be torn apart so as to get at the things (or the nothingness) beyond it" (LSB 1.513-514). He is not long in naming the confining elements in language, just as he is not long in setting a course of anarchistic action. Beckett jeers, "Grammar and style!" as though such things were unbearable impositions, saying that "they seem to me just as outdated [*hinfällig*] as a Biedermeier bathing-suit or the true gentleman's imperturbability" (LSB 1.514). Westbrook follows Esslin's lead in translating Beckett's "*hinfällig*" as "irrelevant," but although "grammar and style" are presented as indeed irrelevant, it should be noted that they are not so by nature (LSB 1.514; Beckett 1984, 171; LSB 1.518). Beckett desires radical renewal. It is not that grammar and style are irrelevant per se. They have become frozen (for this reason Beckett calls them "outdated"). He compares the proprieties of an official, or elevated, literary language to old-fashioned bathing suits and the very model of a modern major gentleman because these things seem to him equally outmoded. What he has in mind, whatever its dark ungainliness, will at least have the virtue of being in step with its times.

In *All That Fall* Mr. Rooney remarks: "Do you know, Maddy, sometimes one would think you were struggling with a dead language" (GC 3.182). The same might be said to the author of those lines. Neither that play nor Beckett's German letter represents the first time Beckett had sought to articulate this sense of senselessness. Beckett's very first piece of published prose contains, aptly enough, a denunciation of the language in which it is written. "It is worth while remarking," he noted in "Dante . . . Bruno. Vico . . . Joyce," "that no language is so sophisticated as English" (GC 4.504). The reader is not left long in the dark as to the value of such sophistication. English has become so sophisticated— or, as Beckett will call it a few years later, "official"—that he sees its life leaving it. English has been "abstracted to death" (GC 4.504). The young Beckett adored Dante and adored Joyce. It should then come as no surprise that he marshals his enthusiasm and erudition to link the two. For Beckett, Dante's *volgare illustre* was to fourteenth-century official Latin what Joyce's illustrious vulgarisms were to the official English of his day. Joyce is progressing toward not only the completion of a work but the revivification of a language. What wakes and sleeps, dies and is reborn, in *Finnegans Wake* is, for Beckett, a language at risk of becoming fixed and frozen into an officious and official form. Beckett's analogy is that the official English of Joyce's day (which is his own) is in a situation similar to the Latin of Dante's, drained of the life that once coursed through it.

The comparison is both clever and distant. In the fourteenth century, Franco Sacchetti recounted how Dante, passing by a blacksmith's shop in Florence, heard a smith singing out verses from his *Commedia*, punctuating the end of each line with a blow from his hammer, and how Dante once observed a peasant driving an ass to market while intoning the *Commedia* with an *"Arri!"* at the end of each line to usher along his charge (Sacchetti 1979, 14, 15). However apocryphal these tales might be, they stress that Dante's language was, or quickly became, that of his people, spoken in streets and shops, in city and country. It is difficult to imagine anything similar occurring for Joyce's crowning work. One of the finest students of Joyce's debt to Dante, Umberto Eco, has noted that of the roughly two thousand words needed to speak Italian with basic functional fluency, eighteen hundred are to be found in the *Commedia* (Eco 2008, 5). *Finnegans Wake* offers no comparison in this regard, and no more than a tiny fraction of the words that make it up would be of assistance on today's TOEFL tests. Beckett is well aware of the limits of his analogy and is clearly not envisaging a future where the language of Shem the Penman has become the lingua franca of the British Isles. He makes no secret of the fact that "no creature in heaven or earth ever spoke the language of *Work in Progress*" (GC 4.507). Nevertheless, he hears something in Joyce's progressing work that has been overlooked. This is how decrepit—or, in his term, "sophisticated"—their native language has become (GC 4.504).[13] Beckett agrees with those critics who claim that "Mr. Joyce has desophisticated language," but, unlike them, he sees this as a grand achievement, one on a par with Dante's, for Joyce is giving English what it desperately needs: *una vita nova* (GC 4.504).[14]

In French and on Style

No single fact about Beckett's writing is so well known or so astounding as that of his having changed literary languages, and it was during this summer when Beckett wrote his long German letter that he began to write with some seriousness in French.[15] It is useful to recall that Beckett's situation bears little similarity to those of other writers of his century who changed literary languages, or who wrote in more than one—such as Conrad, Nabokov, Celan, or N'Gugi. Beckett is unlike Conrad in that he had already written extensively in his native language (as Conrad had never done in Polish, and would never do in French). He was unlike Nabokov in that Nabokov was fluent in his three literary languages (Russian, French, and English) from earliest youth and changed literary language under intense financial, as opposed to aesthetic, pressure. Beckett was unlike Celan in that he started writing in French with nothing of the level of linguistic competence Celan had in German, Romanian, French, English, Hebrew, or Russian, and had nothing of the complex and directly personal sense of his *Muttersprache* being a *Mördersprache*. Had Gaelic been Beckett's native language, or had he even known it at all well, then his situation might be likened to that of N'Gugi's movements between Gikuyu and English, and the colonial pressures it produced, but it was not, and he was not. This is to say that Beckett's situation was unusual even among those unusual cases. When asked about the change of language Beckett replied: "Just felt like it" (Shenker 1956/1979, 148). On another occasion he said it was *"parce qu'en français c'est plus facile d'écrire sans style,"* "because in French it is easier to write without style" (Gessner 1957, 32). Still elsewhere Beckett praised French for having "the right weakening effect" (Blau 1960, 90–91). This had first and foremost to do with weakening his native strength, with diminishing a richness of means at cross-purposes with the aesthetic "impoverishment" Beckett often praised in his essays, novels, letters, interviews and poetry. In 1968 Beckett told Richard Coe that the problem with English was that "you couldn't help writing poetry in it" (Coe 1969, 14). By this he clearly did not mean that so honeyed were his lips and so sparkling his pen that he could produce nothing but sweetness and light, nor that the lure of verse was so great that no prose could be maintained in it. Beckett is referring to the effects of fluency and memory, to all the poetry of his native language so dearly loved and deeply engrained that it was difficult for him not to reproduce it in one way or another.

Beckett remarked that "French represented a form of weakness" not only because it was *not* his mother tongue, but also because "the relative asceticism of French seemed more appropriate to the expression of being undeveloped, unsupported somewhere in the depths of the microcosm" (GC 1.xv). This is a development of an idea long present to Beckett's mind, and long present in his writing. In *Dream of Fair to Middling Women* Lucien "one day let fall nonchalantly, à propos of what we don't know, so nonchalantly that it must have been his and not another's: 'Black diamond of pessimism'" (*Dream*, 47). The phrase embarks Belacqua on a train of thought about the relation of French to style. He finds it "a nice example, in the domain of words, of the little sparkle hid in ashes," intimating that such niceness must first pass through the regions of cliché and commonplace as "the lift to the high spot is precisely from the tag and the ready-made" (*Dream*, 47, 48). Belacqua is speaking about the way cleverness is expressed in French language and culture. This is not done through exuberant elaboration or irreverent innovation so much as through the alteration of familiar formulae ("the tag and the ready-made"). Where Belacqua's thought takes a new turn is in the idea that the "stylist" should not offer his reader such a "lift" (*Dream*, 48). Those writers eschewing style, like "Racine or Malherbe," offer a more varied mixture. Their writing "sparkles" because it does not attempt to shine. Racine and Malherbe have a style "sprigged with sparkles" because "the flints and pebbles are there, no end of humble tags and commonplaces," which leads Belacqua to the conclusion, "They have no style, they write without style" (*Dream*, 48). Which, in turn, leads him to a conjecture: "Perhaps only the French can do it. Perhaps only the French language can give you the thing you want" (*Dream*, 48).[16] This idea is still clearly on Beckett's mind years later as he records in his journal in March 1936 a conversation (as he was traveling through Germany) during which, after having talked about "the nature of language" and the idea of historical evolution—how "every language once ripe, then falls behind, i.e. once congruent with provocation, then eclipsed"— to which he adds, "I boost the possibility of styleness in French, the pure communication" (Knowlson 1996, 257).

Pour faire remarquer moi, or The Need to Be Ill-Equipped

In an unsigned contributor's note in *Transition* magazine in 1948—a note probably written by Beckett's friend Duthuit and translated by Beckett himself—we read:

> Samuel Beckett is a Dublin poet and novelist who, after long years of residence in France has adopted the French language as his working medium. Invited to give some account of his reasons for now writing in French, rather than in his native language, he replied that he

would be happy to do so and seemed then to have some views on the subject. But some months later he wrote saying that he did not know why he wrote in French, nor indeed why he wrote at all. Some considerable time later however, as we chanced to encounter him emerging in unusual good humor apparently from the *Multicolor* in the *Avenue de Wagram,* we begged him to make a further effort, in his own interest and in that of literature as a whole. Drawing us then aside into the little frequented semi-circular *Rue de Tilsitt,* and having first looked round in every conceivable direction to make sure no doubt that we were not observed, he confessed at last in a strong or rather weak Dublin accent: *"Pour faire remarquer moi."* (LSB 2.93)

Pour faire remarquer moi is a richly comic solecism. The simplest and most superficial translation of it would be "to get attention"—tempered and enriched by his saying this in a phrase that is somewhere between awkward and grammatically incorrect. The playful revelation of the great secret that Beckett changed languages for no other reason than that of getting attention is made all the more merry by the statement's being artfully flawed. The joke, however, that Duthuit (and, it seems, Beckett) trust the reader to catch is that the foreigner is so ill-equipped to write in the French language that he cannot even get a simple, if revelatory, sentence out without misusing the language he would adopt. In this light Beer is right to describe Beckett's reply as "facetious" (Beer 1994, 215). And yet it can be read as more than facetious. *Pour me faire remarquer* would have expressed the same sentiment in more proper French—and might have been mildly amusing. But what Beckett is said to have said resonates more fully, not only because the language is misused to comic effect, but because it is misused to another effect. Of the phenomenal burst of creative energy Beckett first experienced in French, the "siege in the room" during which he wrote, on average, an epochal work every six months, he said, "Only then did I begin to write the things I feel"—to speak, at last, clearly of how the *moi* slips from his writing grasp.[17]

Three years before his famous remark that "in French it is easier to write without style," Beckett gave a less famous but no less intriguing response to another enquirer. In a letter to Hans Naumann, German translator and editor of French and Irish literature, that Beckett asked Naumann to keep "confidential" (and which he did not), Beckett says that his change of language was not "deliberate [*raisonné*]," and was done simply so as "to change, to see" (LSB 2.464; 461). Naumann had written to inquire whether Beckett's situation was not that of a Gaelic speaker choosing between two different foreign languages (English and French). Concerning this Irish question, Beckett replies that, on the contrary, "if there is a language truly foreign to me, it is Gaelic" (LSB 2.464; 461). As concerns English, he says simply that "it is my language" (LSB 2.464; 461). At this point, however, Beckett's tone changes:

> You may put me in the dismal category of those who, if they had to act in full awareness of what they were doing, would never act. Which does not preclude there being urgent reasons for this change. I myself can half make out several, now that it is too late to go back. But I prefer to let them stay in the half-light. I will all the same give you *a clue [une piste]*: the need to be ill-equipped [*le besoin d'être mal armé*]. (LSB 2.464; 461; Beckett's emphasis)

At the moment of making these remarks, Beckett had recently completed an astounding outpouring of French prose, having published in the preceding three years *Molloy* (1951), *Malone meurt* (1951), *En attendant Godot* (1952), and *L'Innommable* (1953). At this point Beckett gives his confidential clue: the need to be ill-equipped—or, more literally, poorly armed *(mal armé)*—for the siege at hand.

Beckett is particularly interested during these years in the question of artistic parallels. The literature of his day seems to him not only lamentably behind the times but lamentably behind the other arts. The question is: "Should literature remain alone on the old, fouling paths which painting and music have long abandoned?" (LSB 1.514). Beckett sees the time come for literature to do as the other arts have done—to strike out on its own and strike out against itself. The reader prompted to think of the riotous Joyce in this connection—a reader Beckett anticipates in Kaun—is offered a corrective, as Beckett flatly states, "My sense is that Joyce's most recent work has nothing at all to do with such a program" (LSB 1.515).

ReJoyce

Among the more fascinating aspects of Beckett's career, a close second to his change of literary language is his relationship, personal and artistic, with Joyce. Since the first flickerings of Beckett's fame there has been a natural temptation to see his early years as ones of anxious influence, dead reckoning between the Scylla of Joyce and the Charybdis of Proust. "I simply do not feel the presence in my writing as a whole of the Joyce & Proust situations," Beckett wrote in 1967, but this did nothing to prevent others from doing so.[18] No less an authority than Northrop Frye declared, as early as 1960, that "as a fiction writer Samuel Beckett derives from Proust and Joyce" (Frye 1960, 442). Unsurprisingly, Harold Bloom had a word to say on the matter, claiming that "Beckett's heroic quest has been to go on despite his profound understanding of Joyce, Proust and Kafka, who between them can be judged to have culminated the tradition of Western prose fiction" (Bloom 1985, i). The currency of such literary genealogy can be seen in countless critical studies since Frye, and even in the editorial matter of the standard edition of Beckett's works in English, where J. M. Coetzee's introduction to volume 4 (the volume containing Beckett's early writings) presents Beckett "starting out as an uneasy Joycean and an even more uneasy Proustian" (Coetzee 2006, xiii).[19] Peter John Murphy has suggested that Beckett's relation to Joyce is "the most important as well as most comprehensive case of literary influence in twentieth-century literature" (Murphy 2009, 225). What, we might then ask, is its nature, and what bearing does it have on Beckett's notions of English, French, style, and substance?

To many in the 1930s Joyce's *Work in Progress* strongly suggested nonsense. Even so sensitive, and so admiring, a reader of *Ulysses* as Nabokov would write: "I detest *Finnegans Wake* in which a cancerous growth of fancy word-tissue hardly redeems the dreadful joviality of the folklore and the easy, too easy, allegory," and called it elsewhere a "petrified superpun" and "a formless and dull mass" (Nabokov 1990, 102; Nabokov 1981, 122; Nabokov 1990, 71). In this same vein, Nabokov wrote to his wife in 1936 of how, "in these new things" of Joyce's, by which he meant the *Work in Progress* which was to become *Finnegans Wake* (Joyce kept his title secret until publication was in sight), "the abstract puns, the verbal masquerade, the shadows of words, the diseases of words" make for a whole which "in the end sinks behind reason, and, while it is setting, the sky is ravishing, but then there is night" (cited by Boyd 1990, 425). Nabokov is right in a thematic sense, for, as Joyce himself stressed, *Finnegans Wake* is a book of the night, counterpart and complement to the book of the day that was *Ulysses*. But more importantly for the question at hand is that few before Beckett or since have been able to see so deeply into the darkness as did he. Beckett often spoke with Joyce about the work that consumed the better part of Joyce's writing life; he translated parts of it into French, took dictation of others, and even read galleys.[20] Eco has, not without reason, called *Finnegans Wake* "the most terrifying document of formal instability and semantic ambiguity" our culture possesses, and this terrifying document is one that the young Beckett was better placed to see than almost anyone (Eco 1994, 113). A natural question has thus been, and a natural corollary of the readings of critics from Frye to Coetzee is: Did it frighten him right out of English?

Beckett was perfectly placed to appreciate Joyce's terrific gift, just as he was perfectly placed to grasp its nature, and its idea of nature. Beckett saw Joyce's exuberance as one he could not better, but also as one he would rather not imitate. This did not keep him from imitating it, and he would write of *Dream of Fair to Middling Women*, "Of course it stinks of Joyce in spite of most earnest endeavors to endow it with my own odors" (LSB 1.81). In the same vein he would remark a year later, in 1932, "I vow I will get over J. J. ere I die" (LSB 1.108). Beckett never said anything like T. S. Eliot's remark about *Ulysses*—"I wish, for my own sake, that I had not read it"—but he clearly thought a great deal of it, and about it, and not only in laudatory terms.[21] Beckett remarked to the *New York Times* in 1956 that he was "a non-knower, a non-can-er"—self-descriptions which he clarified by comparing himself with Joyce:

> The more Joyce knew, the more he could. His tending towards omniscience and omnipotence as an artist. I'm working with impotence, ignorance. There seems to be a kind of aesthetic axiom that

expression is achievement—must be achievement. My little exploration is that whole zone of being that has always been set aside by
artists as something unusable—as something by definition incompatible with art. (Shenker 1956, 3)

This is no passing fancy, and this note is consistently struck in Beckett's
remarks on Joyce. When Maurice Nadeau suggested that for Beckett,
Joyce was "an influence *ab contrario*," Beckett concurred, adding, "I realized that Joyce had gone as far as one could in the direction of knowing
more," whereas, "I realized that my own way was in impoverishment, in
lack of knowledge and in taking away, subtracting" (Knowlson 1996, 352;
Knowlson 2006, 47). If the question was how impoverishment might best
be reached, writing in a foreign language seemed a promising start.

In his essay on Joyce, Beckett observes that the English word *doubt*
carries no "sensuous suggestion" of its meaning (GC 4.504). Appealing
to his own senses, Beckett found that the German and Italian terms—
Zweifel and *dubitare,* respectively—do better, having both resisted the pro-
cesses of sophistication and abstraction which ages languages.[22] While
English was farther down the road toward deadening sophistication
than any other living language, it was not alone on that road. Although
German and Italian (not to mention French) might seem to the young
Beckett better off than his own mother tongue, they are nevertheless
subject to the same forces and follow the same lines. The process of
deadening sophistication diagnosed by the young Beckett is not some
pernicious virus that attacks only imperial linguistic powers such as
Latin or English. It is, instead, proper to every language—the reason the
sophistication Beckett diagnoses in his native language cannot simply
be countered by writing in German, Italian, or French. Those other languages were merely at an earlier point on the same continuum. The
process in question is natural, cyclical—and, aptly enough for the matter
and maestro at hand—Viconian. Joyce's idea of at once recapitulating
language's development and renewing its life is what is writ large and
small in *Finnnegans Wake,* from—to borrow one of its characteristic turns
of phrase—"spark to phoenish" (Joyce 1966, 322). The movement of a
drink-slurred spark of a start to a dream-bright phoenix of a finish is
both the form and the content of *Finnegans Wake* (Joyce 1966, 215).[23]

Following the line of millennial thinking that Joyce found so kindred in Vico, Beckett argues that language naturally tends toward "sophistication," thereby departing from its sensuous origins toward the abstraction that will be the death of it. This process explains language's rise from shout, song, and gesture, as well as its decline and fall—just as it explains why artists like Dante and Joyce felt the need to infuse it with new life. This invigorating influx of sensuous suggestion is the common property of genius, and the sensitive senses of the young Beckett find it in the phrase "in twosome twiminds" that Joyce uses instead of the abstracted and official term "doubt" (GC 4.504).[24] It is this same sense that led Shakespeare to use, following Beckett, "fat, greasy words to express corruption," and Dickens to convey "the ooze of squelching" in the his descriptions of land near the Thames (GC 4.504–505).

Beckett does not leave this reflection on the theoretical level, and proceeds to offer demonstrations of a language that is not just about something, but is that thing itself. "When the sense is sleep" in Joyce's writing, "the words go to sleep," just as "when the sense is dancing, the words dance" (GC 4.503). What is more, they are not averse to drink. To this end, Beckett quotes the end of "Shaun's pastoral" from the *Work in Progress*:

> To stir up love's young fizz I tilt with this bridle's cup champagne, dimming douce from her peepair of hide-seeks tight squeezed on my snowybreasted and while my pearlies in their sparkling wisdom are nippling her bubblets I swear (and let you swear) by the bumper round of my poor old snaggletooth's solidbowel I ne'er will prove I'm untrue to (theare!) you liking so long as my hole looks. Down.[25]

Beckett observes how such "language is drunk" and that, consequently, "the very words are tilted and effervescent" (GC 4.504). The champagne trickles down and fizzes up in the phrases, from the neatly concealed bottle to the unbridled bride's cup ("peepair of hide-seeks" conveying not only details of dalliance, but also the maker of the mark, the champagne producer Piper-Heidsieck, which the overwhelmed French tongue pronounces as "peepair hide-seeks"). What happens when Joyce sets his language spinning, dancing, and drinking is, as Beckett says, a "sense which is forever rising to the surface of the form and becoming the form itself" (GC 4.504).

This is why the young Beckett will address Joyce's readers in the terms he does, announcing that "if you don't understand [Joyce's *Work in Progress*], Ladies and Gentleman, it is because you are too decadent to receive it" (GC 4.502). This counterintuitive declaration that it is not Joyce who is impossibly decadent, but those readers unable to understand him, is clarified by Beckett's very personal definition of decadence. The decadence of Joyce's uncomprehending readers is to be measured by the distance they see between form and content. "You are not satisfied," Beckett upbraids them, "unless form is so strictly divorced from content that you can comprehend the one almost without bothering to read the other" (GC 4.502–503). This means that they are so decadent as to have let fall one of the fundamental facts of readerly life: there is no matter without style. The principal finding of Beckett's "exagmination" is that "form *is* content, content *is* form," with, as result, that it "is not *about* something; *it is that something itself*" (GC 4.503; Beckett's emphasis).[26] The problem that this resonant equation raises is its *is*. If form and content are separable enough to deserve distinct names, then in Beckett's reading of Joyce's work they are not two words for one thing so much as two streams so interpenetrated and interpenetrating as to be inseparable. There would thus be no reason to retain the distinction, and yet there it is. As Adam Thirlwell says of Beckett's formula, "it is not just catchy: it is also impossible" (Thirlwell 2008, 14).

Animism

On more than one occasion Beckett pointed to what he called the "considerable animism" of Joyce's writing (GC 4.508). This is at once a direct and a discrete name for what Beckett has in mind. An animistic world is one in which everything is connected and everything communicates. In myth—the literary form where animism rules—everything is alive, and anything may speak, from Achilles's horses in *The Iliad* to the Haida oral epic where a cloak on which the image of an animal is being woven whispers, "Tomorrow again, part of my face will still be unfinished, unfinished."[27] Everything said in the animistic world is heard there—if not by man then by sylph, nymph, naiad, by horse, bear, wolf, raven, or killer whale. That Beckett calls Joyce's writing animistic is fitting insofar as everything there can speak, everything is connected, everything heard, everything very much alive, as when an (unpaid for) bar of soap, deep in *Ulysses*'s Nighttown, ascends:

> (*. . . A cake of new clean lemon soap arises, diffusing light and perfume.*)
> THE SOAP
> We're a capital couple are Bloom and I
> He brightens the earth, I polish the sky.[28]

Bells, kisses, gulls, a fan, and any number of other dumb things speak in that book, and still more unlikely articles speak in its sequel, so that whether applied to *Ulysses* or *Finnegans Wake, animism* may seem a simply descriptive term for the proceedings. And yet it is also, for Beckett, a cutting term. For this everywhere flowing, everywhere extending life in which nature's voice speaks intelligibly to us, is, for Beckett, a lie. Beckett is, in fact, so put off by the notion that nature might have something to say that it leads to the uncharacteristic swipe at Baudelaire mentioned above. In a related vein Beckett will remark of historical writing: "I say the background and the causes are an inhuman and incomprehensible machinery and venture to wonder what kind of appetite it is that can be appeased by the modern animism that consists in rationalizing them. Rationalism is the last form of animism" (Knowlson 1996, 228). Rationalism is animistic, for Beckett, in that it presents an underlying and unifying principle for the mess in which we find ourselves. "Joyce believed in words," Beckett once underlined (Harvey 1970, 249). This is hardly surprising given Joyce's occupation. And yet the belief Beckett had in mind was of a special sort. Beckett told Cioran that Joyce "never rebelled," and that therein lay their difference (Cioran 1979, 337). It might seem that Joyce was as rebellious a writer as ever had been, but for Beckett Joyce's rebelliousness was confined to a dead end. Beckett called Joyce a "biologist of words," as Joyce saw so much life in words, but such "animism" represented, for Beckett, pure invention (GC 4.508). For Beckett, language has no life of its own, and pretending that it does is nothing more or less than "animism."

"In the buginning is the woid," *Finnegans Wake* informs us, "in the muddle is the sound-dance, and thereinofter you're in the unbewised again, vund vulsy-volsy" (Joyce 1966, 378). In the beginning was the word, or the void, or both, and from void to muddle, from the written word to the dancing, drinking one, we move into the light of understanding, so as to be "unbewised again." For Joyce, this round (vice versa it moves, and *vi ricordo* is its motto) is full of strange sound and obscure furies, but always signifies something. "Wear anartful of outer nocense!" Joyce wrote, pointing, wildly, to the fact that we are an artful heart-full of outer and utter nonsense (Joyce 1966, 378). And yet, beneath the outer nonsense is more sense than we could ever imagine, a sense of pure connection between man and nature, myth and history. But Beckett saw all this *animism* as based on the false premise that language is something like birdsong and anything like sacred.

When Beckett told Joyce the epigraph he intended to use for his first book—Leopardi's *"e fango è il mondo,"* "and the world is mud"[29]—Joyce offered, as Beckett recalled, "instantaneous and sole reaction": *"Il mondo—immonde"* (LSB 2.537). A multilingual pun (*mondo* is Italian for world, *immonde* is French for unspeakably bad) produced with prestidigitory promptness, tempering pessimism with good cheer, is what we might expect from Joyce. Recounting this *bon mot* twenty-five years later, Beckett suggested to his correspondent that it might "perhaps suggest to you an exagmination of how in Joyce the form of judgment more and more devoured its gist and the saying of all the saying of anything" (LSB 2.537). Joyce thought the world of speech, and said so. Beckett did not, and therein lay their greatest difference from one another. The question Beckett wanted to pose was how art would be if this sacred sign of life in language were effaced, if art were fully and finally displaced from the sacred space of fine making to the profane level of what he called "willed creative mismaking." This was not to be done without breaking a few things. *Iconoclasm,* being a concept from the sacred sphere, carries a religious charge. So too does that which Beckett modeled on it: *logoclasm. Logoclasm* as Beckett envisioned, and practiced, it involves not merely using language in a few superficially surprising ways; it is to look to the source of its meaning, its *logos,* and to try and break it.

In the first years of his fame Beckett said of Joyce, "I still think him one of the greatest literary geniuses of all time," though he would also add, "but I felt very early on that the thing that drew me [*la chose qui m'appelait*] and the means I could call on were virtually the opposite of his thing and his means" (LSB 2.461; LSB 2.463). Elsewhere, Beckett said that whereas Joyce was a "synthesizer," he himself was an "analyzer" (Knowlson 2006, 47). Beckett saw Joyce as *synthetic* not only in the sense of combining so many colors, characters, moods, manners, languages, traditions, genres, periods, people, places, potions, and purposes, but also in the sense of linking the nature of man and the language of nature. Beckett, by contrast, saw himself as *"analytic"* not only in the Cartesian sense of examining through separation, not only in his reducing literary structures and dramatic scenes to their rudiments, but also in the sense of separating man and nature, voice and language, the imaginary forest of symbols from the real ones in which we go walking.

"It is to be hoped," Beckett wrote in his letter to Kaun, "that the time will come—and, thank God, in some circles it already has—when language is best used where it is most energetically and efficiently misused" (LSB 1.514). In that same language Ingeborg Bachmann would find that "a writer cannot simply use a readymade language [*vorgefundenen Sprache*]—she must, instead, write it apart [*er muß sie zerschreiben*]" (Bachmann 1983, 84). What is remarkable about her declaration, and so helpful for seeing what Beckett speaks of, is the artful prefix she places on writing: a true writer *mis*writes her language. This is an intention to which Beckett's best readers have responded from the first hour. In the first book on Beckett, Gessner enumerated the ways in which Beckett's language takes its world to task, setting out ten distinct "symptoms of linguistic collapse [*Zerfallserscheinungen*]" (Gessner 1957, 44ff.). These include relatively straightforward devices such as "Monologue," "Search for the right word," "Telegram Style," "Excessive Emphasis," as well as more evocative categories such as "Word-piling [*Worthäufung*]" and "word chaos [*Wortchaos*]" (Gessner 1957, 44). Just as Empson's seventh type of ambiguity seems to encompass all others and to stand thereby for ambiguity itself, Gessner's "word chaos" represents linguistic collapse as such. If all language is an excess of language, all use misuse, and all making mismaking, then the goal becomes not clarity but chaos, not graceful concision but loutish logorrhea, not shining success in the artistic arena but failing better, worse, now.

In those same years Adorno identified what he called the "demolition work" of Beckett's "back-sliding language [*die regredierende Sprache*]," and would try for the rest of his life to chart Beckett's "poetic process as erosion [*als Verschleiß*]" (Adorno GS 11.281; Adorno GS 11.283). In much the same vein, and during these same years, Beckett's friend and director Roger Blin described *Endgame* as "a discovery of language [*une découverte de langue*]" whose essence lay—in a formula Blin repeated for emphasis—in "exploding ordinary language [*faire exploser un langage quotidien*]" (an insight predating Cavell's more famous analysis of the "hidden literality" of "ordinary language" in that same play, and of which Cavell appears unaware) (Blin 1957, i). A decade later George Steiner would call this "demolition work" "a formidable inverse eloquence" (Steiner 2009, 178). Closer to our own day, in still another attempt to characterize and account for this same energetic misuse of language, Jacques Derrida would find that Beckett's writing "makes the limits of our language tremble" (Derrida 1989/1992, 60–61).

Animism is a helpful term not only for Beckett's view of Joyce, but for Beckett's view of himself, as his works offer an inverse image of mythic interconnection. In response to the question of why go on in a language incapable of embracing life and communicating experience, Beckett replied, "What, Sir, do you expect? It's the words. We've nothing else [*C'est les mots, on n'a rien d'autre*]" (Gessner 1957, 75).[30] Or, as Beckett says to Kaun: "Since we cannot simply switch off [*ausschalten*]"[31] our language, however much we might wish to do so (which wish becomes the central theme of a number of his later works), Beckett writes that "we should at least leave nothing undone that might contribute to its disrepute [*Verruf*]" (LSB 1.514; Beckett 1984, 172). Wayne Booth wrote of Beckett that "even the most extreme nihilists have not repudiated, as he *seems* to do, the very possibility of communicable speech" (Booth 1974, 276; Booth's italics). "His position," Booth continued, "if it can be called that, seems to me (and apparently to him) self-defeating, illogical and untenable" (Booth 1974, 276). The reader sympathetic to Beckett's endeavor might answer: *as well it should!* If the veil cannot be lifted, perhaps it can be torn; if the mask cannot be removed, perhaps it might be cracked. In this vein Beckett wrote to Kaun, "I cannot imagine a higher goal for today's writer" than to "bore one hole after another into [language] until that which is cowering behind [*das Dahinterkauernde*], be it something or nothing, starts seeping through" (LSB 1.514).[32] Beckett closes his argumentative arc where he began it: uncertain whether there is something beyond language to be got at and exposed, raised high or brought low by the artist's efforts. Here, however, Beckett conceives of a "program" for finding out: a strategy or "method," using silence, cunning, exile, and anything else at hand to tear the veil, shatter the mask, bore holes into literary language until it begins to crumble and he can get at what another unconventional writer had called a decade earlier "Nothing that is not there and the nothing that is" (Stevens, 8).

CHAPTER FIVE

To Hell with All This Fucking Scenery

THE UNNAMABLE begins with what would be, in another novel, a simple question: *"Où maintenant?"* "Where now?" (GC 2.285; 7). In the preceding volume of the trilogy Malone endeavored, more than once, to tell a story with a setting. He related, for instance, how a certain "Sapo loved nature, took an interest," before exclaiming, "This is awful [*Quelle misère*]" (GC 2.185; 27). He is soon back at it, noting, "In his country the problem— no, I can't do it." After another pause he begins anew: "The peasants. His visits to. I can't" (GC 2.190; 35). The narrator of the early French story "The Expelled" pauses in his tale to remark, "That makes sense, cabman, hotel, it's plausible [*vraisemblable*]" (GC 4.257; 35). When Big Lambert's amateur butchery is described in *Malone Dies,* and the fee is noted as lower than that of a professional butcher, the same conclusion is reached: "How plausible [*vraisemblable*] all that is" (GC 2.194; 42). What changed in the interval was not the finding, but the feeling about the finding. Beckett goes from a narrator pausing with something like satisfaction upon observing the verisimilitude of his story to a narrator disgusted whenever he catches anything believable entering his account. As for going on, he can, and will, but with little ease and less success—at least by his own reckoning. Before long he is reduced to describing the room in which he finds himself dying, only to break off with the more emphatic exclamation: "to hell with all this fucking scenery" (GC 2.270; 173).

A clear element in Beckett's artistic evolution (or revolution, or devolution, it amounting to the same so long as no bearings are set) is the elimination of scenery, not because it matters so much whether it is London or Paris, whether dress or dog were gray or black, but because of the question of where to address our imagination. *Dream of Fair to Middling Women, More Pricks Than Kicks,* and *Murphy* were all set in real places (Dublin, Vienna, Cork, London, and so on). *Murphy* went so far as to offer a world as correlated and confirmed in its real-world detail as any of its day. While working on that novel Beckett wrote to a friend in Dublin asking him to make measurements of the exact height of a post office statue against whose posterior one of his characters was to bang his head. Nothing in the Dublin of the work was to be incompatible with the Dublin of the world, just as had been the case when Joyce wrote to familiars in Dublin so as to verify that someone of Leopold Bloom's height, weight, and state of physical fitness could leap down from the area railing at 7 Eccles Street without injury. Joyce drew Dublin from memory, and *Thom's Dublin Post Office Directory* for 1904. Beckett proceeded similarly in *Murphy,* his own prodigious memory assisted by Whitaker's *London Almanack* for 1935.[1] The result is a great deal of detailed setting in strict accordance with the real world it purported to reflect. In *Murphy* we not only have accurately placed posteriors, we have a real place minutely described, and are even made aware of the hair and eye colors of Murphy's love, her height, weight, and a host of additional information (cf. GC 1.9). Beckett's early remarks about not being "Deus ex machina enough" for the job of narrator seem, on the evidence of *Murphy,* to have simply been a matter of growing into the role. This peace with the invented world proves, however, short-lived, and after his next work, *Watt,* Beckett's scenes shift out of the named world, never to return. In *First Love,* we are told that "what constitutes the charm of our country, apart of course from its scant population, and this without help of the meanest contraception, is that all is derelict" (GC 4.236; 26–27). There are many bits of a scarcely veiled Dublin in that story, just as the Irish countryside was semi-recognizable at points in *Watt,* but such elements soon undergo a radical relocation and a prodigious increase in dereliction as Beckett ventured into worlds for which no almanac existed.

Of his creation, Worm, the Unnamable seems at times a spectator:

> Tears gush from it practically without ceasing, why is not known, nothing is known, whether it's with rage, or whether it's with grief, the fact is there, perhaps it's the voice that makes it weep, with rage, or some other passion, or at having to see, from time to time, some sight or other, perhaps that's it, perhaps he weeps in order not to see, though it seems difficult to credit him with an initiative of this complexity. The rascal, he's getting humanized, he's going to lose if he doesn't watch out, if he doesn't take care, and with what could he take care, with what could he form the faintest conception of the condition they are decoying him into . . . (GC 2.353; 122)

Nothing is known except that being believable, plausible, localizable, and human is to lose. As another of Beckett's narrators remarked, "It's enough to make you wonder sometimes if you are on the right planet" (GC 4.291; 108).

In *Mercier and Camier* details were often declared to be of little importance. We find, for instance, "a road still carriageable over the high moorland," which we are told is "a thousand feet above sea level, two thousand if you prefer [*si vous aimez mieux*]" (GC 1.459; 163). We can imagine whatever altitude we like because it is all made up anyway. Spun out a step farther: it is just a story and stories are just words and words are just empty. In *First Love* the narrator pauses to say, "Things may have happened quite differently," before asking, "But who cares how things happen [*Les choses se passèrent tout autrement, peut-être, mais quelle importance, la manière dont les choses se passent*]" (GC 4.232–233; 16; translation modified).[2] Elsewhere, the narrator will wonder "how to express this thing," and before he's reached the end of the sentence declares: "I won't express it, there you are [*je l'exprimerai pas, voilà*]" (36).[3] He will, however, pause to ask himself, "But why these particulars?" (GC 4.240; 37). Molloy, in turn, will "apologize for these details," promising to move more briskly, "and then perhaps relapse again into a wealth of filthy circumstance. But which in turn will give way to vast frescoes, dashed off with loathing" (GC 2.58; 84).

On the first page of the manuscript of *Happy Days* Beckett wrote, in a note to himself, "vaguen it" (cf. Gontarski 1977, 44).[4] Vaguen it he would. Not only there but in all his mature writing Beckett eliminated quite nearly everything that might orient us in the world of the work. The real world does not, however, vanish in the blink of an eye. It is gradually vaguened—or, to borrow another of Beckett's terms for the process, "lessened" (GC 4.389). For a time the scenes are akin to those of the German painter Gerhard Richter: visible in outline but with all localizing details smoothed away. Richter's Jerusalem, for instance, is not recognizable except for those who know its outline by heart. The same is true of the landscapes and skylines of Beckett's final English novel, *Watt,* which an uninitiated reader is no more likely to recognize as Irish than the viewer of Richter's image is to recognize Jerusalem. *Molloy* has copses and bogs, forests and market towns, as well as many other signs of familiar life. This remains, however, worlds away from the streets of *Murphy* or *Ulysses*. In the mature works the places that appear on the maps of this world, and the people known to inhabit them, are recognizable only by special dispensation. When his son proved unsure for whom a certain bicycle was destined, Moran recalls losing his temper: "Who is this bicycle for, I said, Goering?" (GC 2.137; 194). The sharp report of the real world and its violent leaders echoes through the book, but is allowed to take on no more distinct shape. It is, moreover, rare in the trilogy for something from our world to be named (such as Java or the Indian Ocean). This process of lessening and vaguening reference to a real world that begins with *Watt* ends in *The Unnamable,* for there we lose all orientation, just as it is there that we find ourselves closer to home than ever before, as, among the many places where the Unnamable might be located is "the Rue Brancion, never heard of in my island home," true enough of Samuel Beckett, who not only is from an island, but lived around the corner from that address in Paris's 15th arrondissement while writing the novel (GC 2.337; 94).

We might expect the question of setting to be more straightforward on stage. Albright reminds us that "the stage, so good at being any-where, has trouble being nowhere" (Albright 2003, 29). *Endgame* does not give us any information as to where its proceedings are set. It could be London in the future, the Aran Islands in the present, though it is, of course, neither, because it is not set in any here that is not else-where. In *Endgame* we know that it is gray out there, that little life is to be seen, that something is taking its course, somewhere, somehow. But we don't know if this is a nuclear winter or just winter, or a place without winter: a place without seasons because not of this world. This is not to say, however, that the question of setting does not arise—or even that it does not arise for the characters in the play. At one point Hamm places his hand against the wall, invoking the "other hell [*l'autre enfer*]" that lies beyond it (GC 3.110; 39). Is this the great outdoors of the world of the work? Is the "other hell" our own?

The setting of things does not become easier when we check the time. In *Waiting for Godot* Vladimir asks when Lucky became dumb. "*Suddenly furious,*" Pozzo replies in his stead: "Have you not done tormenting me with your accursed time! It's abominable! When! When! One day, is that not enough for you? [*le même jour, le même instant, ça ne vous suffit pas?*]" (*Godot,* 333–334). He calms himself and goes on his way, but the ques-tion remains. The only information we dispose of in the play's case is that at least one of the characters does not believe that the category or concept of time is relevant—although he does find it upsetting. A year after *Endgame*, *Krapp's Last Tape* (1958) begins with the stage direction, "*A late evening in the future*" (GC 3.221). This is not a great deal in the way of precision, but it is nevertheless a time stamp of sorts—and one that seems to indicate that marking time has some meaning—unsurprising given that the play is about love being time's fool. And yet such a sense is fleeting, for we get no more precision in the play that follows—or the play that follows it. *Happy Days* relegates time to another time as, in the world of the play, time markers are a thing of the past. Whenever Winnie catches herself referring to "day" or "night" or using any other term implying succession or progression, she fondly exclaims, "The old style!" (i.e., GC 3.293). One way of reading such statements is as referring to a state of affairs concerning the world of the work. There has been an unnamed catastrophe in that world at some point before the cur-tain on it rises. As a result the time markers no longer have the meaning they have in our world and once did in theirs. Soon after asking, "Where now?" "Who now?" and "When now?" the Unnamable speculates that "one of these days" he will accost a certain passerby (who is, to make things more confusing, perhaps Malone, perhaps Molloy, perhaps neither), before adding, "There are no days here, but I use the expression [*il n'y a pas de jours ici mais je me sers de la formule*]" (GC 2.286; 10). For Worm to move we are told that "the earth would have to quake," although he quickly adds, "it isn't earth, one doesn't know what it is, it's like sargasso, no, it's like molasses, no, no matter" (GC 2.358; 129).

· · ·

A teller of a tale might apologize for an excessive level of detail for the reason that such details threaten to muddle the story's message. But what of a teller who professes to have no message and to have no higher aspiration or expectation than to muddle? What of a work that "ruthlessly drains away the notions of space and location," one where "nowhere" is "not a place" but "a goal, like silence" (Wood 2010, 171)? What stance on the particular is proper in that case? "To tell the truth," we read in *The Unnamable,* "I believe they are all there, at least from Murphy on, I believe we are all here" (GC 2.287; 10). Where, we might well wonder, is *here?* It is a space that becomes a good deal more difficult to locate when he makes clear that "here is my only elsewhere" (GC 2.395; 193). It is not that the narrator is uninterested in where he has been set, in the question with which he begins ("Where now?"), it is that he is made not to know the answer. "Hell itself," he reflects, "although eternal, dates from the revolt of Lucifer. It is therefore permissible, in the light of this distant analogy, to think of myself as being here forever, but not as having been here forever" (GC 2.289–290; 14). How distant is this analogy? From such a passionate reader of Dante, one who named the protagonist of his first two fictions after one of Dante's friends and who had his copy of Dante at his deathbed, it may not seem so distant—that is, if you add to this the fact that the world described is one of endless suffering. In the Whoroscope notebook, kept during the years leading up to *Murphy,* Beckett noted to himself, "But keep the whole Dantesque analogy out of sight" (Caselli 2013, 244). Far from being kept out of sight in this later work, the analogy is underlined as the Unnamable moves through his "hell of stories" (GC 2.373; 155). Of a cold creeping into a story he remarks, "Strange hell that has no heating," which does not tell us that he is in hell, or even that he thinks he is (GC 2.352; 120). It does, however, tell us that inventions in his world are on the model of hell. Being in hell would explain how, without a body, the Unnamable speaks, as well as why he does not believe he is living, why he feels tormented by unseen forces, why he has no other hope than to cease existing, in whatever way he does, why he ends his long aria evoking a "strange pain, strange sin" (GC 2.407; 213). The analogy offers only one conclusion: if this is hell, then hell is indistinguishable from the space of literature. This is, of course, not the end of the reader's worries, for the uncertainty of "Where now?" flows from the question that follows it: "Who now?" (GC 2.285; 7). "I know it's not I, that's all I know, I say I, knowing it's not I, I am far, far, what does that mean, far" (GC 2.398; 197). Far are the windy plains of Troy, far the whale-road and the coast of Bohemia, far heaven, hell, purgatory, earth, self, other, or anything else we might use to situate it in this world or another, for far is the world in which *near* and *far* make sense. It is one thing to say to hell with all this fucking scenery, and another to say to hell with space and time.

In a conversation with Adorno in 1967 Beckett said that his "task" was to "move in an endlessly small space" (Tiedemann 1994b, 24). This remark remained much on Adorno's mind, and finds its way into his *Aesthetic Theory*, albeit without quotation marks, as Adorno finds that Beckett "views his task as that of moving in an infinitely small space toward what is an effectively dimensionless point" (Adorno GS 7.310; 292). In the margins of his copy of *The Unnamable* Adorno linked it to the space of writing: "the unbelievable *abstractness* of the pure *this* [*die ungeheure* Abstraktheit *des reinen Dies*]" (Adorno 1994, 53; Adorno's emphasis). The Unnamable tells us that "the place may well be vast, as it may well measure twelve feet in diameter. It comes to the same thing" (GC 2.289; 13). As for himself, he is "invisible perhaps, or as vast as Sirius in the Great Dog," after which he quickly adds, "These expressions mean nothing" (GC 2.299; 31–32). Such expressions mean nothing because we have, in the words of a later work, "a space with neither here nor there where all the footsteps ever fell can never fare nearer to anywhere nor from anywhere" (GC 4.420).

By the time Beckett wrote his *Texts for Nothing* the earth and the sky are no longer loathed, because no longer known except by hearsay: "the sky, I've heard—the sky and earth, I've heard great accounts of them"

(GC 4.310; 162). The voice seeks to forestall any doubt on the reader's part by stressing that he is merely repeating what he has heard, "word for word" (GC 4.310; 162). The speaker's mind is soon off again, noting, "The sea too, I am conversant with the sea," but the point remains the same: that the natural world is cut off from the unnatural work, leaving what will become in late works such as *Ill Seen Ill Said* and *Worstward Ho* a "Thenceless thitherless there," "A place. Where none," "the inexistent center of a formless space," with their ever-shrinking goal a dimension-less point as fine as the tip of a pencil (GC 4.310; 162; GC 4.473; GC 4.471; GC 4.451; 8–9).

CHAPTER SIX

No Symbols Where None Intended

HAPPY DAYS was not the first of Beckett's plays to inquire into its own meaning. In *Endgame* Clov repeatedly observes that "something is taking its course." On one occasion the reflection is followed by a moment of uneasy silence, after which Hamm asks: "We're not beginning to ... to ... mean something?" (GC 3.114–115; 47; Beckett's ellipses). Clov replies: "Mean something! You and I, mean something! *(Brief laugh.)* Ah that's a good one!" (GC 3.114–115; 47). All uneasy laughter aside, Hamm's concerns are not unfounded. Try as they might, ravaged as their minds, bodies, words, and world might be, *Endgame*'s characters cannot free themselves, or their audiences, from the suspicion that, all appearances to the contrary, they are meaningful parts of a meaningful whole. The figures on stage might be symbols of slavery, of class conflict, of moral, spiritual, historical, technological, artistic, or human degradation. They might be part of a parable. They might offer an artful illustration of Hegel's master-slave dialectic, or of Weber's disenchantment of the world. They might be symbols of the end of metaphysics, the end of humanism, the end of humanity. They might be the means to all sorts of significant ends. But how are we to know which ends, or whether there is an end at all?

Of the arrival of the piano tuners (discussed in the Introduction) we are told that Watt was "obliged, because of his peculiar character, to enquire into what they meant, oh not into what they really meant, his character was not so peculiar as all that, but into what they might be induced to mean, with the help of a little patience, a little ingenuity" (GC 1.227). Watt is not so far gone as to seek a meaning existing on another level than his own, not so peculiar as to seek symbolic significance. The movements of his mind are more solipsistic. It is not into what "the things really meant" that he enquired, but into what, with patience and ingenuity, he might *make* them mean. If the question is why Watt would want to do this, the answer is sanity, for only by attributing significance—somewhere, somehow, to something—can he arrest his slide toward a state where everything and nothing mean everything and nothing. Given the world created for him, that he is unsuccessful is unsurprising. "Watt's need of semantic succor," however humble, cannot be satisfied—a fact which will lead him, as it did Murphy, to an asylum (GC 1.234). Seeing every moment and every event tinkling with a little sound and twinkling with a bit of fury, and yet signifying nothing, proves unbearable even for a creature like Watt.

We are told that "Watt learned towards the end of his stay in Mr. Knott's house to accept that nothing had happened, that a nothing had happened, learned to bear it and even, in a shy way, to like it," though we are also told, "But then it was too late" (GC 1.231). Watt's cross is that he must try to make of the two things one. "That nothing had happened" and "that a nothing had happened" must become synonymous for his vision of a world purified of every trace of meaning, free from every form of symbolism, to persist. Nothing of note happened, and yet things happened which he noted. Next to nothing happened, but his mind made a something of that nothing. That he learns not only to bear this but to like it in his shy way is presented as to his credit, though it does not prevent it from coming too late. The narrator asks, "But what was this pursuit of meaning, in this indifference to meaning? And to what did it tend?," giving as only answer, "These are delicate questions" (GC 1.227). Many questions are deemed too delicate to answer in *Watt*—and these are best reflected in the question marks, centered and set apart by blank lines, noted above. And in one other place.

The most telling remark in *Watt* is also its last. Beckett's last English novel ends with "Addenda"—heterogeneous material about which we are told that "only fatigue and disgust prevented its incorporation"

(GC 1.373). Much is mirror-like in *Watt*, but perhaps nothing so much as its last line. Like an inverted epigraph, the final entry in the "Addenda" is "no symbols where none intended" (GC 1.379). This leads us to the limits of the author's intention and the limits of the symbolic significance of literary language. Of the particular directive "no symbols where none intended," Pilling has noted that the line "looks helpful, but there is of course no authenticated ambience in which it could be so" (Pilling 1994, 37). Hersh Zeifman has likened the phrase to "a pane of glass" in which we see first and foremost our own reflection, with the text glittering indistinctly beyond it (Zeifman 2008, 318). The problem of symbolic significance seemed so great to Gessner that he limited his analysis to *Waiting for Godot, Murphy,* and *Molloy*. Although the entirety of Beckett's trilogy had been published by the time he sat down to write, its second two volumes are left out of account for the frankly stated reason that "the later works, *Malone Dies* and *The Unnamable,* are completely unsuitable as objects of analysis" (Gessner 1957, 35). Their complete unsuitability has nothing to do with quality, and everything to do with the absence of what Gessner could consider representative or symbolic sections. Gessner says that as the two works are so "shapeless" and "without separation and form," "central passages" which the critic might isolate and explicate are quite simply not to be found (Gessner 1957, 35). In the absence of such "central passages" he finds that *any* contention concerning those works "would require citing the entire book" (Gessner 1957, 35).

Were Gessner's an isolated opinion it might be dismissed as a sign of early incomprehension, but the problem he points to could hardly be more pressing, or durable: the problem of exemplarity, of a symbolically representative part expressing a symbolically rich whole, the microcosm reflecting the macrocosm, has lost none of its force. This is everywhere and always a problem confronted by the critic, but Gessner is right that it is present in heightened form in Beckett, and so it should come as no surprise that this was not the last time such an objection would be raised. No less kindred and resolute a reader than Derrida would remark a few months before Beckett's death: "When I found myself, with students, reading some of Beckett's texts, I would take three lines, I would spend two hours on them, then I would give up because it would not have been possible, or honest, or even interesting, to extract a few 'significant' lines from a Beckett text" (Derrida 1989/1992, 61).[1] If the surface is untroubled, then there is nothing to calm. If there are no heightened instances of meaning, no symbolic centerpieces, then all is equally central (and peripheral). Derrida was a self-diagnosed "graphomaniac" and published a truly staggering number of critical studies. He analyzed the mystifying blanks in Mallarmé's poetry, the lacunae in Plato's metaphysics, the silences of Celan, the manuscript Genet ripped into little pieces and tossed in a toilet, but confronted with Beckett's works he had to "give up." Derrida's at once methodological and personal preference for moving from the margins of texts to what had been seen as their centers runs up against a stubborn problem in Beckett: How does one distinguish the central from the peripheral? If the whole is chaos and mess, can any messy part express and explicate the chaotic whole? If the principle of organization was maximal disorder, how might that be measured? For this same reason Adorno, while himself trying to write an essay on *The Unnamable* he would never be able to complete, noted: "B[eckett] arrived at the point of indifference [*den Indifferenzpunkt*] between story and theory" (Tiedemann 1994b, 61). In the margins of his copy of the novel, alongside Beckett's lines "I shall no doubt be launched again, girt with better arms, against the fortress of mortality," Adorno wrote that this was "the key passage," before adding, further down the page, the question: "But to what?" (Tiedemann 1994b, 48).

Mud

As Beckett moves away from familiar places there is one setting which becomes central: mud. "I know there is nothing to be done and that nothing of any value will be done," Beckett wrote in 1930, "but one goes on, driven by the wind, like the accidiosi" (LSB 1.25). Beckett happens to make a mistake in this early letter, but one bearing a hidden felicity in its folds. It is the lustful, not the slothful *(accidiosi)*, who receive Dante's punishment of being "driven by the wind." And yet there seems an echo of the right image as the *accidiosi* Beckett refers to are locked in *"la belletta negra,"* the black muck, mire, and slime of their immobile suffering—and thus the substance to which Beckett's later art would be so drawn. The first sentence of a rejected last story for *More Pricks Than Kicks* begins "in the muck" (Beckett 2014, 3). In *First Love,* we find the narrator "flat on my face in the mud under the moon"—and these are only the first of many subsequent agonists and protagonists to find themselves in a similar position and a similar substance (GC 4.237; 28). No writer has sung so much of mud, from the first words of Beckett's first book—borrowed from another Italian poet: *"e fango è il mondo"*—to the "dark earth sodden" and "black sopping peat" of the *Texts for Nothing* to Winnie's special position in hard-packed mud in *Happy Days* to Beckett's epic of mud, *How It Is.* All of which makes Beckett's slip seem particularly prescient. Striving to explain the way in which his work was "diametrically opposed" to Joyce's, Beckett once remarked, "I take away all the accidentals because I want to come to the bedrock of the essentials" (Knowlson 2006, 47). Beckett said he wanted to get down to "the bedrock," and yet it seems that he found it to have been mud all the way down.

In light of all this mud, Beckett's reader might well wonder what it is meant to mean. And all the more as it is just the beginning. We find, for instance, a narrator in *Texts for Nothing* speak of *"la vase, comme avant la vie,"* and which Beckett enriches in English as "slime, as before matter took ill" (GC 4.300; 141). Beckett's Unnamable, as is often the case, seems to speak for the whole "gallery of moribunds" when he proclaims: "To contrive a little kingdom in the midst of the universal muck, then shit on it, ah that was me all over [*Se tailler un royaume, au milieu de la merde universelle, puis chier dessus, ça c'etait bien de moi*]" (GC 4.292; 119). Mud and all its kindred names and substances—from shit to muck to mire— are present in profusion in the years and pages that follow, and nowhere more so than in *How It Is,* set exclusively in the mud. In *The Image,* the precursor to *How It Is* (some parts of which went unchanged into the final work), the image that gives the story its title is one of being in the mud. Its first line is *"La langue se charge de boue,"* and through it Beckett is able to say, thanks to the fact that *la langue* means at once *tongue* and *language,* that a tongue is moving in mud and that its language is loaded with mire (9). This central image becomes the backdrop for what follows, as *How It Is* unfolds its strange tale of suffering in a mud where

Beckett's creatures crawl for hundreds of pages on end, and where we see no other setting or substance than mud. The end of that terminal tale is not the end of the mud, however, as later radio plays such as *Cascando* wallow in the mud, and *Eh Joe* changes the Biblical "Dust thou art" (Genesis 3:19) to "Mud thou art" (GC 3.395). This is a great deal of mud for one œuvre, and it is consequently tempting to see something significant, something perhaps even symbolic, in it. In a distinctly annoyed review of *How It Is* that John Updike wrote for the *New Yorker,* he wished for the "the END of meditating upon this mud," stressing thereby the difficulty of discovering its point, and the difficulty of putting an end to the search (Updike 1979, 255).

In an early notebook Beckett copied out a passage from Canto Seven of the *Inferno,* where, in Beckett's paraphrase, Dante "sees many fighting and wrangling above the mud, and his guide assures him that there are many sighing beneath it—and hence the many bubbles on the surface. All gurgle a piteous lament."[2] These *"gente fangose,"* these "muddy people," are seen in Dante's poem, "smiting each other not with hand only, but with head and chest and feet, and tearing each other piecemeal with their teeth." Dante's nameless mud dwellers are bubbling and babbling. "Fixed in the slime [*fitti nel limo*]," their chorus forms the words: "We were sullen in the sweet air that is gladdened by the sun," and "now we are sullen in the black mire." Dante's was not, however, the only major reference to mud in Beckett's reading of these years. Plato's *Parmenides* presents a young Socrates. When Socrates explains his idea of ideas which is his doctrine of forms, Parmenides looks for its limits, asking Socrates whether there is an idea of likeness apart from the individual likenesses we perceive. He then asks if there is an idea of the one and the many independent of things, single and multiple, in our world, and is assured that there is. After passing through the cardinal ideas of the true, the good, and the beautiful, Parmenides moves in a different direction, and asks whether there are eternal and immutable forms for even the "vile and paltry things" such as "hair, dirt, and mud" (130). It is with the idea of an eternal and immutable idea of mud that Socrates first feels uncertainty. He responds that no such ideal mud can be thought to exist, though he is also careful not to give Parmenides time to probe further, adding that there are times when he thinks that he should answer that such an idea does exist, times when he thinks that for everything, no matter how vile or paltry, there is an ideally real form, and yet he fears "a bottomless pit of nonsense" in which he might "perish." Plato has Parmenides leave the matter with the prediction that a time will come when "philosophy will have a firmer grasp" on the young Socrates, and that his views on this primal matter will change.[3]

With the question of symbolic meaning in mind, the authors of *The Grove Companion to Samuel Beckett* observe that "sometimes a shelter is just a shelter, a road a road, and mud mud" (Ackerley and Gontarski 2004, 207). They do well to remind Beckett's readers of this. Didier Anzieu had written of "the river of mud whose allegory," beginning with *Molloy*, "will dominate the rest of Beckett's œuvre" (Anzieu 1998, 12). For Anzieu the allegory in question is an "allegory of creation" (Anzieu 1998, 12). Employing a kindred symbolic system, Caselli will claim that the mud of *How It Is* offers a "painfully detailed exploration of the materiality of speech and in its investigation of how repetition and reproduction confer the status of reality upon invisibility" (Caselli 2005, 156). This mud moves for her, however, for when she returns to it, its meaning has shifted: "The mud is also the pleasure of the text itself aspiring to become the materiality of the eroticized body without fissures" (Caselli 2005, 159). Mud thus means the act of artistic creation, the pleasure of language, and the dream of a newly eroticized body. This is, however, only the beginning. The theological note sounded in such phrases as "Mud thou art" leads H. Porter Abbot to find that *How It Is* "recycles both the mud out of which God made Adam, and the Word by which God gave life to the mud" (Abbott 1994, 116). Jackie Blackman, for her part, finds that *How It Is* "evokes the mud, abject violence, and numbering system of the camps" (Blackman 2009, 75). There are thus those who find that the mud is Dante's mud—literary mud; others who see it as the mud of Auschwitz and Hiroshima—historical mud; those who feel it to be the mud of Biblical creation—theological mud; and still others who find it the raw material of expression—creative mud. This diversity of assessment stems from the fact that the mud is both like and unlike the mud of our world. If not an allegory of the concentration camps, if not a nuclear winter's tale, if not the symbol of creation, what then is its story—or is it simply all that remains when you say "to hell with all this fucking scenery"?

That Beckett's first great works were written in the immediate aftermath of World War II, in the same period that information about its greatest horrors—Nazi death camps and the atomic bomb—began to be known, led many to see in Beckett's works a response, even perhaps a warning concerning still darker times to come, of a war far colder than hitherto experienced. In discussing a passage in *How It Is* on, precisely, mud ("the mud engulfs all me alone it carries"), Alain Badiou writes that "you fail to understand the text if you immediately see therein an allegory of concentration camps, of the sick and soiled human animal" (Badiou 1995, 22). This is certainly true, but while Badiou tells us where to turn our eyes *from*, he does not tell us where to turn them *to*. Thirty years before him Hugh Kenner had already remarked of that same book, "Though 'la boue' may vaguely recall the place 'in the Marne mud' where Beckett moved his belongings by wheelbarrow during the hungry winter of 1947, and where nine years later he wrote *Fin de partie,* this information is whimsically extraneous to the present book, the uncertainties of which are not of a geographical order" (Kenner 1968, 191). We need not know whether the mud is French or Irish, Biblical or Platonic, past, present, or future. Creatures crawling through mud, cruelly wielding can openers, are not difficult to visualize, but how it is that they are there in the mud, and what they and that mud are meant to mean, is a more difficult matter.

Mud is ubiquitous, unremarkable, and generally unpleasant. This is the reason that Parmenides suggests it to Socrates. It is not ideal mud that Beckett offers us, but it as little seems real. Can Beckett's mud be the mud of Plato, the mud of Dante, the mud of Genesis, and at the same time the mud of the Marne, the "sea of mud" he found when he arrived for humanitarian work in St-Lô, *"la Capitale des Ruines,"* in August 1945 as part of the Irish contingent of the French Red Cross (LSB 2.18)? Is the mud merely a neutral backdrop against which to show that people want, wait, hurt, need, cry, speak, and are silenced? Or does it offer a different setting, and carry another kind of meaning?

The Gravity of Symbolism

Beckett once referred to Joyce and Mallarmé as authors of "texts into which almost anything may be read" (LSB 2.537). Do things stand differently with his own? Or would it be truer to say that they are texts into which nothing may be read? Beckett often said that he had no interest in symbolic or synthetic analyses, that what interested him were what he called in *Murphy* the "demented particulars" (GC 1.11). In a diary entry he gives his theory of history: "the pure incoherence of times + men + places" (Knowlson 1996, 228). Symbols in the world of a literary work were, for Beckett, like transcendentals in philosophy and unifications in history: efforts to separate what William James called "the muddy particulars of experience" from all of its "muddy instances" (James 2000, 101). Beckett had no desire to remove any mud—on the contrary. And yet it is one thing to tell his audience not to ascend to an empyrean of symbolic meaning, and another thing to block symbolic thought altogether. For our instructions ("No symbols where none intended") leave us squarely before the problem of how we are to locate works which seem to have taken every conceivable pain to disorient us, how to find our way in a world which aspired to look as little like ours as possible.

Elsewhere in the book where he first wrote of Beckett, Blanchot remarked that "the symbolic reading probably represents the worst way to read a literary text. Every time we are bothered by too strong of a term we say: it's a symbol" (Blanchot 1959, 125). But the clumsily symbolic readings Blanchot has in mind represent only one manner of symbolic understanding. For symbolic thought is not only the recourse of lesser minds, and symbols are more than the clutter of the past, more than some attic of art filled with hooded busts and three-legged chairs. One of the greatest twentieth-century scholars of symbolism, from Florentine frescoes to Hopi snake dances, Aby Warburg, saw this clearly. In a note to himself he wrote: "Symbolism understood as (function of gravity in intellectual household)" (Warburg 2010, 615). Warburg was reminding himself that symbolism can as little be banished from our intellectual universe as gravity can be from the physical one. It is a fundamental force of mind, and a fundamental way of understanding art. It can be

used in an endless variety of manners, but it cannot simply be eliminated from the artistic equation.

Seven years before telling himself to "vaguen" *Happy Days,* Beckett
had written to a German correspondent: "I prefer Gegend to Gebiet precisely because it is vaguer" (both terms mean *area*) (LSB 2.548). Beckett
was careful in his vaguening, and the practice can be seen everywhere
in his mature works. The single most famous literary study of the twentieth century, Erich Auerbach's *Mimesis,* begins by distinguishing the
depth and breadth of Homer's world from that of Genesis, and goes on
to trace different reflections of reality from the ancients to the moderns.
Auerbach's analysis—completed as Beckett was writing *Watt*—stops just
short of its contemporaries (the last authors discussed are Woolf, Proust,
and Joyce), but if we were to continue the arc it traces we would find
a quantum leap inward, as Beckett's idea of mimesis is supremely hard
to align with the tradition Auerbach presents. In his mature works
Beckett took great care—both in the writing of his texts and the directing of his plays—to remove anything that might allow them to be
situated. When efforts were made to introduce precision in production
Beckett reacted violently. The result of depriving reader and spectator
of concrete coordinates, of real-world locales in which to imaginatively
set the story, is not, of course, the dismissal of the question asked at the
outset of *The Unnamable,* "Where now?" It is, on the contrary, to increase
its urgency.

Michael Wood reminded Beckett's readers in 1981 that "in spite of
appearances," and even in such late works as *The Lost Ones* (which takes
place in a hellish cylinder), "a good deal of mimesis remains in Beckett.
However broken or derelict, schematic, unlikely or cruel, a *world* is being
imagined or remembered or both, and then imitated in words" (Wood
1999, 34; Wood's emphasis). In a related vein Christopher Ricks would
argue that Beckett could not be farther from "the flaccid assurance that
everything is fictive and verbal, and that the real has finally been shown
the door" (Ricks 1993, 146). Weller in turn noted that in *Dream of Fair to
Middling Women* "there is no sense that art is to be thought as coherent
and unified. Only later will Beckett come to see aesthetic form as
standing in opposition to that which it treats; only later will he abandon
the principle of absolute mimesis" (Weller 2005, 56). This is sharply seen,

and yet leads us to the uncomfortable question of what form of mimesis with what symbolic charge remains. "Repelled by mimesis from his earliest years, Beckett is yet unwilling or unable to abandon representation wholly," remarks still another of Beckett's most influential critics (Gontarski 1985, 1). Wholly abandoning representation is sometimes presented as though, if not quite a bagatelle, at least possible—as though it were an option among others, such as writing in terza rima or setting a story in Killarney. A truly and totally nonrepresentational or nonrelational writing (as distinguished from one where the reference was highly uncertain) is something never yet seen. The ultimate import of deconstruction for the study of Beckett lies less where Ricks rejects it than here. It lies not in separating world from text, for, as Derrida intuited, Beckett's texts require no outside assistance in this regard, but, instead, in linking world and text. For just as deconstruction pointed to the distances between work and world, it showed that this distance could never be unlimited. Not only did Derrida leave no study of the contemporary who seemed most to speak to his concerns, neither did Paul de Man (who never so much as mentions Beckett in any of his published writing), and yet de Man's repeated underlining of the idea that "the notion of a language entirely freed of referential constraints is properly inconceivable" is shown nowhere so vividly as in Beckett's writing (de Man 1979, 49).

Allegory

"Dante, if he can ever be said to have failed," wrote Beckett, "fails with his purely allegorical figures, Lucifer, the Griffin of the Purgatory and the Eagle of the Paradise, whose significance is purely conventional and extrinsic" (GC 4.547). That allegory threatens all art is visible for Beckett in the works of even great poets such as Dante, or the Spenser whose "allegory collapses after a few cantos" (GC 4.547). Beckett adores Dante the way Proust adores Giotto: not for his allegory, but despite it. Beckett will thus say of Dante that "because he was an artist and not a minor prophet" he "could not prevent his allegory from becoming heated and electrified into anagogy" (GC 4.547). What real artists do is burn at an incandescent point that cannot be cooled or compressed into the frozen forms of allegory. Beckett loathed the laziness of symbolism and allegory, but he loathed more than their laziness. He seemed to not only dislike but to dismiss the idea of a level of reference that could be called symbolic. But a world without life beyond parents in garbage cans and a blind master putting his servant through pointless paces is something an audience, come what may, however astutely or awkwardly, is bound to situate.

If the question is what Beckett is then asking of his audience, the answer is not the suspension of the symbolic element in understanding. He does not find it strange that symbols come to mind in connection with his works. "That at any moment Symbols, Ideas, Forms might arise [*se profilent*]," he wrote in 1953, "this is for me secondary—is there anything behind which they do not arise [*derrière quoi ne se profilent-ils pas*]?" "In any event," he continues, "there is nothing to be gained by giving them clear form [*à les préciser*]" (LSB 2.389; 391; translation modified). There is thus nothing nefarious about symbolic reflection per se; it is the act of holding its hand Beckett condemns. "Too much color" was Beckett's frequent, head-shaking objection during rehearsals of his plays, for color suggested symbol, not in the way that green signified hope and red rage, but that coloring speech and scene situated them, and before long the clever viewer knows right where she is, which is the last thing Beckett wanted to see in the theater (cf. Asmus 2012, 257). Writing to Caspari with material that might be of assistance for the latter's 1953 German production of *Godot*, Beckett says of the play's figures that far from being unified symbolic wholes, and far from being placed in a "symbolic play," his characters are marked by the "refusal to tone down all that is at one and the same time complex and amorphous in them [*d'atténuer tout ce qu'ils ont à la fois de complexe et amorphe*]" (LSB 2.389; 391). Beckett will write Alan Schneider early on in their collaboration that the problem actors have in portraying Pozzo "results I think from their efforts to clarify it and to give it a unity and a continuity which it simply cannot receive" (LSB 2.586). Albright saw the result of this process as a situation where "Beckett fringes his protagonists with an iridescence of unmeaning" (Albright 2003, 58). The reason they shimmer is that they oscillate in our understanding, moving between a symbolic suggestion (so too are you) and a literal one (so are you not). In *Ill Seen*

Ill Said the female figure ill seeing, ill saying, is surrounded by twelve indistinct figures, and this emblematic formation is likely to recall the yearly round, the zodiac which marks it, the apostles, and other kindred formations without the slightest hope of fixing one in place.

Is *Endgame* about Auschwitz and about Hiroshima and about the master-slave dialectic and the arrested march of history and an allegory of artistic creation here on what Krapp calls "this old muckball" (GC 3.228)? The characters onstage in *Endgame* suspect that "something is taking its course," but none of them pretends to know what, or why, and all would prefer to know no more than they already do. Things stand differently for us. As Wolfgang Iser first noted, there is an almost axiomatic relation to be found in this regard, as the less Beckett's characters care about their condition, the more we do. It should come as no surprise that the most passionate viewers of *Endgame,* such as Adorno and Cavell, seek to see their way clear. They are far too curious to say along with the characters that it does not matter, that nothing is of any importance. They feel that they are being shown a kind of meaninglessness, a representation of meaninglessness, even a parody and burlesque of meaninglessness, but that this meaninglessness is not ultimate and final, and beneath the seeming meaninglessness they sense a meaning, and not just any meaning, but one as powerful as ever conveyed onstage. This would be a triumphant state of affairs if they agreed, even approximately, as to what this was. Each sees something strongly tinged by their situation. A German Jewish polymath forced to flee his country by a regime attempting to destroy all he had ever loved sees the remnants of Auschwitz and the misery of philosophy on stage in *Endgame.* Cavell sees there not Germany's genocide, but his own country's moral catastrophe, Hiroshima, and the "the phenomenology of the Bomb" which it engendered—along with the madness of philosophy. The question *who is right?* might better be posed as *who could be wrong?* No mention is made in *Endgame* of death camps or nuclear weapons. No mention is even made of weapons or war. These things are heard in the silence Beckett said he wanted to have pouring into his drama as into a sinking ship.[4] Both philosophers find that the characters on stage would only speak and move and hope and despair as they did if they were confronted with the remnants of Auschwitz—or with the phenomenology of the Bomb—for nothing else in their world could produce such desolation. But that, of course, presumes that the movements on stage reflect those of history. *Endgame* is, as Beckett was careful to remind audiences, only a play, merely a play, purely a play. It is not real—and so no cucumber sandwiches, no election reform, no marriage theme or revenge plot, no progression or regression, and thus no Auschwitz, no Hiroshima, nothing of our world—or so, at least, Beckett said. Not for nothing have two other of Beckett's great early critics (Vivan Mercier and Hugh Kenner) compared his works to Rorschach blots (Mercier 1977, vii; Kenner 1968, 66).

There is a long tradition of seeing Ludwig Wittgenstein as holding a key for Beckett in this connection, from Hoefer (1959) to Cavell (1969), Kawin (1984), Perloff (1996), to still others, none of them perturbed in the slightest by Beckett's own stance on the matter, which was, in his own succinct words: "Don't understand a word of Wittgenstein" (LSB 3.262). Beckett first read Wittgenstein late (in 1959), and it did not hold him. Whence then this conviction? Those for whom Wittgenstein's writings in all their brilliant and fragmentary desperation are a key to all mythologies may presume a general applicability (in a way analogous to Heideggerian interpretations). But they are a minority. There are, of course, striking affinities between the two men, and each has become an icon of austerity, humility, uncertainty, and principled misery. The most recent of these Wittgensteinian readings of Beckett is also the most radical. Andre Furlani takes up one of Wittgenstein's fondest dreams and presents it as a model: to "stop interpreting." Furlani tells his reader that, in the case of Beckett, "interpretation is neither inexorable nor always desirable," and that we should stop (Furlani 2012, 38). Interpretation may not be desirable (when it disappoints expectations), but it is most certainly inevitable. Furlani interprets Wittgenstein's injunction "Don't think but look!" as saying the same thing as Beckett's (German) note to self while directing *Waiting for Godot: "Zuerst Wahrnehmen dann Kommentieren"* ("First perceive, then comment") (Wittgenstein 2009, 36–37; Beckett 1994, 1.202). Wittgenstein's statement is radical and reproving. It is also presented as an alternative: you can *think* and you can *look* and you should choose *looking* over *thinking.* Beckett's note to self presents something different. He is (in a remark never intended for publication) affirming the natural order, reminding himself of the most common-sensical of matters: that we should observe before we comment and think before we speak. As such it is no more or less compatible with Wittgenstein's logical positivism than with phenomenology, pragmatism, Platonism, or any philosophical approach that respects empirical observation. But the essential element is that interpretation is for both Beckett and Wittgenstein inevitable. That in Wittgenstein's case it is even desirable can be seen in the very passage from which Furlani draws his phrase, and which includes Wittgenstein's famous interpretation of the "family resemblances" shared by the different things called "games" and "play" (36–37). When presented with Wittgenstein's declaration in the *Tractatus,* "Whereof one cannot speak, thereof one must be silent," Beckett remarked that he "fervently disagreed" (Knowlson 2006, 218).[5] To this he added: "That's the whole point, we must speak about it." Beckett does not say this because it is the philosophical thing to do, or the ethical thing to do, but because it is the only thing to do. Furlani finds it significant that Wittgenstein wrote parts of his *Philosophical Investigations* in Ireland—not in contact with Beckett, not while Beckett himself was even in Ireland, but Beckett being Irish, and the Irish being Irish, it is deemed relevant for accounting why it is Wittgenstein to whom we might turn for assistance in understanding Beckett. This is, of course, interpretation. That Furlani exempts himself from his own interpretive ban is of far less importance, however, than the way in which it underlines an essential element of Beckett's art, which is that our curiosity concerning what world the one on stage refers to is not under our control. Furlani's frustration with critics' symbolic overreach is not hard to understand, or to share, and yet it presumes that what Beckett called the "mad wish to know" might be silenced by force of will, something Beckett's writing goes to great pains to disprove (GC 2.330; 83). It is beyond the audience's power to suspend all questions of reference except by genuine indifference. If you go see *Endgame* and are not engaged, are bored and distracted, eager for it to end and relieved when it does, then the question of what it might all have been meant to mean is unlikely to be a burning one. But if, like Foucault, seeing one of Beckett's plays was the decisive event of your intellectual life, or if, like Adorno, Cavell, and a long list of others, you see the most pressing concerns of your time and place on stage, you will, whether you want to or not, try and make sense of them: to interpret a relation, even if a shifting one, between the world on stage and the one surrounding it.

In *Molloy* Moran, on the orders of Youdi, is to find Molloy, which he fails to do. Nussbaum hears in this master's name: "You die" (Nussbaum 1990, 298). Critchley takes issue with this view, asserting that Youdi is instead "Yahweh" (Critchley 2004, 167). Such a symbolic game of the name was not unique to Youdi, as many of Beckett's names are bluntly suggestive, and much has been sought in them. Watt seems only to need a question mark. Molloy is both mollified and mollifying. When we first meet him Moran has all the hallmarks of the moron, including thinking he is not one. Malone's voice speaks of *Me alone*. Mercier both thanks and pleads for grace. Murphy recalls axiomatic pessimism, to begin with.[6] Youdi presents particularities of another order, however. In *Molloy* Youdi's messenger is named Gaber and, for Critchley, he is "all too obviously the Angel Gabriel" (Critchley 2004, 167). This, however, is perhaps not too obvious for all. Gaber, after all, thinks primarily of beer and not only remembers nothing but understands nothing of what is charged to him, making him perhaps an ironic angel—or, just as easily, no angel at all. Gaber is a messenger and, *angelos* being Greek for messenger, the symbolic register is within reach. Precision is had through Gaber's name sounding a bit like Gabriel (albeit less than Godot sounds like God, and it may be recalled how that ends). Moreover, a clearer echo would be the German for gift and giver (*Gabe* is German for gift, and *Geber* is German for giver), not irrelevant given that far and away the most substantial statement Gaber gives is about the gift of life. And yet even if we deem these reservations too slight and suppose that Critchley is right and that this is an angel, the question becomes: what sort of a God sends this sort of an angel? We are told that Youdi finds, like Keats, life to be "a thing of beauty" and "a joy forever" (GC 2.158). In the original life is *"une bien belle chose," "une chose inouïe"*—"a truly lovely thing," an "unheard-of thing." This message sounds, however, so absurd to the character hearing it that Moran interrupts the angel Gaber to ask whether he means human life. Keats's poetic voices find that life is exceptionally painful, but that its exceptional beauty makes it worth living is never in question. Beckett's protagonists see matters differently. To a man and a woman they find life "an excrement." Sometimes they say it in subtle ways, just as sometimes they say it more directly, as where, in not one but two works we are told the moral of the story: "Fuck life" (GC 1.475; 204; GC 3.470).

This does not, of course, mean that Beckett cannot be allegorized. On the contrary. Is the story of Hephaestus's net in Book 7 of *The Odyssey* an allegory of creation? Are Aphrodite and Ares symbols of contrary principals held in union by the net of the Empedoclean *logos* (as suggested in *Heracliti Allegoriae Homericae*)? Allegory is foreign to Homer's modes, and so one good answer is *no*. Beckett's writing is also foreign to allegory, but not because it is ignorant of or indifferent to it. It is, instead, allergic, most aggressively so, to all forms of allegory. Nabokov was also allergic to allegory, said so, and laid many refined, and many not so refined, traps for allegory-searchers. The result has been relatively little allegorical response. Few see Nabokov as the whisperer of Derrida or the code-changer of Wittgenstein, the prophet of being of Heidegger, the raving id of Freud. Whereas all of these things can be found in abundance in writing on Beckett. This makes for the great irony of Beckett's situation: the author who most thoroughly attacked ideas of symbolism is regarded as the most symbolic writer of his century, perhaps rightly.

In the last sixty years Beckett has been the subject of a variety, intensity, and quality of critical writing without modern parallel. From Blanchot to Frye, Kenner to Bataille, Gilles Deleuze to Bruno Clément, Badiou to Albright, Iser to Nussbaum, Guy Davenport to Pascale Casanova, George Steiner to Hélène Cixous, great critic after great critic has attempted to find a critical form that accommodates the mess. Many of those critics do their very best writing on Beckett (nowhere, for instance, does either Adorno or Cavell write better about literature than when writing about Beckett, and they are far from the only critics for whom Beckett is uniquely inspiring). What then is the result of all this indisputably excellent writing for a shared understanding of Beckett's mismade art? The answer is almost nothing. For there is no greater consensus today concerning ideas of meaning and making in Beckett's writing than there was sixty years ago. If anything, there is less. The question that poses to today's critic is whether there is reason to believe that there may be any more shared understanding sixty years hence.

What is at issue is the operative mode of mimesis: where the work stands with respect to the world in which it is experienced. It is more common today to see in Beckett's works an expression of deconstruction than existentialism, of logical positivism than phenomenology, but that has far more to do with prevailing philosophical winds than any critical agreement about the coordinates for answering questions of meaning and making in Beckett's writing. Beckett's is the most uncertain œuvre in Western literary history, by aspiration and design. Uncertainty is not just one element of its aesthetic vision, it is the main element. It is then natural that the question of nature, of all things natural—beginning with art—has proven so difficult to answer. For the very thing that invites symbolic speculation, philosophical parable, psychoanalytical revelation, and mythical resonance also prevents those things from taking hold in a shared understanding of the work. The symbolic surface of Beckett's mature writing is so smooth, its details so vaguened, its form so deformed, and its art so mismade, that no symbolic significance encounters enough friction to come to rest there, and so off everything attracted goes, back into the space of speculation.

CHAPTER SEVEN

The Psychopathology of Character Creation, or The Series

IN 1973 Beckett's first great critic in English, Hugh Kenner, observed that, "surprisingly," Beckett's had already become "an old-fashioned coherent *œuvre*" (Kenner 1973, 183). After Beckett's death in 1989 his first great French critic, Maurice Blanchot, came to the opposite conclusion, finding that, "*il n'y a pas d'œuvre chez Beckett*" "Beckett's is not an œuvre" (Blanchot 1990, 636). Blanchot did not, of course, mean that taken as a whole Beckett's writing was anything less than an astounding achievement, but that this achievement was not rounded, bounded, and intelligible as œuvres had hitherto been—so much so that it was perhaps something else entirely.

An œuvre is, of course, not merely a list of publications. It is an idea about an author, and a story about the creative life. In one respect Beckett's is a classical œuvre, for it tells a classical story. Even if you leave out taking Joyce's dictation, making a tree with Giacometti, winning the Nobel Prize, directing Buster Keaton, driving Andre the Giant to school— even if you leave out the whole life—you are still left with one of the most riveting and reversal-rich stories in literary history. An Irish author with nowhere to turn in his own language enters the French Resistance and in the process so deeply acquires the language that within a decade he counts among the greatest writers in its history—in two separate domains, drama and fiction. For his next act he becomes a great English writer through translating his French novels and plays, after which more original English writing follows. The torrent then becomes trickle as he writes ever shorter, ever barer, ever bleaker, ever more stifled and staccato works, for the stage and radio and film. His last work is a poem he wrote after a terrifying, and terrifyingly emblematic, bout of aphasia, titled "What Is the Word."[1] As all good stories do, Beckett's presents a clear beginning, middle, and end as the author seeks his voice, finds it, raises it, strains it, looses it, finds it again, exeunt.

Beckett's is an œuvre recognized in virtually every way a culture—or, more precisely, two cultures—can do so. And yet what made Blanchot quite justifiably raise the question is that each of Beckett's works not just lightly or slightly but vehemently and volubly rejects, denounces, and generally spits fire from afar at the ideals of competence, coherence, completion, development, progression, aspiration, and achievement on which the notion of œuvre rests. That Blanchot was far from alone in sensing something strange about this œuvre can be seen in that the single most influential inquiry of the last fifty years into the question of what an author is, that of Michel Foucault, both begins and ends with words from Beckett ("What matter who's speaking?"), and draws the limit of its exploration at what Foucault names the "curious unity called by the name œuvre [*qu'on désigne du nom d'œuvre*]."[2] Nor should it surprise that the finest study in French on Beckett, that of Bruno Clément, is titled *L'œuvre sans qualités* (*The Œuvre without Qualities*). If œuvre is a bit too masterful a name for ease of use in Beckett's case, and neither *canon* (despite Ruby Cohn's superb *A Beckett Canon* [2001] and Paul Auster's repeated nonironic use of "the Beckett canon" to discuss editorial decisions in the standard edition of Beckett's English works) nor *corpus* is likely to replace it, there is a term to which no objection can be made, if only because it was Beckett's own: *the series*.

The Series

Watt is wildly funny and full of a dry, crackling cleverness, but its flatlining tone and exhaustive serial permutations led both to its comparative neglect and to Beckett's low opinion of it. "It is an unsatisfactory book," he wrote in 1947, "But it has its place in the series. As will become clear over time, as will perhaps appear over time" (LSB 2.55). In point of fact, and as Beckett makes clear in more than one letter, it was not the first, for "the series [had] begun with *Murphy*" (LSB 2.71). "*Molloy* is a long book, the second last of the series," wrote Beckett (LSB 2.71). Not long thereafter he invokes its successor: "I am now retyping, for rejection, *Malone meurt,* the last I hope of the series Murphy, Watt, Mercier & Camier, Molloy, not to mention the 4 Nouvelles & Eleuthéria" (LSB 2.80). Beckett's works thus formed for him something of a *series.* They proceed—at least to his mind—in a line, following one another not just in chronology but in conception. If we compare Beckett's "series" to what we might more customarily envision under the heading we do not find many points of convergence. The books are not, for instance, linked by the same protagonist, as is common for those in Moran's trade (detectives such as Sherlock Holmes or Jules Maigret). Nor are the books in "the series" linked by their sharing the same time and place, as in Balzac's human comedy. And yet Beckett's readers did not need to await the publication of his letters to sense there was something deeply *serial* about his books, or, for that matter, to comment upon it. It has been, in point of fact, in French and English, one of the most common responses of critics from the 1960s to the present, for it is easy to see the respect in which it is as though each book were written so as to teach you how to read the next. A story whose veracity is called into question in its last lines *(Molloy)* is followed by one in which that veracity is called into account in its first lines *(Malone Dies).* This, in turn, is followed by a work that never gets within a mile of the world of veracity *(The Unnamable).* At the outset of the trilogy, in *Molloy,* there are forests, plains, ramparts, regions, towns, men, animals, north, south, and more. Readers rightly found that novel minimalist when compared with its predecessors: with the teeming Dublin and London of *More Pricks Than Kicks* and *Murphy,* their worlds awash in "demented particulars." When compared with its successors from *The Unnamable* to *How It Is* to *Imagination Dead Imagine* (1965), however, it is lush, lavish, and baroque in its trappings. Molloy eats and sleeps, walks and talks, rides a bicycle, kills an animal, abuses a butler, is himself abused by several policemen, commits grievous bodily harm upon an unsuspecting forest wanderer (who may or may not be someone we will be getting to know quite well in the next book), all against a backdrop of leaves and forests, plains and hills, houses and cities, and even a purpose into the bargain, a primal one: to find his mother. *Molloy*'s first words are "I am in my mother's room. It's I who live here now" (GC 2.3; 7). About his mother Beckett had written, privately: "I am what her savage loving has made me" (LSB 1.552). The biographical critic could not, without effrontery, ask for more. But doing any more of this sort of real-world correlation is about to become a good deal more difficult.

2 to 3

Within moments of receiving his assignment *Molloy*'s Moran finds that "the color and weight of the world were changing already" (GC 2.92; 131). The change proves great. And yet, losing sense of relations—with self, with other, with nature, with culture—as Moran does is light fare when compared with the experience reserved for the Unnamable, for whom it is not that the color and the weight of the world changes, it is that they have disappeared. In the first parts of the trilogy there is a quite impressive parrot, a dog is killed, there is a very pretty photo of an ass in a straw boater, but the animals are then cleared out, followed by the humans. Beckett had not always meant to go too far, nor had the trilogy always been one. His initial plan was for two books. As we saw, Beckett called *Molloy*, in 1948, "*the second last* of the series," just as he referred to *Malone meurt* as "*the last* I hope of the series." That there were to be only two books is not, however, something for which we must rely on private communications. At the outset of *Molloy* we read: "*Cette fois-ci, puis encore une je pense, puis c'en sera fini je pense, de ce monde-là aussi*" (8). This was altered in translation to "This time, then once more I think, then perhaps a last time, then I think it'll be over, with that world too" (GC 2.4; 7). This cannot make an abundance of sense for the first-time reader. Molloy is moving fast in his strangeness and only several hundred pages later does the remark become something approaching clear. What Beckett changed in translation, however, was the number of elements. In the French *Molloy* there would be one more time; in the English there would be two. For by the time Beckett was working on the

English translation of *Molloy* he had already finished *L'Innommable*, and thus knew that his hopes had been disappointed and that when he could not go on, he did.

The trilogy is so masterful that it bears comparison with Beckett's lifelong reading companion, Dante's *Divine Comedy,* and this quite naturally obscures the fact that it would have made perfect sense as a diptych, ending as it would have with the terrific finality of Malone's death rattle. What better place to end than where he had burned all realistic bridges and all symbolic ships, with the speaker dying into the bargain? *L'Innommable* was written in a notebook like the ones in which Beckett had written *Molloy* and *Malone meurt,* and he began as he always did, as everyone always does, with the first page, recto. And then he stopped and turned the page over and proceeded to write the entire rest of the book, filling completely two notebooks, on the verso sides of the pages (cf. Van Hulle and Weller 2014). The part he had always left blank was the only part now made full—in more ways than one.

The Unnamable is what a novel looks like from the other side. Adorno, who excelled at naming, called *The Unnamable* a *wahrhaft ungeheurliche* work (Adorno GS 11.426). His English translator renders this as "genuinely colossal,"[3] which is not wrong, but is only the more decorous half of the spectrum, for Adorno's remark literally means "truly monstrous." Both translations are true of the work. In the first book of the trilogy the mollified Moran leaves open the question of whether he merely invented a few picturesque details (rain, night) or the entire tale. In the second book the question shifts to whether it matters. The dying Malone asks himself, "How many have I killed, hitting them on the head or setting fire to them?" (GC 2.229; 103). The demented demiurge creates new life—such as Sapo and Big Lambert—but his heart is so little in it that he soon stops to exclaim, as had the narrator of *Mercier and Camier,* "What tedium [*Quel ennui*]," "Mortal tedium [*Mortel ennui*]," "This is awful [*Quelle misère*]," followed by similar cries and whispers (GC 2.181; 20; GC 2.211; 71; GC 2.185; 27). These exclamations resemble nothing in the history of Western letters so much as the marginalia of another mind, as in medieval manuscripts where scribes would pause to note such personal matters as "Thank God, it will soon be dark," or "For Christ's sake give me a drink."[4]

Despite the fact that Malone seems to have passed away in the last lines of *Malone Dies,* he is soon back at it, in *The Unnamable.* "Malone is there," we read; "of his mortal liveliness little trace remains" (GC 2.286; 9). Malone's attitude toward his creations, toward those whose story he tells, seemed desultory at the very best—until we meet his successor, who significantly raises the bar for not believing in one's creations by seeing himself as one, and not believing. "I, say I. Unbelieving," is something he goes to some pains to convince us he means (GC 2.285; 7). Where he begins to show himself is in what he will not do, that to which he will not stoop, he does not know why. The *gran rifiuto* of the Unnamable concerns pretending to be real. Some force or forces, in all probability malevolent, want him to believe he is real, but he will not have it. "I've swallowed three hooks and am still hungry," he boasts (GC 2.332; 86). In some initial respects the Unnamable's situation resembles Malone's. "I shall have company," he says. "In the beginning. A few puppets. Then I'll scatter them to the winds" (GC 2.286; 8). But not only will the Unnamable tell us his own characters will soon be scattered to the winds, he points to Beckett's earlier characters and says "all these Murphys, Molloys, Malones do not fool me" (GC 2.297; 28). How he is able to see them is never disclosed, for it is never known. Moreover, he sometimes sees his relationship with "my compatriots, contemporaries, coreligionists and companions in distress" very differently (GC 2.320; 66). He will express varying degrees of uncertainty—unsure as he is whether Malone is his invention or another's, unsure whether Mahood, the voice that tells him he knows things, was things, should be things, is a voice from within or without; whether Worm and the other "miscreated puppets" are parts of himself, or the means by which "the dirty pack of fake maniacs" behind the whole thing are trying to get him "to sign his life warrant" (GC 2.319; 63; GC 2.361; 136; GC 2.351; 119).

For this is the other matter: he is very upset. Who "they" are and why he is upset are not easy questions to answer. "I'll impute words to them you wouldn't throw to a dog," he says, and does (GC 2.373; 155). They (don't ask who) want something of him (don't ask what.). And though he does not know what it is he is not about to grant it, or even understand it. "It is they who dictate this torrent of balls [*ce ramassis de conneries*]," he tells us, and that is enough to give him a low opinion of them

(GC 2.329; 81). As to who they are, he as little knows as his predecessor, Malone, although he knows he does not like the sound of them, "proper cunts whoever they are" (GC 2.262; 158). Not that he pretends to know how they speak and he hears, or what they are, or how any of it works. "But who, they? Is it really worthwhile enquiring? With my cogged means? No, but that is no reason not to. On their own ground, with their own arms, I'll scatter them, and their miscreated puppets" (GC 2.319; 63). The problem with this plan is that not only is he one of the puppets, he knows it. Knowing it creates a singularity in the universe of his fiction. For the Unnamable has access to files which should be secret, ones of which he should have no conception. "Am I clothed? I have often asked myself this question, then suddenly started talking about Malone's hat, or Molloy's greatcoat, or Murphy's suit. If I am, I am but lightly" (GC 2.298–299; 30). Unlike his predecessors, all those Murphys and Malones who do not fool him, he is not fooled by character, and thus not by himself. The Unnamable is more lightly than any character before him, for not only does he see through the illusions, the inventions of Molloy and Malone and Mercier and the rest, he sees through his own, he sees that he is but lightly, that he is separated from them by the thickness of a sheet of paper, just as he sees that he has no greater amplitude than the point of a pencil. In this same breath Beckett has him issue a verdict on making. Just as Moran will find that all language is an excess of language, he will find that all making is mismaking. It is willed creative mismaking, and the will is out of his control. The book is thus a series of singularities, black holes that would lead to the real world, were aesthetic space not curved in upon itself. In an exceptionally charged letter from 1948 from Dublin to Georges Duthuit in Paris, Beckett wrote of *"une pensée autophage et maigrissante,"* "a self-devouring, thinning thought," and the trilogy is its result (LSB 2.83; translation modified).

Beckett had nothing good to say about allegory, even in the hands of such masters of it as his beloved Dante, or Spenser. And yet he is the modern writer who makes most use of its ambidextrous model of meaning. More than any other work in our culture it blurs the lines of invention, more than any other does it present itself as the poorest, unfictionalized truth, before, a moment later, recalling that it is a fiction. Beckett is as close to allegory as modern literature comes. For the point of allegory is not for us to know error is bad; we knew that already (it being named error). It is, instead, the experience of thinking about something with an abstract component, such as what is the right way to live, or whether there is one. When the Red Cross Knight attacks Errour and it vomits foul black poison "full of bookes and papers," alive with "loathly frogs and toades, which eyes did lacke," we are in a highly detailed abstraction (*Faerie Queene,* 1.20.6–8). Its point is clearly not that error is imaginary. Error is real, but in our world it hides its destructive face in a "darksome hole." It is a distinct and truly terrible element with which we would like to have as little to do as possible, and which, if not opposed, spreads quickly, thus the need for knights. For modern readers unschooled in its modes, allegorical writing seems childish, straining against itself, for the more it calls upon our sense of the substance of the world, the farther it seems to move from its message. But that is simply because we are out of practice. It is prolonged because it is more than a message. For were it somehow enough for Spenser to say *Beware error,* or for Dante to say *Stay on la diritta via,* there would be no need for so many cantos. The same is true of Beckett's works. If the point were merely to say that the world is a terrible place, or that every person ever to live found themselves in a world not of their making, or that the language you use is not your own and as much controls you as you control it, he might have made short work of the matter. Beckett's allegory is not of error, it is of creation—experienced as error.

> HAMM: Scoundrel! Why did you engender me?
> NAGG: I didn't know.
> HAMM: What? What didn't you know?
> NAGG: That it'd be you. (GC 3.126)

This is what the Unnamable has to say of his creations, and his book consists of the dialogue he carries out with the creative act—an act which Beckett subjects to more withering scrutiny and which is denounced with more sustained vehemence than anywhere in Western literary history.

The result is something like allegory, but it is an allegory carefully mismade, one that does nothing to naturalize the singularity at the center of the system. Just as Dante's lion is not *either* Pride *or* an animal so fearsome that the air before it seems to tremble, Beckett's Unnamable is not *either* a teller of tales *or* a prisoner of them. He is both, sometimes in alternation, sometimes in one mad breath, and it is at such dimensionless points that the quantum state of his character becomes something like clear. The book is constantly setting its question marks deeper (as Wittgenstein recommended), all the while asking, why "this stupid obsession with depth"? (GC 2.287; 10).

Logoclasm

When wrestling with Menelaus, Proteus changes himself into a lion, a dragon, a leopard, a wild boar, running water, a tree, and yet for all that he cannot compare with the Unnamable for changeability. The first volley of questions—"Where now? Who now? When now?"—is followed by a second salvo: "What am I to do, what shall I do, what should I do, in my situation, how proceed? By aporia pure and simple? Or by affirmations and negations invalidated as uttered, or sooner or later?" (GC 2.285; 7). The answer proves to be both, and the practice of proceeding by aporia will continue quite literally through to the last line: "I can't go on, I'll go on" (GC 2.407; 213). "I should mention before going any further," the Unnamable stresses, "that I say aporia without knowing what it means" (GC 2.285; 8). Directly on the heels of this admission is, however, the still more learned rhetorical question (and joke), "Can one be ephectic [*éphectique*] otherwise than unawares?" (GC 2.285; 8). He shares this uncertainty with his precursor, as Malone had found himself "back at my old aporetics," before asking, "Is that the word?" and answering, "I don't know," and so neither do we (GC 2.175; 10).

Bare ruined choirs of cultivation are not only visible in the Unnamable's deft and darting syntax. He has all kinds of knowledge which, in the world where we read the text, are obtained only through study and travel. He knows, for instance, the exotic, at least what we had hitherto thought of as such: "perhaps I had left my leg behind in the Pacific, yes, no perhaps about it, I had, somewhere off the cast of Java and its

The Psychopathology of Character Creation • 117

jungles red with rafflesia stinking of carrion, no that's the Indian Ocean, what a gazetteer I am, no matter" (GC 2.311; 51). He also knows the classical—about "thousand-breasted Tellus" and that *"De nobis ipsis silemus,* decidedly that should have been my motto" (GC 2.309; 86). He knows the period of Prometheus's punishment, as well as all sorts of things that are thought of as the privilege and province of intellectual refinement. "There's no denying it," says the Unnamable, "I'm confoundedly well-informed" (GC 2.310). There is not only no denying it, there is no explaining it. The result is that we do not know where he is, except in words. "I'm in words," he says, as one might be in tatters—a desperation still stronger in the French: *je suis en mots* (GC 2.379; 166). Like the last line of *Molloy,* "I am in words" sends a shockwave through the book, and through those that preceded it. Something must be feigned in fiction, and this seems unfeigned—which is, in the revolution of the circle, the feint.

But even as diminished a tale as the Unnamable's must have opposition, must have an *agon,* and for that *aporia* will not do. The *agon* of *The Unnamable* is language. Beckett's term *logoclasm* is a quite accurate one for what ensues, as the Unnamable is in open revolt against anything he can name. What made him this way is not known. Was it the world? Or was it being a character? He is out to find the answer, after his fashion. Sometimes he seems to be fighting for character rights, at which moments he describes himself as "a kind of tenth-rate Toussaint L'Ouverture" (GC 2.343; 104–105). At other times he is in it for himself, whatever he is. He is in the position of the partial amnesiac trying to figure out what happened, and keeps happening. He is, however, quite unlike, say, Jason Bourne in this regard, as he has no body—none that works, at least. What works just fine is speech—for he is an exceptionally able sayer and missayer of things, an inspired breaker and stormer of words, a guerrilla fighter against *logos*—aided by the gifts of irreverence, irascibility, fear, and fury. His only way of figuring out who or what he is fighting, and thus perhaps why, is to observe his instincts, his tactics, observe how he opposes this thing he feels he must oppose. And in this respect he does with his combative words what Jason Bourne does with his movements: as he fights he interprets those movements so as to divine who or what made him this way. For in both cases there has very manifestly been a great deal of training, but no memory of why, or what for. All the Unnamable has to interpret, all that might lead him back to whatever started the whole "wordy-gurdy [*la chasse aux mots*]," is his own oppositional instincts (GC 2.392; 187). And as he lays into them we learn something more important than whether or not he was born in Bally, which is how he resists. He is vindictive, but not at individual entities, he does not want to shoot any messengers, he wants the leader, the *logos,* of it all. He has a few words for that thing.

Despite the fact that he seems to be making up his stories as he goes, Malone casts doubt on this by regretting that certain things in his stories are not as he would like, as where he wishes that Jackson had had a cat, or a young dog or, still better, an old dog, instead of a gray and pink parrot he had taught to say "Nihil in intellectu" (GC 2.211–212; 72). That said, what more could one with his aspirations wish for than such a beast? With the Unnamable they might succeed in hammering words into his head, sometimes even elegantly antiquated ones ("they gave me some lessons in pigsty latin too, it looks well, sprinkled through the perjury"), but he will not mean a word of it (GC 2.323; 71). Being a parrot is his fondest dream: to have nothing verbal in mind, even when speaking, even when saying such things as "Nihil in intellectu." By interrupting the famous phrase in its middle it separates the mind from the senses *(quod non prius in sensu),* the mind from the world, precisely the connection through which all trouble comes. And so it should come as no surprise when he himself comes around to this view, exclaiming: "A parrot, that's what they're up against, a parrot" (GC 2.329; 82).

"It is to be hoped," Beckett wrote in his word-storming German letter, "that the time will come—and, thank God, in some circles it already has—when language is best used where it is most energetically and efficiently misused [*missgebraucht (sic)*]" (LSB 1.514). This is no passing concern. Beckett's best uses of language, his most incisive, artful, adventurous, creative, and compelling language, could be no better described than in the terms used in this letter: as language energetically and efficiently misused. One question such misuse raises is *how,* another is *why.* It is in *The Unnamable* that we first glimpse an answer. In one of the arias of uncertainty and rage that make up that work we read:

I'm all these words, all these strangers, this dust of words, with no
ground for settling, no sky for dispersing, coming together to say,
fleeing one another to say, that I am they, all of them, those that
merge, those that part, those that never meet, and nothing else,
yes, something else, I'm something quite different, a quite different
thing, a wordless thing in an empty place, a hard shut dry cold black
place, where nothing stirs, nothing speaks, and that I listen, and that
I seek, like a caged beast born of caged beasts born of caged beasts
born of caged beasts born in a cage and dead in a cage, born and then
dead, born in a cage and then dead in a cage, in a word like a beast, in
one of their words, like such a beast, and that I seek, like such a beast,
with my little strength, such a beast, with nothing of its species left
but fear and fury . . . (GC 2.380; 166–167)

Words define, but that is not all they do—they confine and cage the
beasts who use them. Beckett's speakers cannot help but suspect that
they are at once much more and much less than the words they bring
up. But the unspeakable intuition that he is nothing but words is reserved for the Unnamable. One of his few convictions is that expression
in language is not free: it is, instead, the deepest form of coercion.
The reason this can be both so funny and so unsettling is that in one
respect his experience is universal, for our words are never quite our own,
whether we know how to weave them together to our satisfaction or not.
Words precede us and are not of our making. The Unnamable's addition to this chain of reasoning is that, as a result, they mismake us at
every turn. This gives us a *how*, as well as the beginning of a *why*, for his
manner of proceeding. Writers stand, of course, in a special relationship
to language—an extreme, dynamic, evolving, frequently fraught, and
sometimes frightening relationship to the common means of communication. Consequently, a wide range of passionate attachments and
dispassionate claims about language are to be heard from them. But
no writer expresses such suspicion of language, such resistance to its
movements, so strong a desire for its stilling and silencing, as does
Beckett—and none before him had ever placed this problem at the dead
center of an entire œuvre.

In the Introduction we saw Watt perplexed by a painting of a broken
circle and a dot. His subsequent symbolic search goes no better. "Watt's

stay in Mr. Knott's house," we read, "was less agreeable, on this account, than it would have been, if such incidents had been unknown, or his attitude towards them less anxious" (GC 1.227). As he stares at the painting on the wall, "Watt's eyes filled with tears that he could not stem" (GC 1.273). From here on out it is rough sailing. Things had been slipping from Watt for some time, but now his very words began behaving strangely. "Watt now found himself in the midst of things which, if they consented to be named, did so as it were with reluctance" (GC 1.232).

> Looking at a pot, for example, or thinking of a pot, at one of Mr. Knott's pots, of one of Mr. Knott's pots, it was in vain that Watt said, Pot, pot. Well, perhaps not in vain, but very nearly. For it was not a pot, the more he looked, the more he reflected, the more he felt sure of that, that it was not a pot at all. It resembled a pot, it was almost a pot, but it was not a pot of which one could say, Pot, pot, and be comforted. It was in vain that it answered, with unexceptionable adequacy, all the purposes and performed all the offices, of a pot, it was not a pot. And it was just this hairsbreadth departure from the nature of a true pot that so excruciated Watt. For if the approxima-tion had been less close, then Watt would have been less anguished. (GC 1.232–233)

Curiously, it is not when things seem utterly unlike what they are, or are said to be, that Watt experiences problems. It is when they are indis-tinguishably close to what they are said to be, when appearances seem *not* to deceive him, that a shrinking suspicion arises, and his isolation begins. "The pot remained a pot," we learn. "Watt felt sure of that, for everyone but Watt. For Watt alone it was not a pot, any more" (GC 1.233). Watt knows that the pot is a pot and thus called one. And yet, as though he were struck with the linguistic equivalence of Capgras syndrome, the word has ceased to serve. The link between word and feeling is broken (just as those suffering from Capgras syndrome no longer have the feeling about familiar people that they had in the past, and therefore deduce that these familiar people are imposters).[5] In a related sense, Watt with his pot is like an indolent linguist, glaring at what Ferdinand de Saussure called the "arbitrary nature of the sign." "The closer you

look at a word, the farther it looks back at you," Karl Kraus once remarked (Kraus 1965, 3.291). Watt, however, does not merely realize that
the linguistic sign is arbitrary, that the word is just a word, independent
of the thing it signifies, he also feels isolated in his realization. For the
others *pot* continues to mean *pot*—only for him has it ceased to do so.
Language may have an arbitrary side, but it is one we share—so long, of
course, as we can.

Slight Excesses of Language

Molloy's Moran remarks that "anger led me sometimes to slight excesses
of language," which in turn leads him to reflect, "It seemed to me that
all language was an excess of language [*que tout langage est un écart de langage*]" (GC 2.111; 158). This reflection (that all language is an excess of
language—or, in the original, a "swerving" of language) takes on a life
of its own in that work and its successors—becoming one of the very few
truths Beckett's creations hold to be self-evident. In the next volume of
the trilogy Malone, suddenly mild, remarks: "There is no use indicting
words, they are no shoddier than what they peddle" (GC 2.189). (In the
original Beckett wrote: *Ils ne sont pas plus creux que ce qu'ils charrient,* "They
are not emptier than what they cart"; 34.) However final a judgment this
might seem, it is accompanied by no resignation and is soon succeeded
by the deviant, defiant, vengeful, and triumphant tones of the Unnamable, who declares, "I'll fix their gibberish for them [*Je vais le leur arranger,
leur charabia*]," and finds:

> Not to be able to open my mouth without proclaiming them, and our
> fellowship, that's what they imagine they'll have me reduced to. It's a
> poor trick that consists in ramming a set of words down your gullet
> on the principle that you can't bring them up without being branded
> as belonging to their breed. [*M'avoir collé un langage dont ils s'imaginent
> que je ne pourrai jamais me servir sans m'avouer de leur tribu, la belle
> astuce.*] (GC 2.111; 63)

The Unnamable is careful to add about this "gibberish" that "I never
understood a word of it in any case, not a word of the stories it spews,

like gobbets in vomit [*Auquel je n'ai jamais rien compris du reste, pas plus qu'aux histoires qu'il charrie, comme des chiens crevés*]" (GC 2.111; 63). The Unnamable's control over language, if not its foundations, is, however, impeccable. He is artful beyond words. Cohn and Van Hulle and Weller wrongly describe *The Unnamable* as a work that "almost dissolves syntax itself," for one of the few things held fast to is indeed not self or other, world or work, life or death, reason or madness, but *syntax*—over which the Unnamable has amazing control, in French and English (Cohn 2001, 185; Van Hulle and Weller 2014, 27). This point is relevant because the very fact that the Unnamable has such syntactic mastery spurs our search to understand what happened to this creature, with his wild way with words, to so turn him against the language he deftly employs.

His target extends well beyond "grammar and style," diction and syntax: it is self, other, reason, love, purpose, language, meaning, and, perhaps, mother. The revolt of the Unnamable aims not to say *je est un autre*, or, as does *Watt*, on a strange channel: "*Ot bro, lap rulb, krad klub. Ot murd, wol fup, wol fup. Ot niks, sorg sam, sorg sam. Ot lems, lats lems. Ot gnut, trat stews, trat stews*" (GC 1.303). He aims to unseat the whole thing, even if he has no idea what it is. For Beckett's speakers language does not come naturally. It is social—suspiciously so—and no sooner do they begin using it than it begins using them, telling the tale of a tribe they want no part of. "But what they were most determined for me to swallow," the Unnamable reports, "was my fellow-creatures. In this they were without mercy" (GC 2.292; 18). His fevered pitch, like the vast majority of speakers Beckett will create in his wake, is directed against speaking itself, and is born of the deepest suspicion concerning language's purpose and nature. To speak a language is to belong to a linguistic community, even if only at its cutting edge or lunatic fringe. The mouth opens and here comes everybody, a trillion generations of conception and consensus weighing down on him, through one language and another, none of it his. The isolation felt by Watt with his pot has evolved, serially. The Unnamable suspects that anything he might think he is saying for and of himself, he is saying for and of others. At many points he sees language as part of an insidious plot designed to discipline and punish its speakers, and all the more insidious because there is no point but confinement and no escape because nowhere to go—

nowhere, that is, except a silence he can as little conceive as maintain, made as he is of words. This suspicion will persist for the remaining three decades of Beckett's writing as voices, such as that of *How It Is,* hear in their statements "scraps of an ancient voice in me not mine," which they can as little trace as silence, and as little silence as stomach (GC 2.411; 9).

Viewed as a collective, Beckett's "gallery of moribunds" has a common problem: they cannot stop talking (GC 2.132; 187). Not because it is so pleasurable, commanding, or clarifying to speak—on the contrary. Nothing muddies their waters like their muttering, and yet on they go. Watt experiences in the passage on the pot a transformative event, a moment where the word seems suspended from its congeners. Once isolated from its fellows, and unmoored from its meaning, however, it starts pulling the rest of language along in its wake. As sense and statement increasingly part ways so too does Watt's feeling of connection with his fellows, or those who might present themselves as such. Hand in hand the desire to speak clearly and the ability to do so disappear—followed, as will often be the case in Beckett's writing, by a wildly willful attempt to misuse language with extreme prejudice. What is for Watt a transformative event is a fait accompli for his successors, and Molloy will supply something like a motto for the trilogy when he declares, "No things but nameless things, no names but thingless names" (GC 2.27; 41). For him, as for his creator, word and world seem to have parted ways; they still shadow one another, but the tie that binds them is frayed. And far from seeking to mend it, Beckett's speakers hack and gnaw away at it for all they are worth.

This is the motivation for what Beckett called, in still another arresting phrase from his logoclastic letter to Kaun, a "literature of the unword [*Literatur des Unworts*]" (LSB 1.515; LSB 1.520). If all language is an excess of language, if all making is a mismaking, two possibilities present themselves. One is to try to make things better, to help and heal; the other is to exacerbate, to make them hurt, hoping that "the unworsenable worse" will either reveal the root problem or eliminate the need for further searching (GC 4.480). In *Worstward Ho* we find the starkest instructions and most radical ground rules for such energetic misuse: "Say for be said. Missaid. From now say for be missaid" until the speaker reaches the "unworsenable worst" of the equation: "Said is missaid" (GC 4.471; GC 4.480; GC 4.481). In writing of the painter brothers Van Velde, Beckett pointed to "a path forward" offering "half-glimpses in the absence of relation and the absence of object a new relation and a new object" (Beckett 1984, 137). The truth of language's faultiness will out, but Beckett has his creations accelerate the process, to spread word of its unword.

Such imperatives allow us to contemplate a paradox, and a pathology, that Beckett represents more strikingly than any Western artist of his century. That paradox is choosing pathology: how someone, in Albright's words, "possessing the most remarkable literary equipment of his age, spent a lifetime learning how to write like a mental defective, in a toothless, broken-jawed, goggling idiom, maniacal and compulsive" (Albright 2003, 17). Why choose artful misuse over artful use? Why use one's creative energies to *mismake?* Mismaking and misuse are, of course, relative terms. The dozens of inventions which Shakespeare introduced, from *madcap* to *eyesore,* from *faint-hearted* to *fool's paradise,* might all be classified as instances of misuse, like all poetic inventions. Literary language lives from misuse, removing as it does what Coleridge called "the film of familiarity" (Coleridge 1983, 2.7). This is to say that the creative use of language can always be accused of misuse, especially if one does not like it. But what Beckett is advocating here is of another order: to find the innermost form of thought itself, the *logos* at the heart of language, and trample it underfoot. The Unnamable is at once Beckett's greatest and most enigmatic creation, his Hamlet, and his character is developed solely through opposition to an environment exactly like that of every one of his literary forebears in being made of words. But unlike every one of them, he not only knows it is made of words, he is out to get them.

As a young man Beckett once summarized the stances that could be taken with respect to language's nature: "the materialistic and the transcendental views; the one declaring that language was nothing but a polite and conventional symbolism; the other, in desperation, describing it as a gift from the Gods" (GC 4.500–501). Beckett presents a third way. Still elsewhere in the German letter to Kaun, Beckett refers to an *Unnatur des Wortes,* an "unnature of the word," corresponding with the "literature of the unword," and which he qualifies as "very desirable" (LSB 1.514; LSB 1.518; LSB 1.515; LSB 1.520). The Unnamable as little understands what language and its speakers want of him as Molloy understands the desires of the local police. And yet he does not need to know very precisely what they want of him to resist, for wanting him to be human is more than sufficient to incur his wrath. For all he knows they may be gods. "I alone am man and all the rest divine," he declares, just as he will declare, "I am Matthew and I am the angel, I who came before the cross, before the sinning, came into the world, came here"—which is immediately followed by "I add this, just to be on the safe side," for he has no idea who or what or when or where or why he is, nor is he made to know (GC 2.295; 24). One thing about which he is sure is that nothing should be permitted to matter in this regard besides resistance. God or man, they are not to be trusted. If they are gods and language is their gift, or their punishment, they are obviously a nasty, perhaps Gnostic, lot, the less said about the better.

> The fact that Prometheus was delivered twenty-nine thousand nine hundred and seventy years before having purged his offense leaves me naturally as cold as camphor. For between me and that miscreant who mocked the gods, invented fire, denatured clay and domesticated the horse, in a word, obliged humanity, I trust there is nothing in common. (GC 2.297; 27; translation modified)[6]

Nearing his end the Unnamable says, "There was never anyone but me," and that "all these stories about travelers, these stories about paralytics, all are mine" (GC 2.395; 193; GC 2.405; 210). This is a point he had approached before: "When I think, that is to say, no, let it stand, when I think of the time I've wasted with these bran-dips [*ces paquets de sciure*], beginning with Murphy, who wasn't even the first, when I had me, on the premises" (GC 2.384; 173). As Clément writes, "nothing more closely resembles an author than a Beckettian narrator" (Clément 1994, 46). All that is said in the work seems said about the work: about thinking, imagining, creating, about all that is required to write a novel, all that has to be given, all that has to be taken, all that has to be revealed and concealed, all the truths and lies one must invent when playing God. As the trilogy progresses we see the removal of more and more elements, more and more artifice, and it may seem we are moving closer and closer to the singularity that separates truth from fiction, work from world, and thus the point of stories. The rhythm, musical and mental, of the book is set by such moments where it seems as though the Unnamable is about to shed the final vestige of fiction and at last be real, removing the barrier between art and life, ceasing to be unnamable, and taking the name of Samuel Barclay Beckett. But then something interferes, the rage returns, and words get in the way.

For these reasons *realism, narrative,* and *mimesis* prove to be very unwieldy terms for describing the situation (consequently they are often debated, customarily blunted or sharpened by a *post-* or an *anti-*). And so it is little wonder that there should be such recourse to bespoke terms like *vaguening, unwording, logoclasm,* and *mismaking.* "The fiction is at once the appearance of a story," writes Badiou, "and the reality of a reflection on the writer's work, its poverty and grandeur" (Badiou 1995, 6). True enough, it would appear, but what makes that reflection realer than the story it interrupts? Is one really *realer* than the other? Moreover, how do we conceive of the Unnamable writing? Malone was forever telling us about his pencils and notebook and what he did with them, but, given he has neither hands nor the power of speech, with what would the Unnamable write, "to consider only the manual aspect of that bitter folly" (GC 2.295; 24)? The one bit of fictional bedrock is in the necessity of going on—as the one thing that does not waver in the book is the indomitable will to go on. Beckett remarked of Bram Van Velde that he "paints, since he is obliged to paint," prompting his interlocutor to respond:

D—Why is he obliged to paint?
B—I don't know. (GC 4.560)

No more is known of the Unnamable, but the one thing not broken in his logoclasm is the will to break, and so perhaps we have in him the verso of the oldest poetic thing in the world: the unnamable desire to do things with words.

How It Will Be

In *That Time* (1975) a voice tells itself: "turning-point that was a great word with you before they dried up altogether always having turning-points and never but the one" (GC 3.420). There is in the story of Beckett's œuvre a decisive turning-point: the "siege in the room" which Beckett also called "the frenzy of writing" lasting from 1946 to 1950 and during which Beckett wrote his first French fictions, the trilogy of novels *Molloy, Malone Dies,* and *The Unnamable,* the *Texts for Nothing,* and *Waiting for Godot.* "It was always submission with me," Beckett noted, "until I overdid it, with *L'Innommable,* I mean beyond the joke" (LSB 2.544). What came before seems to prepare for and presage it; what followed seems to convalesce from it. Beckett was fond of calling *Texts for Nothing* "the afterbirth [*arrière-faix*] of *L'Innommable,*" specifying that they were "not to be approached [*inabordables*] directly" (LSB 2.299; 300). And indeed they seem to take up the most fundamental elements in *The Unnamable* and first explore and then explode them. In 1951 Beckett wrote his French publisher that he was happy *L'Innommable* was moving quickly toward publication, as "it is this last work that I am most attached to, although it has left me in a sorry state [*dans de sales draps*]" (LSB 2.234). He does not expand upon his state—whether it is physical exhaustion, or something far more difficult to name—noting merely, "I'm trying to get over it. But I'm not getting over it" (LSB 2.234). Two and a half years later, with the French trilogy in stores, Beckett wrote, "I feel more and more that I shall perhaps never be able to write anything else. *Niemand wandelt unbestraft* [*sic*][7] on the road that leads to *L'Innommable,*" to which he adds, "I can't go on and I can't get back" (LSB 2.434). Beckett closes the matter, saying, "Perhaps another play some day"—and given that the play was to be *Endgame,* any reports of demise will sound exaggerated. The abbreviated allusion—*Niemand wandelt unbestraft*—Beckett uses to underline this point is one he trusts his friend McGreevy to recognize, not easily done given that it is missing its trees, and thus its meaning. In a fragment of a letter to another close friend Beckett spoke of a special solitude seen in the paintings of Bram Van Velde, and of a desire "to be alone with impunity, to wander beneath the palm trees

without being shat upon by the vultures" (LSB 2.78; 79). Here too
Beckett trusts his addressee to catch the reference. In Goethe's *Elective
Affinities* Ottilie remarks, "Nobody wanders under palm trees un-
punished, and one's opinions must surely change in a country where
elephants and tigers are at home [*Es wandelt niemand ungestraft unter
Palmen, und die Gesinnungen ändern sich gewiß in einem Lande, wo Elefanten
und Tiger zu Hause sind*]" (Goethe 1972, 173). Ottilie is made to say something which travelers (and exiles) often note: that travel does not simply
broaden horizons, it changes them, and a new nature nurtures new
thinking. The exotic wilds in which Beckett had been wandering in *The
Unnamable* are not those of a far-off place—not palm-ringed Tahiti or
tiger-wild India. There are in *The Unnamable* no elephants. There are
barely people, although where Beckett has wandered is nonetheless a
harrowingly foreign place.[8] The "afterbirth" of *Texts for Nothing* followed
The Unnamable, and then night. It was a beautiful night, a night at the
theater, as *Endgame* was played, *Krapp's Last Tape, Happy Days,* and much
more amazing work. Beckett's next, and last, long narrative work, *How It
Is,* came a decade later, and makes *The Unnamable* seem like a rollicking
tale of intrigue and adventure by comparison with its unpunctuated
pain, muddy wastes, and mired artifice. The thing that had been fluid in
Beckett's writing was now frozen, and while it would occasionally warm
again, it would never lose the chill in its voice. Kenner would say of *The
Unnamable* that it is "the book that, of all the fictions we have in the world,
most cruelly reduces the scope of incident, the wealth of character"
(Kenner 1973, 112). Were he to seek a rival for this title, he would need
go no farther than Beckett's next long fiction. Far into Part Two of *How
It Is* we read:

> the proportion of invention vast assuredly vast proportion a thing
> you don't know the threat the bleeding arse the cracking nerves you
> invent but real or imaginary no knowing it's impossible it's not said
> it doesn't matter it does it did that's superb a thing that matters.
> (GC 2.462; 113)

The speaker does not pretend to be in a privileged position as regards
his own actions or inventions. He crawls cruelly through the mud, tor-
turing a fellow traveler with a can opener, but does not pretend to know

whether he is really doing so, or whether it matters. Beckett's contemporaries and first critics often experienced the long diminuendo of the last decades of his writing as a commentary on the changed status of the work of art in modern times, as though it were a raised finger at the proliferation of bright vacuous images inundating our culture. The titles alone of these shrinking works and worlds seem to tell a tale of woe, whether of the earlier works, or the modern times: *From an Abandoned Work, All That Fall, Fizzles, Enough, All Strange Away, Imagination Dead Imagine, The Lost Ones, Ill Seen Ill Said, Worstward Ho, Stirrings Still,* and Beckett's final poem, "What Is the Word." What truly makes Beckett's œuvre unlike any other is his trampling upon the idea of a sanctifying role for art: a relation of art to life where art, from on sacred high, tells us how to live, eat, grow, be brave, marry, and die. In this light Blanchot's sense of œuvre ceases to seem so outlandish.

The voice of Malone is like the voices of Molloy and Moran who preceded him in the trilogy, only more frank about what is being invented, and why. The voice of the Unnamable, in turn, is like Malone's voice, only raised, now that he has nothing but language to die into. But the voice of *How It Is* and the voices from *All Strange Away* to *Stirrings Still* have a different tone entirely. *The Unnamable* is as relentless an expression of emotion as any work of the century. There is a departure at this point in Beckett's aesthetic development which is often seen as a progression, as though there were no other conceivable routes, as though Beckett merely stayed on a worstwardly course from *The Unnamable* onward. And yet the leap is great, for *How It Is* takes place on another planet of expression—one unlike all that precede it, and like all that follow it. What has changed is emotion. While the themes and situations are the same as in *The Unnamable,* the emotional register has been thinned to a hard line. Feeling and fluency disappear. There is no longer anything natural or positive about expression, or resistance. What goes missing with this huge truncation of register is humor. The Unnamable furiously, and funnily, resists a voice dictating to him a torrent of balls about how to be, do, and think. In *How It Is* the voice is no longer resisted, and so there is no more questioning (there are precisely zero question marks in *How It Is*—a diacritical mark with a life of its own in Beckett's writing—concerning which the reader might think of the question marks which roam free, uncoupled from any statement, in *Watt*). The voice we hear no longer resists, it only quotes: "how it was I quote before Pim with Pim after Pim how it is three parts I say it as I hear it" (GC 2.411; 9). And whereas *The Unnamable* would begin with aporia and maximal uncertainty about the means of going on, *How It Is* has everything laid out from the beginning, for, even if we cannot recognize it right away, we have been offered in this first line a total summary of the following, which is indeed in three parts, moving from how it was to how it is, before, with, and after Pim, all "ill-said ill-heard ill-recaptured ill-murmured in the mud" (GC 2.411; 10). How it is for the voice in *How It Is* is very different from how it had been hitherto. The voice of the Unnamable was, by definition, undefeatable (given his position on losing). Not so his successors. The faculty of fluid expression, which the Unnamable, for all his disorientation, possessed so greatly, is gone as well. Whereas the Unnamable thrilled in excelsior outrage ("ah fuck all that"), this subsequent voice is curbed, cowering, caged (GC 2.392; 187). With the resistance of these voices goes their humor. Whatever has happened to caring in this world is cataclysmic, such that the voice of *How It Is* makes the Unnamable sound like Shelley: "sudden series subject object subject object quick succession and away" (GC 2.415; 16). This is no criticism of Beckett (or Shelley), but it is a fact that demands understanding, and a place in the series.

Conclusion

Aesthetic Pessimism

Critics, Bastards, Shutting Off

In *Waiting for Godot* Vladimir and Estragon argue about who interrupted whom, with tempers rising until one calls the other a "moron." Estragon, thus addressed, is pleased. "That's the idea," he says, "let's abuse each other." The two then exchange insults, with Vladimir calling Estragon an "Abortion!" and a "Sewer-rat!" and Estragon replying with "Vermin!" and "Curate!" The debate ends when Estragon exclaims, *"with finality,"* "Crritic!," after which Vladimir is seen to *"wilt, vanquished"* (*Godot*, 268–269).

Beckett had little use for literary criticism, his own or others'. His friend Cioran tells of one evening in Paris during which a by-then famous Beckett was posed "uselessly erudite questions" which so exasperated Beckett that he fell silent, then picked up his chair and literally turned his back on the gathering (Cioran 1976, 46). Beckett was more patient, and verbal, with those who were producing his works, and yet when one of his directors proposed writing a critical article in 1957, Beckett inveighed first against "these bastards of journalists" who keep asking the same questions, before turning to worse: "I feel the only line is to refuse to be involved in exegesis of any kind. That's for those bastards of critics" (LSB 3.82).

Beckett's first published words were "The danger is in the neatness of identifications," and this was a danger of which he remained, for the ensuing sixty years of writing, keenly aware (GC 4.495). "I don't feel this need to explain things," he remarked while writing *How It Is,* "or to make quite sure that the dear listener will not be left with the hideous feeling that the two old chaps are slightly unlikely" (LSB 3.259). He found that those with a need to explain such things could only be fixed upon "mysteries of their own making," and that, "if people want to have headaches among the overtones, let them" (LSB 3.82). When, decades later, he sat down to write *Catastrophe* (1982), he depicted a related situation. The director-figure of the play is an instrument of an utterly corrupt state (like the one then imprisoning the play's dedicatee, Václav Havel). But he is a director nonetheless, and when his assistant suggests a gag for the prisoner, the director explodes: "For God's sake! This craze for explicitation [*Cette manie d'explicitation!*]. Every i dotted to death!" (GC 3.487; 77).[1] Beckett may be far from that figure's political allegiances, but he could hardly be closer as concerns the dangers of dotting.

The first draft of *Happy Days* began with the announcement of a nuclear catastrophe. Beckett not only removed it, he kept it out. Some saw on his stages the remnants of Auschwitz, others the fallout of Hiroshima, still others ecological catastrophe, the master-slave dialectic, the urges of the unconscious, and much more. But both in the writing of his texts and the directing of his plays Beckett worked against any orientation, symbolic or otherwise, of the sort. When productions such as a notorious 1984 *Endgame* in Cambridge, Massachusetts, sought to give a bit of explicitation (the A.R.T's stage suggested the aftermath of a nuclear catastrophe), Beckett reacted with personal outrage and legal action. Nine years earlier Beckett had himself considered projecting the faint shadow of bars on the floor of the stage in Berlin's Schiller-Theater for a production of *Waiting for Godot,* before rejecting even that as an i too many dotted (Beckett 1994, xxii).

This then was Beckett's view of the search for symbolic significance, but can it be ours? The last words of Beckett's last drama, *What Where* (1983), are:

Time passes.
That is all.
Make sense who may.
I switch off. (GC 3.504)

Where Beckett's voices switch off is where ours switch on. Where their search for sense ends ours begins. Beckett found the state of maximal confusion the most creative one he knew or could envision knowing, but in our thinking we will, to the degree we care about it, see into that confusion and seek to understand it. Beckett's perspective was that of what he called "the dark and fumbling of making" (LSB 3.511). We, in turn, are in the dark and fumbling of meaning. It is natural for these spaces to be different, just as it is natural that a new making relation, such as Beckett's, should produce a new meaning relation.

The meaning of Beckett's works is not some secret concealed so that it might one day be plucked and presented to the wonderstruck public, for it is not that kind of meaning (no literary meaning is). While Clov stares at the fourth wall with his telescope Hamm employs other means to gain perspective. He imagines "a rational being come back to earth [*une intelligence, revenue sur terre*]" about whom he asks, "Wouldn't he be liable to get ideas into his head if he observed us long enough?" (GC 3.115; 47). Hamm then imagines himself such a being: "Ah, good, now I see what it is, yes, now I understand what they're at! [*Ah, bon, je vois ce que c'est, oui, je vois ce qu'ils font!*]" (GC 1.3.115; 47). This idea is the most chilling one in his entire world. "To think perhaps it won't all have been for nothing! [*Dire que tout cela n'aura peut-être pas été pour rien!*]" (GC 3.115; 48). What sends shivers down his spine is not meaninglessness, but meaning. As with *Watt*, in *Endgame* what is truly terrifying for Beckett's characters is not that life is meaningless, but that it might be meaningful. Hamm seems to have lived as though there were no point to it, no sense or significance to the endless endgame he found himself in. If he were wrong, if there were a meaning, if the endgame were purely of his own making, then this would mean an incalculable waste and intolerable pain. Immediately thereafter Clov discovers a flea on his person, and Hamm's mobile outrage switches focus: "A flea! This is awful! What a day!" (GC 3.115; 48).

Fail Better

In *Happy Days* Winnie finds that "words fail, there are times when even
they fail" (GC 3.284). She, however, is in the minority, for in Beckett's
worlds the time when they fail is, as a rule, every time. "I don't mind
failing, it's a pleasure," volunteers the Unnamable, and he has company
(GC 2.304; 39). At the end of Beckett's œuvre failure is given a great ral-
lying cry. *Worstward Ho* presents a series of throttled imperatives, chief
among which is "Fail better" (GC 4.472). The phrase has often been
seen as a motto, pointing as it does directly at the central paradox of
Beckett's writing. *Fail better* has even moved into the swirling spaces of
popular culture (it is the name of a literary magazine and a video
game company, it is tattooed on the left forearm of the, at the time of
writing, third-ranked men's tennis player in the world, etc.[2]), and it is little
wonder as no other phrase more succinctly states Beckett's aesthetic
aim. And yet at the same time it is a phrase that no one could claim
to understand fully, for if Beckett or his creations have failed well, at
what have they failed? At art? At orienting us in an intelligible universe?
At making a harmonious, unified, beautiful work where life has a value
and mankind a place? The image of Beckett as valiant failure, as a knight
of the night, has been the dominant one, both in French and English,
concerning stage as well as page, from academia to the Association of
Tennis Professionals—so much so that it is easy to forget that this is
praise, not analysis, so long as we cannot say at what Beckett failed. And
indeed what could something fail to do that had never aspired to anything but failure?

Beckett's idea of failure is, to begin with, free from all concern for
audience. Writing to director Alan Schneider to console him for the
commercial and critical failure of the American premiere of *Waiting for
Godot* in 1956, Beckett encouraged him not to mind it too much, saying
that for his own part he was "much more at home" with "failure,"
"having breathed deep of its vivifying air all my writing life up to the
last couple of years" (LSB 2.594). Beckett is not being disingenuous here,
and yet the failure he discusses in his works is of another nature entirely.
In a letter to Duthuit Beckett wrote of *"la seule beauté de l'effort et de*

l'échec," "the single and/or solitary beauty of effort and failure" (LSB 2.127).[3] That there is a beauty proper to failure is clear, but not how it is best conceived. Three years later the addressee of this letter found himself asking: "what does this term failure really mean today?" (Duthuit 1993, 39).

Just as the failure at issue is not financial or critical, it is also not one Beckett keeps to himself. He notes, for instance, how Hölderlin ended in "a kind of failure" (Bowles 1994, 31). This is something that is observed by virtually every commentator of Hölderlin, and yet those commentators invariably mean something quite different. For them, the failure in which Hölderlin ended was that of the poet's madness and the increasingly disjunctive writings accompanying its onset. The failure is the loss of his ability to write intricate and evocative verse as he had hitherto done. Beckett, however, will say of Hölderlin that "his only successes are the points where his poems go on, falter, stammer, and then admit failure, and are abandoned. At such points he was most successful. When he tried to abandon the spurious magnificence" (Bowles 1994, 31). For Beckett, Hölderlin only succeeded when he failed: when he conceded failure, when he stammered and faltered and abandoned himself, there was he great, there had he failed well.

In one of the stories Malone tries to tell, a woman raises and lets fall her arms, "Then she began to move them about in a way difficult to describe, and not easy to understand" (GC 2.196; 46). The next sentence is one Beckett omitted from his English translation of the novel: *"Elle les* [her arms] *écartait de ses flancs; je dirais brandissais si j'ignorais mieux le génie de votre langue"* (46). "She lifted her arms from her sides—I would say that she wielded them were my ignorance of the genius of your language better." It is not surprising that Beckett chose not to translate this sentence given the difficulty of finding terms with the right resonance. Moreover, "your language" could of course be understood in the narrow biographical sense that the Anglophone pushing the pencil was addressing a Francophone public. But the work is fiction, the speaker a character, and the situation more complicated. "The term failure," Duthuit wrote, as he began to answer the question his friend had asked of him, "can no longer serve to evaluate, only to define—to give us the precise formula for the rift between the subject and the object of expression" (Duthuit 1993, 40). If failure is a given in the artistic equation it can no longer be positive or negative, nor can there be any more sense in trying to judge it or wish it away than to judge or wish away gravity. In a letter to the Israeli writer Matti Megged from 1960 Beckett remarked:

> I understand—I think no one better—the flight from experience to expression and I understand the necessary failure of both. But it is the flight from one order or disorder to an order or disorder of a different nature and the two failures are essentially dissimilar in kind. Thus life in failure can hardly be anything but dismal at the best, whereas there is nothing more exciting for the writer, or richer in unexploited expressive possibilities, than the failure to express. It was some realization of all this and what it involves that enabled me to go on (about 15 years ago) in a situation probably very different from yours, but certainly no less critical. (LSB 3.377)

The unprecedented and unrepeated burst of creativity Beckett experienced fifteen years prior stemmed, at least in his own view, from seeking not to narrow the gap between expression and experience but to widen it. "No time now to explain," says Malone, "I began again. But little by little with a different aim, no longer in order to succeed, but in order to fail. Nuance" (GC 2.189; 34). That trying to succeed and trying to fail are only a nuance away from one another in Malone's world, and yet remain distinct, is what makes it so elusive. Failure only makes sense when it is measured against expectation. If, however, the expectation is failure the scene shifts suddenly, which is, of course, the goal.

In the "Three Dialogues" with Duthuit Beckett remarked that "the only thing disturbed by the revolutionaries Matisse and Tal Coat is a certain order on the plane of the feasible" (GC 4.556). This would seem to be a great deal for a revolutionary to achieve, and Duthuit quite naturally asks, "What other plane can there be for the maker?" Beckett concedes, "Logically none," before adding, "Yet I speak of an art turning from it in disgust, weary of puny exploits, weary of pretending to be able, of being able, of doing a little better the same old thing, of going a little further along a dreary road" (GC 4.556). As in his German letter to Kaun, literature seems to Beckett here like a road, and the most interesting thing is to leave it. Duthuit asks what should be preferred. The response is the most explicit description Beckett ever gave for his work then in progress: "The expression that there is nothing to express, nothing with which to express, nothing from which to express, no power to express, no desire to express, together with the obligation to express" (GC 4.556).[4] The rest of the dialogue is as follows:

> D—But that is a violently extreme and personal point of view, of no
>   help to us in the matter of Tal Coat.
> B—
> D—Perhaps that is enough for today. (GC 4.556)

This is as it should be. But how are we to understand it? As a joke between friends? A few moves from an endgame? As a violently extreme and personal point of view which is of considerable help in the matter of Samuel Beckett?

In the last of these dialogues Beckett distinguishes "mere misery" from "ultimate penury" and explains the distinction by noting that "there is more than a difference of degree between being short, short of the world, short of self, and being without these esteemed commodities" (GC 4.561). What Beckett sees in Bram Van Velde's paintings is how, by concerning itself with "the acute and increasing anxiety of the relation itself," an art might "submit wholly to the incoercible absence of relation"—becoming thereby not "short on world," but without it (GC 4.563). This is a transition from a strained relation to none at all; from a work "short of the world" to a work without that esteemed commodity. It is at this point in the dialogue that Beckett raises the question of *failure*, for Van Velde is presented as "the first to admit that to be an artist is to fail, as no other dare fail, that failure is his world and to shrink from it desertion, art and craft, good housekeeping, living" (GC 4.563). To this Beckett adds: "I know that all that is required now, in order to bring even this horrible matter to an acceptable conclusion, is to make of this submission, this admission, this fidelity to failure, a new occasion, a new term of relation" (GC 4.563).

Negative Capability

A friend of Beckett's recalls a late evening in the 1970s:

> I mentioned the "Negative Capability" passage to Sam, who, of
> course, had read it when he studied Keats; when I came to "when a
> man is capable of being in uncertainties, mysteries, doubts, without
> any irritable reaching after fact and reason" he became tense with
> attention, suddenly sitting bolt upright as though pierced by an
> electric current, and asked me to read it again at the table, and
> repeated excitedly, "irritable reaching after fact and reason—that's it,
> capable of being in uncertainties." (Atik 2001, 70–71)

That an intimate of Beckett's would be put in mind of the phrase
"Negative Capability" in his connection is as unsurprising as how
warmly Beckett responded to the lines. He had, after all, an exceptional
interest in nothing. One of his favorite phrases, woven into a number
of his letters, as well as into two novels written in two different languages, is Democritus's "nothing is more real than nothing." In *Murphy*
there is "the Nothing, than which in the guffaw of the Abderite naught
is more real" (a turn of the syntactical screw typical of Beckett's early
English writing) (GC 1.148). The (fifth-century Greek) philosopher (born
in the Thracian city of Abdera) will also bring nothing to Malone's
mind:

> I know those little phrases that seem so innocuous and, once you let
> them in, pollute the whole of speech. Nothing is more real than
> nothing. They rise up out of the pit and know no rest until they drag
> you down into its dark. But I am on my guard now. (GC 1.148; 30)

Beckett's reticence to encourage "those bastards of critics" even knew
an exception on this point. "The heart of the matter," he wrote to one
critic, "if it has one, is perhaps rather in the *Naught more real than nothing*
and the *ubi nihil vales,* already in *Murphy*" (LSB 2.427; Beckett's underlining). These are coordinates which will remain constant for decades
as, although extremely wary about giving authorial indications, Beckett
will repeat them. He will write in 1956 of his work, "If there is a queer
real there somewhere it is the Abderite's mentioned in *Murphy*" (LSB

2.669). Beckett notes, concerning the above remark, "I suppose these are its foci and where a commentary might take its rise. But I really do not know myself," and he is quick to add, "and don't want to know" (LSB 2.669). However much he might not have wanted to know, he continued to aid others, writing more than thirty years after the novel's publication to an inquiring student, "If I were in the unenviable position of having to study my work, my points of departure would be the 'Naught is more real . . .' and the '*Ubi nihil vales . . .*' both already in *Murphy* and neither very rational"—to which he added, kindly, "*Bon courage quand même*" ("Good luck all the same") (Kennedy 1971, 300; Beckett 1984, 113; Beckett's ellipses).

Although Beckett is careful to attribute the thought, and the phrase, to Democritus, it bears noting that what Democritus said is at least slightly different, is perhaps very different, and is in either case quite nearly untranslatable.[5] For it contains, like Beckett's *Wörterstürmerei*, a cleverly disorienting neologism: *den*, a negation of *hen*, "one," but not a customary one (these are *ouden*, an objective negation, and *meden*, a subjective negation). The standard edition of Democritus in Beckett's day, Diels and Kranz's 1903 German one (where is it Fragment 156), translates the phrase as *Das Nichts existiert ebenso sehr als das Ichts*, inventing the German term *Ichts* (related to but distinct from the standard negative *Nichts*), and which Beckett more elegantly, and with more license, rendered "Naught" (Diels and Kranz 1935, 174).[6] Beckett is neither the first nor the last major thinker to be singularly intrigued by it (Lacan was to discuss it at a key point of his 1964 seminar *The Four Fundamental Concepts of Psychoanalysis*), but what is essential for Beckett's negative capability is that Democritus's neologism could with as much justice be seen as saying *not nothing, but something very strange and small as nothing*. And so it is little wonder that Beckett adds, *Bon courage quand même*.

This second assisting phrase is an abbreviation of *Ubi nihil vales ibi nihil velis*: "Where you are worth nothing, there you should want (or will) nothing," also found in *Murphy* and taken from the seventeenth-century Occasionalist philosopher Arnold Geulincx's *Ethics*.[7] What the two phrases ("the 'Naught is more real . . .' and the '*Ubi nihil vales . . .*'") share is an attempt to present a negative like none before it. Geulincx's phrase means something quite different in its native habitat—his *Ethics*—than in Beckett's hands. For Geulincx worthlessness is relative, for Beckett it is absolute. Geulincx thinks of God, compared to whom we are nothing. Beckett arrives at the same conclusion without need of comparison. His approach to the idea of negation and of its creative possibilities was so unfamiliar, and so striking, that from the first years of his fame there sprang up the liveliest debates around whether he was denouncing, trouncing, nullifying, and negating all things artistic, perhaps even all things human, or, on the contrary, whether this was an unprecedented mode of affirming those very same things. A great many philosophically trained critics (beginning with Adorno) saw in Beckett's work a negation so sweeping that it effectively blew out the circuits of the dialectical power plant, or hooked up to another grid (as was the dream of Blanchot and the assumption of Deleuze and Badiou). The reason this was possible was because the negative activity, the *mismaking, vaguening,* or *logoclasm* in question, so little resembled art of the past, and took such different stances on the ideas of *success, completion, totality, unity, structure,* and *progression,* that it could with equal justice be seen as attack or defense, a positive charge or a negative one. As the Unnamable says on such occasions: "Into the dossier with it in any case, for whatever side you fancy" (GC 2.338; 96).

This should not lead us to forget, however, that the reason Beckett sat bolt upright upon being reminded of Keats's words was another. For in his remarks on Negative Capability Keats is not talking about metaphysics, or even about reading, but about writing. "I had not a dispute but a disquisition," the twenty-two-year-old wrote in the letter from 1817, during which

> several things dove-tailed in my mind, and at once it struck me what quality went to form a Man of Achievement, especially in Literature, and which Shakespeare possessed so enormously—I mean Negative Capability, that is, when a man is capable of being in uncertainties, mysteries, doubts, without any irritable reaching after fact and reason.[8]

These lines, the most famous of any literary letter in English, address something so intuitive that it is easy to lose sight of the strangeness of the phrase. The thing in question seems, after all, singularly *positive*. It is positive in value, but negative in nature, as, for Keats, genius entails negating the need to know.

Great works convey, subtly but thoroughly, what is generative in them. In *Ulysses*, for instance, this is *love*. Bloom's bravery, in the moment corresponding to Odysseus's escape from the cave of the Cyclops, takes place in a pub where the anti-Semitic nationalist into whose verbal clutches Bloom has fallen will not leave him in peace. And so Bloom tells the Citizen, "it's no use" to talk as he does, for "Force, hatred, history, all that. That's not life for men and women, insult and hatred. And everybody knows that it's the very opposite of that that is really life." When asked what that is, Bloom replies, simply, "Love" (12.1481–1485). It is in this respect as much as in any other that Beckett became Joyce's opposite. Love has all but left the worlds of his mature work. Where it survives is in echoes, like the hauntingly beautiful one Krapp is made to hear, with the blue fire of lost eyes and the movement under him of the water whose lesson he could never learn (all changes). *Murphy*'s great chain of amorous being that could unite Ireland and England will not just be broken, it will disappear. Beckett's first book could end romantically enough, with Alba and her bottle and her fire, come what may. By the time we have *Enough* (1966) unfeeling fellatio is the full extent of amorous contact, and as for amorous feeling, it has become a joke. "Farewell to love" is how Krapp describes the chapter under review (GC 3.223). *Not I* and *That Time* are distinctly audible points in the farewell, where love is considered, shuddered at, dismissed. The totality of Beckett's mature creations either profess not to be personally acquainted with the idea of love, or bring a definitional dementia to the task. "But is it true love, in the rectum?" wonders Molloy (GC 2.52; 76).

In an unfinished essay posthumously published as "Every Generation Is the Dumbest," Ingeborg Bachmann wrote that "The world has no accredited holidays, for it itself is a holiday. And time is a slow, secret celebration" (Bachmann 1978, 334). Whatever the pain in the worlds of Bachmann's works, however perilous or cruel they proved, they remained places of intense hope, promise, and joy—and in this they differ utterly from Beckett's. Sophocles has the chorus of *Oedipus at Colonus* rate as the highest good not being born and the second highest a swift and early death. Beckett concurs. His chorus says that being alive is a standing affront and will affront them so long as they stand. They are, moreover, granted no holidays and whatever celebrating goes on is kept quite secret indeed. Readers have, understandably, not been eager to dwell upon this point in any other form than categorical rejection (as done, most famously, by György Lukács). Adorno and Badiou, for instance, are utterly unsparing critics of the consoling illusions of their times, and yet each quails before the possibility that Beckett might actually have meant what he said about the world, the life to be led in it and the art which would allow it to understand itself. Beckett has been represented not only as artistic anti-matter, but as artistic antidote. And yet is it not surprising that such healing faith is placed in the most sweepingly pessimistic writer in the history of either French or English literature, one who makes the great pessimists of the century before his, such as Leopardi and Schopenhauer, seem positively dewy-eyed by comparison? Both Leopardi and Schopenhauer rate art, as do so many, as, if not the antidote to all that is wrong in the world, at least a respite from it, and a sign that there exists the possibility of a higher order and a better ordering. This is because while they are moral and epistemological pessimists they are not aesthetic pessimists. Beckett refuses to set art apart from the general condemnation—on the contrary, it is placed front and center.

"Because what has happened since the Gods of our world went too far," wrote Cavell in his essay on Beckett, "is that what used to seem life's leaven, the sources of meaning and coherence, the shelters from chaos and destruction, have now grown to shut out existence; morality, art, religion and the rest, lead lives of their own, grown out of hand, that shear man's existence from him" (Cavell 2002, 149). That the question of meaning in Beckett's writing is inseparable from the question of the autonomy of art is one of Cavell's great insights, for Beckett's works present an autonomy like no other. The subject of greatest uncertainty in Beckett's writing, and the point on which his critics are least in agreement, is how we are to relate the bad in the work to the bad in our world. In "Possibilities," Wisława Szymborska notes, "I prefer the hell of chaos to the hell of order." Beckett's speakers seem to say that they have no opinion on the matter, provided it's hell. After the Danish pre-

miere of *Waiting for Godot* in April 1956, Beckett wrote to the play's translator, "Let people laugh by all means, and then be reminded it is no
laughing matter" (LSB 2.617). There is no mention of whether this should
be so because that is how the play works best, or because that is how
the world most is. Of the same play Beckett wrote to a friend that while
he was glad she had seen it in England, "the French production was more
like what I wanted, nastier" (LSB 2.611).

Democritus (for whom naught was more real than nothing) traveled
widely, lived to a great age, went mis- or unrecognized by celebrated contemporaries such as Socrates, and had his atomic theory of matter as
well as his theories of an infinite universe and multiple, finite worlds
lose out (for a long time) to the Aristotelian conceptions of a single,
finite, and eternal universe with unified principles of teleology. He was,
in short, a man after Beckett's heart. Dante refers to him as *"Democrito,
che 'l mondo a caso pone,"* "Democritus who set the world at chance" (*Inferno* 4.136). This induced in him legendary cheerfulness, such that he
became a major iconographical figure, traditionally depicted as beaming
or laughing (just as his emblematic foil, Heraclitus, was depicted as
weeping).[9] But this is not the equanimity and good cheer we find on
Beckett's stages. Laughter is present, but it has little to do with good
cheer, and a great deal to do with tears. As Nell reminds the audience
in *Endgame,* "Nothing is funnier than unhappiness [*Rien n'est plus drôle
que le malheur*]" (GC, 1. 206–207; 31).

Another of Beckett's first great critics, Iser, undertook an effort to
understand this laughter. Attending performances in Germany, France,
and England, he watched the watchers, and found their laughter strange.
"In Beckett's theater no chain reaction of laughter can continue," he
wrote. "It is the interrupted laughter of individuals, not the freeing
and communal laughter in which the laughing community mutually
affirms its reaction" (Iser 1979, 6). Iser saw audiences, whether in French,
German, or English, begin laughing together, only to break asunder,
and break off, as though ashamed. This isolating effect of laughter,
not fed by one's fellows but, on the contrary, fueled by one's isolation
from them, brought on, in Iser's observation, "an unprecedented degree of unease which finally strangulates the laughter [*den Lacheffekt
shließlich stranguliert*]" (Iser 1979, 7). As is always the case with sociological

data, Iser's is open to interpretation. But it bears noting that those audiences were reproducing what they saw on stage. When Vladimir has the idea of repenting, without going into for what, Estragon suggests they repent "being born," at which point Beckett's stage direction tells us, *"Vladimir breaks into a hearty laugh which he immediately stifles."* "One daren't even laugh any more," he says, and will serve as example (*Godot*, 8–9). On Beckett's stage no laugh can last long, as in play after play it catches in the players' throats—by design. What then happens is, from the side of humor, sad. Beckett ceases to be funny, which is to say he ceases to write in that comic mode, except on rare occasions. The removal of this register is even inscribed into Beckett's next major prose work after *The Unnamable*, *How It Is*, where we read:

> fire in the rectum how surmounted reflections on the passion of pain irresistible departure with preparatives appertaining uneventful journey sudden arrival lights low lights out bye-bye is it a dream

> a dream what a hope death of sack arse of Pim end of part one leaving only part two leaving only part three and last Thalia for pity's sake a leaf of thine ivy. (GC 2.436; 59)

The muse of comedy (Thalia) is implored in vain. The author of the greatest comic masterpieces of his century is, after *The Unnamable*, almost never funny in prose again, and on stage the humor will not hold out long, with works for the stage whose emblem is *Not I:* a red raw mouth, harried and horrified by a voice inside too cruel for it to be a joke.

In critical studies of Beckett—and of modernism, more generally—the aforementioned Lukács is often led out so that shafts may be rained down upon him for finding that modernists like Beckett "glorified," with or without laughter, "perversity and idiocy" (Lukács 1979, 26). This response is not hard to understand, for Lukács argues himself into a corner, and it is unpleasant to see what he does there. The conclusion he draws is based on an extreme, but not insane, supposition: that art should serve life, and, more precisely, should serve the project of a more equitable distribution of resources and rights in society. That he chose to work in the service of a (Stalinist) system that murdered millions of his fellow party members has sufficed, in most quarters, to disqualify his position. It is thus easily forgotten that the "perversity and idiocy" he finds "glorified" in Beckett's writing concern not some individual set of practices or group of figures, but, instead, rational action and emotional connection. In Beckett's works expression is never a positive force, never a clarifying one, never one that brings love, comfort, reason, or happiness to the shelter, cylinder, mudpit, or late evening in the future. Badiou is, on this point, not the opposite of Lukács so much as the opposite of the painter in *Endgame*. Shown mud and ashes he sees shimmering fields and herring fleets. "It is indispensable," he writes, "to take Beckett at his word—at the word of beauty [*Prendre Beckett à la lettre est indispensable. A la lettre de beauté*]" (Badiou 1995, 17). Beckett is "the constantly attentive servant of beauty"; he who "seeks to beautifully ravish" the "fragments of existence"—and so on (14; 12). This is said in an imperious manner, as though he were conceding something we did not quite deserve, which obscures how very strange a reaction it is. Not, that is, to find Beckett's writing beautiful, but to find it so fully about beauty. Others have approached the question of pessimism more directly. With undisguised disdain Terry Eagleton has written of how "there are always critics on hand to scour these remorselessly negative texts for the occasional glimmer of humanistic hope, in a world where rank pessimism is felt to be somehow ideologically subversive" (Eagleton 2006, 1). Both things Eagleton says are true, the question is whether they are related. Critics are naturally on the qui vive for hope. Who would not like to find that, in the last analysis, his or her activity had meaning and value? Rank pessimism, moreover, can most certainly be ideologically subversive, but only if the implication is that the pessimism concerns something which might be changed. "Like Heraclitus, the Irish have always held that nothing is quite as real as nothing," remarks Eagleton. He means Democritus, but the real problem lies in explaining Beckett's pessimism away as an Irish peculiarity (Eagleton 2006, 3). If it does not make sense to hear Beckett channeling the voice of being, as Eagleton (contra Blanchot) insists, it cannot make much more to have him channel the voice of Ireland.

The inevitable result of severing emotion from communication is the loss of love. But what is harrowing about Beckett's late writing is not merely the loss of love, it is the estrangement of emotion and the quieting of laughter. To see, as in *Not I,* the stage frozen to a bright mouth that has no idea what it wants or what happened to it, but that most assuredly has been broken on the wheel of the world, is harrowing. But such explosive emotion is rare in the writing of the last three decades of Beckett's career. The Unnamable's speech was afire with emotion which is soon to go out. It is not that life is given a different principle than love (such as hate), it is that life is presented as utterly unprincipled. What is then generative in Beckett's literary universe, his negative capability, is the dark matter and dark energy of the seriously contemplated possibility that this all might really be for nothing.

Aesthetic Pessimism

When Ezra Pound first saw *Fin de partie* in Paris he leaned over and whispered to his neighbor, *"C'est moi dans la poubelle"* ("That's me in the garbage can") (Kenner 1971, 556). There is much to recommend this phrase, including the possibility that Pound was recalling his having spoken rudely to Beckett about his literary aspirations twenty years earlier. Did Pound see himself in the movements on stage because he too was old, because he too had been wrong about the future, because he too was locked in a game that brought no relief, or simply because he too was human? For no work, ancient or modern, is it harder to answer the questions: *Does he mean us? Is this about us?* For if it is, it does not look good. And if it is not, it looks strange. As with another great French writer of prodigious invention, Rabelais, with Beckett it is no easy matter to know, when he mocks, whom he mocks. It is of the nature of readers to estimate themselves in the fortunate camp of those who also understand, those who agree that the others, whoever they are, have not understood, whatever it is. *We* may say *we,* believing, but we do so with the knowledge that the case is under appeal. Consequently, this view does not orient us and the question shifts. *Did we do this to you?* becomes *Has this been done to us?*

As John Banville once observed, Beckett has "more than something of the night about him" (Banville 2006, 92). How is it that an œuvre so dark has been welcomed with such warmth from so many quarters and in so many languages is a question without clear answer. One possibility is that it only seems dark. Another is that it is a darkness visible, and never having seen in the dark before, we are drawn to it. The question becomes harder, however, when we note what can be made out in the darkness. For what would an anthropologist from another culture think we were feeling about a work where love was absent except in the cases where it could still be cruel? Why would we be understood to so enjoy a story in which nothing changes? Have we grown out of progression? One option is to view the bleak and the barren as formal factors of no special interest. It happened to be torture by can opener, but it might just as well have been a picnic on Howth Head, for all we are following is a formal line and a musical shape, far away from this world's emotions of love or loss.

In a notebook entry from the fall of 1887, entitled "Chief Symptoms of Pessimism," Nietzsche included the stenographic "aesthetic pessimism l'art pour l'art" (Nietzsche 1999 12.409). He immediately turned to more pressing business—anarchism and nihilism—but it is not difficult to fill in the blanks. If art can do nothing to or for the world, the result is an art detached from that world: *l'art pour l'art.* Viewed from the other side of the equation, the idea of *art for art's sake* is inherently pessimistic, as it takes a dim view of the ability of art to engage the world in which it was made. What was a (grave) diagnosis for Nietzsche was, for Beckett, a (grave) inspiration. Beckett mismade plays and novels where world and work were so far apart, so hard to correlate in detail, that it became impossible to tell whether their pessimism more concerned the world or the attempt to reproduce it. Proust's and Joyce's projects, to limit the examples to writers on whom Beckett himself wrote, both offer the most fundamental of affirmations: that this world, taken the right way, is enough. Beckett's vision is less warm, for he is as explicitly an *epistemological* and *moral* pessimist as can be (time and again he indicates that neither the true nor the good are attainable because neither is real). He is also, moreover, an explicit *aesthetic* pessimist in a sense related to, but distinct from, Nietzsche's. For he will try to mismake on purpose, to mismake by design: this will be his goal, sometimes in so many words. In his art he will seek the *pessimum,* the very worst. But he will be careful to reject all the while the idea that art is any better than the world in which it is mismade. There was no idea to which Beckett remained so allergic as that language and art have a sacred force or function. He was so sensitive on the matter that he was easily irritated, as he was by Goethe's idea that poetry is inherently ennobling. He was, in point of fact, so sensitive on the matter as to find false positives, such as Baudelaire. But the greatest proponent of the naturalness of language, of a faith in language's secret sacred heart, was one it was given to Beckett to see at exceptionally close range, over a long period of time, and who was, moreover, too good at it and having too much fun to begrudge him the exercise, not to mention the results, which were astounding.

This idea which so bothered Beckett in Joyce, Baudelaire, Goethe, and many others—one name for which is "animism"—is what his aesthetic pessimism was made to oppose. If art were more than life, if it had some power to correct and guide us—to allow us, instead of turning in circles of animal bloodshed, to become more reasonable and just— then art would be our culture's most precious possession, the one thing that was more important than all the rest and be, like fire, the ravaging necessity of culture. But if art is neither better nor worse but simply of the world, the sacred side of the equation is cancelled. Aesthetic autonomy is to Beckett's purposes only if it refrains from placing art upon a pedestal. If art involved a sacred autonomy, an elect, select separation from life, he wanted no part of it. Who could ever want to dignify this world with a work? That would only encourage it.

How History Works

Kenner sets aside many of the problems posed by *Waiting for Godot* through a rephrasing of what Beckett had said about Joyce: "the play is not 'about,' it is itself; it is a play" (Kenner 1973, 31). Were Kenner a less brilliant reader this would end in pedantry—the equivalent of saying, Have you forgotten that this is art and not life? And were Kenner to remain at that point, it would be false pedantry, for although plays are indeed never merely about things, asking what the things on stage might mean is not an aberrant reaction. Kenner concedes that his claim sounds "impossibly arty" so long as we fail to recall that this is what always happens with works of art—it is only that, as a rule, it takes much, much longer. Kenner reminds his reader that "dynastic irregularities in Denmark" no longer especially interest even Danes, though *Hamlet* does

(Kenner 1973, 31). Comparing *Waiting for Godot* to the tragedies of classical antiquity, Kenner describes the process by which, over time, dramatic events such as the murder of Agamemnon and the unheeded prophesies of Cassandra "acquired the authority of powerful abstractions" (Kenner 1973, 31). Beckett's abstractions have become comparably powerful—speaking, as they do, to an incredibly broad range of audience. This happened in the space not of centuries or millennia, but more or less immediately. "The effort of Beckett's play in suppressing specific reference, in denying itself for example the easy recourse of alarming audiences with references to the Gestapo," writes Kenner, "would seem to be like an effort to arrive directly at the result of time's work" (Kenner 1973, 31). That Kenner himself acquired the habit of hearing the Gestapo in Beckett's harsher voices weakens his position, but not on this point. Beckett discovered the means, it would seem, for speeding up the clock of historical reception by stripping the world's work—to borrow *Endgame*'s stage instruction—to a "bare interior."

Kenner's claim becomes still clearer if we compare it to the 20th century's most famous description of the relation of art to its times. A few years before Beckett's first books were published Benjamin wrote of enduring works of art that "the beholder who contemplates them long after their own time finds the realia all the more striking in the work as they have faded from the world" (Benjamin 1996–2003, 1.297; Benjamin 1974–1989, 1.125; translation modified). This is a natural enough thing to observe, although it takes a more than casual attention to see it with lucidity. In Beckett's work the *realia* are not striking because they have faded from the world, but because they were never in it, because they claim not to be *realia* at all. This is the reason for the difficulty of entering Beckett's hermeneutic circle. The audience might easily wonder whether these are not the *realia* of our world after all—displaced, distorted, radicalized, and thus, at last, fully realized—"disfigured," in Elfriede Jelinek's evocative phrase, "into recognizability" (Jelinek 1995, 49). Just as we did not murder our father and wed our mother, or plot the deaths of Rosencrantz and Guildenstern, we do not stand at a crossroads contemplating how best to kill ourselves. Or do we? We have not relegated our elders and their accumulated wisdom to garbage cans. Or have we? Our world is not ruined or ravaged. Or is it?

Benjamin developed his intuition into a distinction between the task of the commentator and that of the critic. The fading of *realia* over time provides what Benjamin calls "an inestimable criterion of critical judgment," as "only [then] can the critic ask the basic question of all criticism—namely, whether the work's shining truth content is due to its subject matter or whether the survival of the subject matter is due to the truth content" (Benjamin 1996–2003, 1.297; Benjamin 1974–1989, I.125). It is for this reason that he made his celebrated comparison:

> If, to use a simile, one views the growing work as a funeral pyre, its commentator can be likened to the chemist, its critic to the alchemist. While the former is left with wood and ashes as the sole objects of analysis, the latter is concerned only with the enigma of the flame itself: the enigma of being alive. Thus the critic inquires about the truth whose living flame goes on burning over the heavy logs of the past and the light ashes of life gone by. (Benjamin 1996–2003, 1.298; Benjamin 1974–1989, I.126)

We may see Beckett's works burning brightly but acknowledge that they have not burned long enough for us to analyze the ash, and so we cannot know how much of our interest is born of the chemistry of contemporary concern and how much of the alchemy of art. We are not interested in the House of Atreus or dynastic irregularities in Denmark in the same immediate way that we are interested in the cataclysms of our time; the injustice and the suffering of the more or less remote past do not speak to us in the same way as do concentration camps, atomic bombs, ecological catastrophe, or the society of the spectacle, and we cannot, therefore, see the artistic matter as distinct from the historical. We might throw up our hands, or warm them over the fire of the glowing work but, either way, a decision is required.

The Human Condition

Fresh from seeing *Fin de partie* in Paris in 1957, the French philosopher Jean Wahl concluded a conference on Edmund Husserl and phenomenology in Royaumont by saying: "These last days were interrupted by my having seen a play. I recall a few phrases, a few exchanges, and I'd like to read them to you." He then proceeded to do so, from memory (making a number of mistakes, but effectively conveying the strangeness), adding: "I don't know their exact relation to our subject."[10] Wahl shows great delicacy in not claiming to know what bearing Beckett's plays have on the questions raised by Husserl and phenomenology. What is exemplary is his conviction that whatever the play might mean, it most certainly has *something* to do with the things that most concern him, and might concern all those interested in the study of philosophy. A few years later Adorno and Cavell would continue this tradition, as would a long list of later philosophers who have shared their sense that whatever Beckett's works might mean, they have some bearing on philosophy—some meaning, message, or mission—without being sure of much besides that whatever it says to philosophy, it is reproving. There are many small reasons for this, and one large one, which is that in Beckett's mature writing the particulars which might render philosophy's approach to literature difficult have all been removed, so vaguened as to invite philosophical definition. But just as that which renders philosophical abstraction difficult has been removed, so too has that upon which it might catch.

Two general possibilities present themselves. The first is that Beckett is presenting the human condition, the second that he is presenting a historical one. The question is thus how to understand what Beckett once called "the time-honored conception of humanity in ruins" (Beckett 1995a, 278). Beckett's friend A. J. Leventhal saw in the international collective of names of *Waiting for Godot* (Russian Vladimir, Italian Pozzo, French Estragon, and English Lucky) "a world condition in which all humanity is involved" (Leventhal 1965, 49). Lukács saw the same sweep, but with the value inverted, as he denounced Beckett for "the adoption of perversity and idiocy as types of the *condition humaine*" (Lukács 1979, 26). No critic, however, offers a more resounding response to the question of whether Beckett's writings present a timeless given or a sign of the times than, however, Adorno. In an essay on—or, more precisely, *against*—Lukács, Adorno eschews the most common response to those who had seen Beckett's works as had Lukács. Instead of claiming that between the lines of perversity and idiocy are encrypted signs of purity and brilliance, courage and renewal (as did, and do, many of

Beckett's readers), Adorno upbraids Lukács for missing the artistic, philosophical, historical, and social points. Adorno found that Beckett was emphatically *not* presenting a timeless human condition but, instead, something that merely looked like one. He saw Beckett denouncing a *historical* situation characterized by the very totalitarian systems of discipline and control in whose socialist service Lukács had chosen to work, and whose most insidious achievement lay in disguising a historical condition as a human one.

Had Beckett not existed, it seems as though Adorno would have had to invent him. In the same years Beckett's "siege in the room" was laid, Adorno wrote *Minima Moralia: Reflections from Damaged Life* (1951), whose blunt epigraph might have come from the Unnamable's mouth: *Das Leben lebt nicht* ("Life doesn't live"). In that work, written before his first encounter with Beckett, Adorno claimed that "the goal of art today is to bring chaos into order," and that "the comfortable citizen wants art to be luxurious and life ascetic; the opposite would be better" (Adorno GS 4.251). Such statements seem made to measure for the ascetic art Beckett was pioneering. Beckett would be the first artistic figure Adorno personally sought out after the war, and would be the writer who most influenced his aesthetic theory.[11] Following a first meeting with Beckett, Adorno published "Understanding *Endgame*" with the dedication: "To S. B. in memory of Paris, Fall 1958" (Adorno GS 11.281). The essay's title in the original, *Versuch, das Endspiel zu verstehen,* stresses the degree to which what Adorno saw himself undertaking was at once an *attempt* and an *experiment* (the term *Versuch* has both meanings—like *essay*). The end of the essay was not, however, the end of the experiment, and Adorno's attempts to understand Beckett continued for the rest of his life. Beckett is discussed at key moments in *Notes to Literature* (1958/1961), in *Negative Dialectics* (1966), and in the works in progress Adorno did not live to complete: the unfinished essay on *The Unnamable* and his (posthumously published) magnum opus, *Aesthetic Theory* (1970), which, as mentioned earlier, he planned to dedicate to Beckett.[12]

What were the findings of Adorno's experiment in understanding? If understanding is about ascertaining and ascribing meaning, then the first step in "Understanding *Endgame*" would seem to be the last, as he says of Beckett's works that "their meaning is meaninglessness [*ihr Sinn sei Sinnlosigkeit*]" (Adorno GS 11.293; 128; translation modified). This meaninglessness is, for Adorno, however, only the beginning, as meaninglessness, once recognized as such, acquires a certain meaning. "Understanding the play," Adorno says of *Endgame*, "cannot be anything other than understanding its incomprehensibility: that is, concretely reconstructing the meaningful context through which it expresses that it has no meaning [*Es verstehen kann nichts anderes heißen, als seine Unverständlichkeit verstehen, konkret den Sinnzusammenhang dessen nachkonstruieren, daß es keinen hat*]" (Adorno GS 11.283). In a kindred vein, Cavell (to all appearances unaware of Adorno's essay) wrote six years later that "solitude, emptiness, nothingness, meaninglessness, silence—these are not the *givens* of Beckett's characters but their goal, their new heroic undertaking" (Cavell 2002, 156; Cavell's emphasis). Simon Critchley, in turn, described the notion as one of "meaninglessness becoming an *achievement* rather than a fact, meaninglessness becoming the work of Beckett's work" (making it thereby something like the performance art of failure) (Critchley 2004, 178; Critchley's emphasis).[13] How to respond to this meaninglessness becomes the central question. And it can be seen in the diametrically opposed stances of Adorno and Cavell as concerns critical mastery. There is no more masterful, no more daring, imperious, and relentless philosophical critic of Beckett than Adorno. And there is no *less* masterful a one than Cavell—by design. Cavell does not pretend to be up to the task, or even that it is the kind of task to which one may be up to. He does not pretend to have read what one would expect him to have read—such as Beckett's trilogy of novels (which had been available in English for years when Cavell wrote his essay), or any other works besides *Endgame* and *Godot,* or even essays such as Adorno's or Blanchot's, then on the tips of most tongues interested in Beckett. He does not pretend to know about the theater or French. His essay, among his most famous, and among the most famous on Beckett, is, if one follows purely argumentative lines, a mess. It is associative and garrulous and exchanges more than passing glances with paradox. Cavell knows this, and shows that he knows it in subtle ways, as well as not so subtle ones. After a long bit of close reasoning he concludes: "Perhaps I hallucinate" (Cavell 2002, 121). A little later, at the close of another argumentative arc, he will concede, "Though it is hard to be reasonable" (124). At still another point we are told, "This can't, I think, be the right track" (148). He is a critic, in short, after Malone's heart. One of the unexpected virtues of Cavell's essay is how the reader can quite literally watch Cavell let go of mastery, watch him lose interest in his initial aim (an argument arising in ordinary language philosophy), and embark on his real journey. In what is a wonderful plot turn in the essay the deepest problem turns out to be not Beckett or the descendance of Noah or "the phenomenology of the Bomb," but philosophy. For, Cavell finds, "It sometimes looks as if philosophy had designs on us; or as if it alone is crazy, and wants company" (126). "The misery of the participants in *Endgame*," Adorno had written before him, "is the misery of philosophy" (Adorno GS 11.295; 253; translation modified). Where Adorno saw philosophy's misery and miserliness, Cavell saw it as quite simply out of its mind.

One way of understanding that *Endgame* is meaningless and yet resonates so strongly for so many is through what has been the most consistent category employed in the play's interpretation: the *absurd*. In the notes for the unfinished essay on *The Unnamable* Adorno declares that he is "against the term 'absurd'" (Tiedemann 1994b, 69). He is in good company as, in *The Unnamable,* we hear: "That the impossible should be asked of me, good, what else could be asked of me? But the absurd! Of me whom they have reduced to reason" (GC 2.331; 84). Adorno's reason for being against the absurd is that it clarifies so little, for it "presupposes the meaningful as the normal state," which is precisely what Beckett's works placed so squarely in question (Tiedemann 1994b, 69). The problem with absurdity is thus not that it is inexistent, but that it is unexceptional. With his countryman Martin Esslin's famous phrase *theater of the absurd* in mind, Adorno wrote that "Beckett's plays are not absurd thanks to the absence of meaning therein—for in this case they would be simply irrelevant" (Adorno GS 7.230). Distinguishing Beckett from the then-reigning existentialists, Adorno finds that for Beckett "absurdity is no longer a diluted Idea [*zur Idee verdünnte*]" and "no longer an illustrated finding concerning a mere mental state [*bebilderte Befindlichkeit des Daseins*]" (Adorno GS 11.281).[14] For Adorno, what Sartre and company fail to do is to fail at all. They play dexterously with failure, they represent failure with artistry, but without taking its measure, running its risks, or letting it into their language. They remain at a safe distance. The characters on the existentialist stage are made to realize the most devastating things imaginable, and yet their ability to experience and express that devastation is curiously unimpaired. In Adorno's pitiless view, existentialist dramatists make no effort to express the contradiction which is the condition of their expression, and so end up failing to express anything fundamental at all. This argument, more influential than any other for the understanding and interpretation of Beckett, had, however, a precedent: in the reading of Kafka which Beckett shared with Adorno.

Reading Kafka, or Serenity and Disaster

Upon reading in Kafka's journal the entry: "Gardening. No hope for the future," Beckett remarked, "At least he could garden" (Knowlson 1996, 601). It is the rare reader who finds Kafka, on the whole, sanguine on the existence question—and fortunate into the bargain. Asked by a German correspondent for his ideas on Kafka in 1953, Beckett replied, "All I've read of his, apart from a few short texts, is about three-quarters of *The Castle,* and that in German—which is to say, missing a great deal" (LSB 2.464). There is an exaggerated dose of modesty here, as Beckett's German was more than good enough to find a great deal in Kafka. To this Beckett adds something more to the point: that in reading Kafka "I felt at home, too much so—perhaps that is what stopped me from reading on. Case closed there and then" (LSB 2.464; 462). As a young man of letters Beckett did not shy from immersing himself in *Finnegans Wake, In Search of Lost Time,* or any of a host of other modern masterpieces where he might have felt at home, too much so. Here it seems that a relatively small dose of Kafka, however, proved too strong and Beckett closed the case, there and then.

Fortunately, the case was reopened by Beckett himself. In reading Kafka he found himself bothered by the "imperturbable aspect of [Kafka's] approach [*le côté imperturbable de sa démarche*]" (LSB 2.464; 462; translation modified). He then gives his deepest reason for resistance: "I don't trust disasters that can be presented like a statement of accounts [*Je me méfie des désastres qui se laissent déposer comme un bilan*]" (LSB 2.464; 462; translation modified). This is something about which the supremely reticent Beckett felt strongly enough to repeat more than once—and not only in private. He told the *New York Times* in 1956 that *The Castle* was "difficult for me to get to the end," as well as why:

> The Kafka hero has a coherence of purpose. He's lost but he's not spiritually precarious, he's not falling to bits. My people seem to be falling to bits. Another difference. You notice how Kafka's form is classic, it goes on like a steamroller—almost serene. It *seems* to be threatened the whole time—but the consternation is in the form. In my work there is consternation behind the form, not in the form. (Shenker 1956/1979, 148; Beckett's emphasis)

In his first meeting with Adorno, two years later, Beckett used the same terms, speaking of Kafka's "serenity" (Tiedemann 1994b, 23; 27). In *The Unnamable* we read: "No cries, above all no cries, be urbane, a credit to the art and code of dying, while the others cackle, I can hear them from here, like the crackling of thorns, no, I forgot, it's impossible, it's myself I hear, howling behind my dissertation" (GC 2.308; 46). A form that corresponds to the mess is a form harrowed and shaken by devouring black silences and sounding fury. It is also one where the howls behind the dissertation are distinctly audible. Beckett's characters, at least in his great works, are anything but serene, anything but imperturbable— despite the non-negligible fact that they profess to care about nothing. "Nothing ever troubles me," says the Unnamable. "And yet I am troubled [*Rien ne me dérange jamais. Néanmoins je suis inquiet*]" (GC 2.287; 11). One might say that Beckett's reading of Kafka is unfair, that Beckett mischaracterizes Kafka's approach, that to each his own unease. There is in Kafka a preternatural calmness, an entrancing serenity in the storm. As with Joyce and Proust, Descartes and Schopenhauer, as with all the authors important to Beckett, the point is, however, less whether Beckett's critical judgment was fair than what his assessment says about his own works.

Adorno's diaries show both that this is a distinction Beckett conveyed to him personally, and that it was one with which he did not agree. He would continue to think of Beckett and Kafka in the most kindred manner. After the notation *f* (for fortissimo), "Kafka" is, by my count, the most common marginalium in Adorno's copy of *The Unnam-*

able. Adorno found that Kafka's parables "expressed themselves not through their expression but through their refusal, through their inter-ruption." "Each sentence," he added, "says, 'interpret me,' and yet none will tolerate it" (Adorno GS 10.255). There is, however, another level, a deeper intolerance, that Adorno found in Beckett. For Adorno *Endgame* is the morality play philosophy would write, were it able. If it presented philosophy in a miserable light, however, Adorno bore it no grudge. When he claims that in *Endgame* the absence of *any* "positive metaphys-ical meaning" leads to "a devastation of form that extends into the very structure and texture of Beckett's language itself," he is offering the highest praise he knows (Adorno GS 11.282). The reason for this is that, like Beckett, he saw those forms, that structure, that texture, and that language in need of devastation.

In seeming contradiction to his earlier views, Adorno, in the prepa-ratory notes for his article on *The Unnamable,* included a reminder: "Do not silence the simplest thing: experiencing existence as absurd" (Tie-demann 1994b, 28; 161; translation modified). To this maxim Adorno added a precision: "but this experience is not ontological, it is histor-ical" (Tiedemann 1994b, 28; 161; translation modified). *The ontological absurd* would be simply, and timelessly, how it is. *The historical absurd* is a screaming injustice which we might alter. This was why the category of the absurd was, for Adorno, worth fighting over. Where others saw a timeless human condition, he saw something that looked for all the world like it, and was the last thing but it. He called this the "ideology of the *condition humaine*": a historical state of affairs masquerading as a natural one, and thus a pure product of oppression (Tiedemann 1994b, 28; 161).

In *Endgame* there is every indication that the absurdity portrayed is the human condition. The first draft of *Happy Days* begins with the announcement of a nuclear catastrophe, but Beckett was careful to re-move it, and all historical indicators like it—and to do so not only in that work, but in all his mature work, for stage and page. The most natural conclusion to draw from Beckett's works is that ours is not a passing nightmare. Cioran once said of Beckett that he was "one of those be-ings who make you realize that history is a dimension one could have dispensed with" (Cioran 1979, 335). Adorno readily concedes that it indeed *seems* so. Beckett's diagnostic genius, which was also, for Adorno, his artistic genius, lay in showing us the hard, bright edge of that seeming: in "capturing the appearance of the ahistorical, of the *condition humaine,* in historical images," thereby replacing "the ideology of the *condition humaine* with dialectical images" (Tiedemann 1994b, 28; 161; translation modified). During a television roundtable a year before his death Adorno said of *Waiting for Godot* that it "represents the deluding totality in which we are trapped" (Tiedemann 1994b, 89). The term he used was *Verblendungszusammenhang,* a highly characteristic word of his own crafting, and which has been translated as "veil of delusion" and even "blinding element" but which is more literally "deluding totality."[15] The delusion in question is that a historical state of affairs is mistaken for a timeless one: something that is *not* a totality masquerading as one. Its causes, for Adorno, were many. He attributed it to "the loss of belief in Providence," "the explosion of cosmology," "the problematization and obsolescence of meaning-producing structures," and, finally, "the threat to the survival of the species"—in short, the usual suspects of modern history (Tiedemann 1994b, 28; 161; translation modified). This array of interrelated causes has robbed modern life of its ability to attribute meaning and value. Mary Bryden has written of the "apparent ahistori-cism" of Beckett's work, and the *apparent* side is precisely what Adorno wishes to argue (Bryden 2009, 41). What is decisive is that such historical reasons for the seeming meaninglessness of existence "*necessarily appear* ahistorical, *appear* ontological," and that this is the crucial element in the *Verblendungszusammenhang* which, for him, Beckett represents (Tiedemann 1994b, 28; 161; Adorno's emphasis; translation modified).

Adorno finds in Beckett a system of control which disguises the contingent as the necessary and the changeable as constant. "Beckett photographs society's bad side," Adorno wrote, "in which everything is but a part of a function-fixed whole [*in der alles Funktionszusammenhang ist*]," and thereby shows "what we become in this functionalized world [*dieser funktionalen Welt*]" (Tiedemann 1994b, 91). He is careful to stress that it is *society*'s (not mankind's) bad side, and wrote that "the historical fever of situation and speech" in Beckett "is not the concretizing, *more philosophico,* of something ahistorical" (Adorno GS 11.319). Adorno does not tire of repeating that the matter is *historical,* for the reason that historical matters are changeable: they start and they can end. Beckett's works are of such power, and hold out such hope, for him because they help us see through the illusion that the problem with life is life.

And yet if Beckett meant to speak of history, why did he go to such pains to omit all trace of it? Adorno found that Beckett addressed the horrors of their times the only dignified way possible. He wrote that Beckett "does not even indict society. Precisely not, and this is exactly the tip of the spear he aims at it" (Tiedemann 1994b, 31; 169; translation modified). In a similar vein, Adorno remarked elsewhere that "the moral element" in Beckett's works was to be found in the fact that they were "completely undefiant" (Tiedemann 1994b, 118). These remarks give a sense of the ways in which Adorno is willing to interpret absence. Adorno may not have said, as he is often credited with having done, that poetry after Auschwitz is impossible, but he did say that "after Auschwitz, writing a poem is barbaric," as well as that "Auschwitz irrefutably demonstrated culture's failure," and even that "all culture after Auschwitz, including its urgent critique, is garbage" (Adorno GS 10.30; Adorno GS 6.359; see also Adorno GS 6.355). Auschwitz presented a problem for artists that Adorno saw Beckett as the first to truly address: by not saying a word. In *Negative Dialectics* Adorno wrote that "Beckett responded to the situation of the concentration camp—which, after the manner of a ban, he never names—in the only fitting manner. What is, he says, is like a concentration camp [*Was ist, sei wie das Konzentrationslager*]" (Adorno GS 6.373; 380). Beckett did not act as though Auschwitz had never happened and did not write lyric poetry as though the air were not full of cries. But he also did not name the historical horror. And this, for Adorno, is how it should be. In response to a questionnaire on literary themes in contemporary society sent to him in 1960, Adorno informed its sender that he was unable to respond to the questions posed, but deigned to note that "in Beckett's novels, in which not a word is said about the historical horror of our times, I find this horror incomparably more precisely portrayed" than any work he knew (Tiedemann 1994b, 137). For Adorno, Beckett did the noble thing—as a man and an artist—which was to refrain from writing anything at all about the concentration camps (in which many close to him were murdered), and to write of absolutely everything else as though it were one.

Critical theory, aesthetic theory, historical materialism, negative dialectics, and the other names Adorno gave to his enterprise are carried out in the name of seeing through the veil of delusion raised not by a cabal of absolutist monarchs or corporate villains, but through fantastically complex social ensembles that create the conditions of possibility for exploitation, suffering, and even genocide. "Art means," Adorno wrote, "to resist the course of a world that unceasingly holds a gun to mankind's chest" (Adorno GS 11.413). Hume once remarked to Berkeley that his arguments admitted of no refutation and produced no conviction. A reader of Adorno's interpretation of Beckett might be tempted to say the same. Standard evidentiary models do not easily admit the absence of evidence as evidence, and one cannot therefore examine or refute Adorno's claims in any customary manner. While it is clear that Adorno's argument admits of no standard refutation, it might of course still produce conviction. What is at issue here is seeing social criticism present and intelligible at the level of *form*. "If it is still possible," Adorno wrote in his unfinished final work, "social criticism must be elevated to form, dimming down any manifest social content" (Adorno GS 7.371; 354). Except for the odd bicycle or bowler, Beckett's mature works are free of even vague historical markers. Adorno's deduction is that this seeming timelessness, this mythic never, is the opposite of what it seems, that this is a denunciation *not* of the meaninglessness of human existence per se, but a denunciation of a relatively recent historical and social movement toward total control of individual lives by the powers that be. Adorno's debate with Lukács on this point is irresolvable because each had a conviction which was profound and unprovable. Lukács thought that holding a faithful mirror up to a corrupt and abusive society would lead individuals to unite and change it. Beckett's mirror was, for him, too strangely shaped, and directed, for such purposes, isolating far more than it unified. Adorno, on the other hand, thought that precisely such a jarring and distorting mirror was best suited to release the creative energies necessary for revolutionary change.

Appropriately enough, the ontological view preceded the historical one, beginning as it did with Blanchot's early essay on Beckett. Do Beckett's books come from where all books come from? If that is understood as a writer in a room, then yes, and if it means pure pulses of being, a fire in the heart of language, the answer is, of course, that it will depend on whether one believes in those things. As with Beckett's, Blanchot's writings made distinctions such as fact/fiction seem provincial. And they made history disappear. Both men's books presented fictions that seemed searingly personal without revealing the least personal, or presenting the least historical, detail. Blanchot's Beckett wrestled with a timeless problem: language. French criticism has been far more ontological than historical (whether Blanchot was its cause or its expression is uncertain) and has been intensely focused upon the space of language and the lies language cannot help but tell. (Thanks to the concerted efforts of two exceptional critics—Clément and Casanova—this ontological view has begun to shift.) Making the source of Beckett's dark view of things something specific, even if only somewhat, is a great temptation. Because he is harsh and unsparing, Adorno has been called a pessimist, but he is, in this respect, the brightest of optimists, unwilling as he is to entertain the notion that life could be life's problem. Our difficulties are, for him, many and terrible, but they are also all contingent, the fruit of twists and turns in history. Adorno finds that if power and wealth were distributed differently, and the dinning of an industry selling superficiality were quieted, we might be happy on this earth. Seeing this as Beckett's message requires, however, a very liberal interpretation of Beckett's own silences and statements on the matter.

At the beginning of this book I spoke of Beckett's difficulty, and have since dwelt upon some of its facets. As is obvious, Beckett's difficulty is one of description and discernment, not, of course, enjoyment. From the first hour his works—from the uneducated to the hyper-educated, on stage and page, in French and English, from Paris's left bank to San Quentin prison—were acclaimed as immediately and as universally as any œuvre of the century. Beckett's critics have not been wrong about there being something unprecedented going on in his works. But what this unprecedented thing is has been a subject of the purest uncertainty. The work of sixty years of criticism in French, English, and other languages attests to how difficult it has been to define and describe those worlds and works. One question is what everyone is enjoying so much, and why. For they cannot all be seeking to acquire cultural capital, not all seeking to seduce by obscurity, and not all performing aesthetic penance. They are obviously enjoying themselves at the same time as they are experiencing acute uncertainty concerning art's relation to life, action's relation to desire, language's relation to truth, and humanity's possibilities for happiness. The work evidently speaks to acute uncertainty concerning the limits of our experience, the nature of our language, and the meaning of our being. Any answer to the questions raised by critics depends upon how one sees art's relation to anarchy. Art is perhaps in its essence and by its nature anarchic. Just as it is perhaps in its essence and by its nature order. What is clear is that a hallmark of modern art is a pronounced anarchic, disorderly, and even aggressive attitude toward the means of expression—in music, in the visual arts, in drama, and in literature. Lying through images has always been a human concern but the society of the spectacle in which Beckett wrote presented unprecedented changes in this regard, and unprecedented reason for alarm. But it is impossible for Beckett's reader to say—without a leap of critical faith—whether the charges are leveled at art or the culture which so debased it—or both. Here the question of history meets the question of pessimism. If things have ever been thus, then the best response is acceptance, given the givens. If, however, they have simply become thus, not by any historical necessity, but because we were poor custodians of what should have been most dear to us—our means of reflecting on who we are and how to live with one another—then action is demanded. Happily or unhappily, Beckett offers absolutely no assistance on this point. He tells us that he chose the negative. He does not say it was right for all, only that it was right for him. The question thus remains open of whether this is a fact about the age, or merely about the artist. Did Beckett work so closely with negations because there was nothing left for the creative individual born in 1906 to do besides work in the negative? The only work was in the mines. So he worked in the mines. Unless he chose them out of an unusual love, and in the hope of bringing up something never before seen.

The answer to such questions determines our sense of what lies ahead. Could mismaking, disorder, chaos, and the mess be the future of art? Is mismaking only compelling against a backdrop—a long and rich backdrop—of fine making, and consequently can only be enjoyed at distant intervals and in small doses, in which case mismaking like

Beckett's is a saturnalia of art and its forms, not a new calendar? Or might mismaking become a major mode and dominant form? Here the question rejoins that of Beckett's chess partner Duchamp, for both make their audience decide how separable context is from content and art from anarchy, and both leave the questions uncomfortably open.

We should have at least as much of a problem assimilating and characterizing Beckett's works as those of Duchamp. As the media are different, so, of course, are the methods, but the question is identical: How close to life can art be? Can it be simply anything? Will just anything work? How are we to understand the work that goes into the work of art? Is the goal to efface the line between art and life, so that art's creative energies might flood outwards into life, like the Nile, rendering life fertile again? And what of the fact that the moment in Western history when a torrent of images began to flow which has not ceased, or even slowed, saw the arrival of its most iconoclastic, and logoclastic, writer?

The Christmas Tree

It would be hard to find a better gloss of Beckett's position than St. John of the Cross's description of the steps of the spirit on the path of Mount Carmel: "Nothing, nothing, nothing, and even on the Mount nothing." The positive does not indeed seem to abound in works with elders kept in garbage cans, figures buried to their midriffs in mud; with blind, maimed, mud-bespattered, wounded, and warped individuals; with cruel masters and crazed servants for whom speech is a chore, thought a joke, communication an impossibility, life a burden, and love long since cancelled. On occasion Beckett alluded, guardedly, to "a chance of renovation" to be grasped through artistically embracing "the mess" (Driver 1961, 23). "One cannot speak anymore of being," Beckett once remarked, "one must speak only of the mess. When Heidegger and Sartre speak of a contrast between being and existence, they may be right, I don't know, but their language is too philosophical for me. I am not a philosopher. One can only speak of what is in front of him, and that now is simply the mess" (Driver 1961, 23). Instead of an artist confronted with a mess he will order, clarify, and interpret is one who aspires to do no more than circumscribe the mess, uncertain whether the mess comes from within or without or is made the moment they meet, in the artist, in the work.

After a meeting with Beckett in Berlin in 1967 Adorno recorded Beckett's "seriously puzzling remark on the positivity to be found in pure negativity," to which he added "my own idea that even in [Beckett's] plays the curtain lifts as though revealing a Christmas tree" (Tiedemann 1994b, 24). This is a strange image for anyone to see on Beckett's stage, and all the more strange for one of the century's most outspoken Marxist—and Jewish—intellectuals. Adorno's cryptic note to self is clarified if we look to his essay from these same years "Is Art Light-Hearted? [*Ist die Kunst Heiter?*]." The title was a jab at Schiller, who had written, "Life is serious, art is light-hearted [*Ernst ist das Leben, heiter ist die Kunst*]." The idea that art should offer a respite from life, a vacation from its seriousness, a sort of mental spa, is one Adorno dismissed. In the place of such light-heartedness he finds something deeper and fuller: that even in the most extreme "expression of despair," art, in and by its very nature, "allies itself with a promise of happiness" (Adorno GS 11.600). Adorno then draws upon an image become dear to him: "even Beckett's plays raise their curtain as though upon a room at Christmas time" (Adorno GS 11.600).

The withered tree of Beckett's *Waiting for Godot* seems a far cry from a Christmas tree aglow with warm light and ringed with presents—as do the opening images of all Beckett's works. In his copy of *The Unnamable* Adorno again and again underlined Beckett's variations on the theme of "going on," and stopped at one point to write in the margins that "going on is a fundamental category. And it is a *critical* one" (Tiedemann 1994b, 56; Adorno's emphasis). Adorno wrote elsewhere that "through the seemingly Stoic 'going on' is silently screamed that things should be different" (Adorno GS 6.373). If you must go on and you cannot go on, and yet on you go, then you follow a path supremely difficult to chart, but not therefore meaningless. It might be a dull compulsion to go on about which you can know nothing because there is nothing to know, just as it might be radical means taken to say a radical thing. For if you see mismaking not as aimed at blunting or blurring capacities, but at sharpening them, then you are in another world, a world of brilliant and desperate dedication, with the scream that things should be different, and the belief that they might be. In such a case you would be at home right where you were, and what you saw before you, even if it appeared to be but a withered tree in a dead land, would reveal a different outline.

Notes

Introduction

1. That Mr. and Mrs. Shower (or Cooker) stand in for the audience is as obvious (and ironic) as such a thing can be. "Shower & Cooker are derived from German *schauen* & *kuchen*," Beckett told his friend and director Alan Schneider (Harmon 1998, 95). (*Schauen* means to look. As for the second term, Beckett meant the slang term *kucken*, sometimes spelled as *gucken*—not the word Schneider transcribes, *kuchen*, which means *cake*.) To make the matter absolutely clear, Beckett also told Schneider, "They represent the onlookers (audience) wanting to know the meaning of things" (Harmon 1998, 95).

2. For one—authoritative—example among many, see Arthur Danto's claim in *The Abuse of Beauty: Aesthetics and the Concept of Art* that "it is the mark of the present period in the history of art that the concept of art implies no internal constraint on what works of art are, so that one no longer can tell if something is a work of art or not" (Danto 2003, 17).

3. "The Insufficiency of Language: A Study of the Decline of Form and the Lack of Relation in Samuel Beckett."

4. For ease and clarity of reference I will use the term *trilogy*, as is customary in Beckett studies, for the three novels *Molloy* (1951), *Malone Dies* (1951), and *The Unnamable* (1953), written (in French) between 1947 and 1950, published individually (in Beckett's translation, with initial assistance from Patrick Bowles) in English in 1955, 1956, 1958, and collectively in 1959. In English these novels have been readily available as a single volume. In French they have never been published as a single volume. It bears noting that Beckett,

for his own part, had reservations concerning the term and limited himself to referring to "my so-called trilogy" (cf., especially, Ackerley and Gontarski 2004, 586).

5. The joke not intended concerns *fundament*'s anatomical meaning *(anus)*.

6. Cited by Esslin (1969), 12. Schneider's recollection is almost identical: "That very first time, I asked Sam who or what Godot was, though luckily not what it 'meant'; and he told me, after a moment of deep reflection in those seemingly bottomless blue-gray eyes, that if he had known, he would have said so in the play" (Schneider 1986, 243).

7. Beckett liked this phrase so much that he used it again, in the final lines of his first book (cf. GC 4.554).

8. Cf. LSB 2.xix.

9. Given that the *Grove Centenary Edition* of Beckett's writings is the first to offer an authoritative text for the novel, it is unsurprising that volume 1 of that edition should have an image of this painting on its cover. What *is* surprising is that it is misdrawn (the circle is broken at its *highest,* not lowest, point). Also surprising is that this is not the first time, as the first edition of *Watt* also chose to place this image on its cover, and also misdrew it, albeit differently (on that first edition see Ackerley 2010b, 128).

10. See Beckett (2006b), 97–99.

11. The man was Axel Kaun, and the circumstances surrounding the letter are discussed in Chapter 4.

12. The translators are, respectively, Martin Esslin and Victoria Westbrook (cf. Beckett 1984, 173; LSB 1.520).

13. Beckett had spent a great deal of time during the preceding six months looking at pictures—a significant number of which were the victims of a modern iconoclasm under way during his trip as the Nazi bans on "degenerate art" went into effect (through a curious legal loophole, foreigners such as Beckett were permitted to see "degenerate" works held in galleries and museums that were off limits to German citizens). Beckett read widely in art history during this period—as his notebooks attest—making him amply familiar with the *Bildersturm,* or iconoclasm, debates of sixteenth-century Germany (as well as earlier ones, such as the Byzantine).

14. This period of astounding productivity lasted from 1946 to 1950. During it Beckett wrote his first French fictions, the trilogy of novels *Molloy, Malone Dies,* and *The Unnamable, Texts for Nothing,* as well as *Waiting for Godot.* (For Beckett's use of the phrase, cf. Bair 1990, 346, and Kenner 1961, 24—although the latter uses the phrase without quotation marks, in all likelihood an oversight.) Cronin, one of Beckett's three Anglophone biographers, interprets the expression as referring to Beckett's sense of being besieged and thereby cut off from resources (resources ranging from his native language to standard storytelling; Cronin 1997, 364). This is indeed one possibility, but a more consistent one is that Beckett was as much laying siege as besieged.

1. First Forms to Accommodate the Mess

1. Beckett always celebrated, if that is the right word for it, his birthday on this date, as did his family and friends. His birth certificate gives his date of birth as May 13, 1906, a discrepancy that was likely the result of a clerical error. For more on the matter, see Knowlson 1996, 24, and Cronin 1997, 1-2.

2. Beckett's psychoanalysis with Wilfred Bion (a student of Melanie Klein and follower of Freud) from 1934 to 1936 involved an effort to recover such memories. Whether or not Beckett was successful in any traditional sense, the "wombtomb" was to prove a recurrent image in his writing, from Belacqua's declaration, "I want very much to be back in the caul, on my back in the dark for ever," to the addendum to *Watt,* "never been properly born," to Murphy's reasoned refusal to wear a hat (*Dream,* 45; GC 4.94; GC 1.374). Beckett sought out Bion because of "pavor nocturnus [night terrors]" and "somatization" (including tachycardia, tremors, boils, and abscesses). Bion believed that Beckett's problems stemmed primarily from his fraught relationship with his mother. In the important French reference work *Dictionnaire de la psychanalyse* the authors note that Beckett sought treatment for "severe respiratory problems, headaches and various chronic complaints linked to alcoholism and a certain vagranticization [*une certaine clochardisation*]" (120). One can only imagine that Beckett would have been pleased by the last item on the diagnostic list.

3. First published posthumously (in 1992).

4. Sheila Jones (née Dobbs) and Moira Symons (née Neill) in Knowlson 2006, 53, 55.

5. Beckett 1984, 169. Jean du Chas was the subject of Beckett's 1930 presentation to the Modern Languages Society of Trinity College, *"Le Concentrisme."* It is unclear to what extent Beckett's audience was duped, just as it is unclear to what extent the intention was to dupe them.

6. Cf. Knowlson 1996, 73 ff.

7. Shortly before his death in 1989, Beckett told James Knowlson that he "still regretted" publishing it (Knowlson 1996, 183).

8. *More Pricks Than Kicks* elicited few reviews (though those it did tended to note an affinity with Joyce that did not, at the time, stand Beckett in good stead) and sold few copies (Colm Tóibín gives the endearing figure of two copies sold by 1936; Tóibín 2006, xi). Six months after its publication it was banned in Ireland. It eventually sold five hundred copies of the first edition. After it went out of print Beckett kept it there for more than thirty years, referring to it, when refer he must, as a "fiasco" (e.g., Ackerley and Gontarski 2004, 381; LSB 3.633). Krapp will note of a work of his own, "Seventeen copies sold, of which eleven at trade price to free circulating libraries beyond the seas. Getting known" (GC 3.228).

9. Not only did Beckett wonder darkly at the "bathos of style & thought" in Balzac, he dismissed traces of it in writers he treasured, such as Proust (LSB 1.145). In rereading *Le temps retrouvé* in 1932 Beckett finds the whole "Balzac gush" of Morel and Charlus unreadable, but is careful to note that "surely

the first 100 pages [of volume 2 of *Le temps retrouvé*] are as great a piece of sustained writing as anything to be found anywhere" (LSB 1.145).

10. A novel from 1936 written by Jack Yeats, which Beckett was reviewing.

11. Beckett's tutor, the philosophy professor A. A. Luce, recommended Beckett pursue either law or chartered accountancy upon enrollment at Trinity College (Knowlson 1996, 69). Despite these references to Austen and Dickens, Balzac is seen as far and away the chief offender in this realist regard. Beckett will have positive things to say elsewhere about the other two writers, as where he writes to McGreevy that Austen "has much to teach me" or where he praises Dickens's powers of sensual description (LSB 1.250; GC 4.504–4.505). Chesterton once wrote of Dickens's depictions of London streets that "he did not stamp those places on his mind; he stamped his mind on those places" (Chesterton 1965, 46). Beckett seems to come to a similar conclusion, albeit with a different valuation.

12. Gerry Dukes "How It Is with Bouncing Bel," *Irish Times*, October 31, 1992, cited by Knowlson 1996, 147.

13. The poem was ultimately published in 1935 under the title "Eneug I" (an "Eneug II" had since been written) with the slightly altered ending: "the silk of the seas and the arctic flowers / that do not exist" (GC 4.13).

14. On this point see especially Smith 2002.

15. Beckett was to write in 1959 of this essay that it was "perhaps ce qu'on a fait du mieux [the best that anyone's done] on that gruesome subject [Beckett's own writing]," to which he adds: "I think he's on to something very important which he probably over-systematizes" (LSB 3.222).

16. My translation. Beckett is a breathtakingly good translator of himself, but, as would anyone, he nods. For reasons hard to grasp, Beckett's English translation of this novel (the last thing but a labor of love) becomes, as though fatigued, unusually literal at this point: "Don't tell me he is all that rancorous."

17. *Godot*, 141–142. Two of the finest playwrights active today find a point of departure in this passage. The "skull the skull the skull the skull in Connemara" which recurs at the end of the monologue gives Ireland's greatest living playwright, Martin McDonagh, a title (and, intermittently, a tone), *A Skull in Connemara* (1997). Were one to seek a template for the ceaselessly brilliant dramatic monologues of the French playwright Valère Novarina one would need seek no further.

18. Calder claims that "there is not a single character in Beckett's novels or plays who is not a religious believer" (Calder 2012, 11). This can only be true if "religious believer" is understood in an unprecedentedly elastic sense.

19. In these pages Calvino misquotes the last line of *Ohio Impromptu*, replacing the "Nothing is left to tell" with "Little is left to tell" (which is the play's first line) (GC 4.473; GC 4.476; Calvino 1995, 753). Caselli claims that by doing so Calvino is "indicative of the way in which even one of the main figures of twentieth-century Italian letters needs to keep alive Beckett's humanism" (Caselli 2009, 216). While there being little left to tell is perhaps a more heartening idea than that there is nothing left to tell, Caselli's conclusion that this

is Calvino giving in to humanism's siren song through such a misquotation (in an unfinished and posthumously published text) involves a great leap of probabilistic faith.

2. The Will to Mismake, or Fish and Chips

1. The phrase is borrowed from Beethoven's last quartet and its recurrent *Muss es sein?* Beckett alluded to it often (cf. Knowlson 1996, 193).
2. The mystery of the *M*'s can have no definitive solution, though a great many hypotheses have been advanced, from those focusing on anonymity, such as Kenner's, who saw in the *M*'s an evocation of an everyman inherited from Joyce's HCE (Here Comes Everybody), to Leventhal's noting how the *S* of Sam in Beckett's handwriting "looks like an M standing on its side. And therefrom stem the dissyllables Murphy, Molloy, Malone, Mahood" (Leventhal 1965, 48). By the end of Beckett's career, the letters are reduced to their reversible rudiments, with the company (in *Company* [1980]) offered by characters named M and W, one "a hearer," the other "a character" (GC 4.442; 58).
3. This line conjoins Hume's relative certainty (that the sun will rise tomorrow) with Beckett's absolute certainty that, once it does, nothing under it will be new. Shortly after finishing *Murphy,* Beckett employed a variation of this same expression in *Mittelalterliches Dreieck: Es dämmert, weil es nicht anders kann:* "Dusk came, having no alternative" (Beckett 2006b, 123).
4. In September 1935 Beckett wrote to McGreevy of visiting "Bedlam" and how he "went round the wards for the first time, with scarcely any sense of horror, though I saw everything, from mild depression to profound dementia" (LSB 1.277). As has often been wrongly reported—including in the blurb for an English paperback edition of the novel—Beckett at no time shared Murphy's employment (though he often shared his unemployment) (Knowlson 1996, 209).
5. In this connection it bears noting that both *brooding* and *reflecting* are used with something approaching systematic precision in Beckett's work, early and late—something on prominent display in *Act Without Words I* and *Act Without Words II.* In the former, the tantalized mime again and again "reflects" on the fleeting objects that descend from above before trying, in vain, to grasp them; in the latter, the response to the goad extending from the wings is, again and again, "brooding" (see GC 3.191–194 and GC 3.215–217).
6. Cf. for instance "The will itself, or man himself, insofar as his will was evil, was, as it were, the corrupt tree which brought forth the evil fruit of those evil deeds" (Augustine 1998, 604).

3. Nature Painting

1. Lois Oppenheim writes that "Beckett's concerns had little to do with the idea of what art qua art *is* and even less to do with its meaning," bearing instead on "process—the means of discovery, the disclosing of a relation of human

to world prior to its falsification by the limits of cognition and the representational modes of consciousness" (Oppenheim 2000, 2).

2. "... and the dying spit of a Paduan Virtue, / for alas she has stripped her last asparagus." Cf. Beckett 1977, 38. The Paduan Virtue Charity is, for Proust, embodied by a kitchen maid (sadistically made to peel asparagus, to which she is allergic).

3. "... *ed ora ha Giotto il grido*" (*Purgatorio* 11.95).

4. Walter Benjamin, writing a year earlier, saw the relationship between Baudelaire and Proust in the same terms as Beckett, but inverted. Benjamin declares that the reader who "penetrates to the heart of Proust's world" finds "the world in a state of similarity, and in it the *correspondances* rule; the Romantics were the first to comprehend them and Baudelaire embraced them most fervently, but Proust was the only one who managed to reveal them in our lived life" (Benjamin 1996–2003, 2.244; Benjamin 1974–1989, 2.320).

4. The Alibi of a Foreign Language

1. Coetzee writes of his "surprise" that "this letter to a comparative stranger" should be so revealing (Coetzee 2009, 7). The matter might be seen in the opposite light, however, as it is in all likelihood precisely the freedom offered by writing to a relative stranger, in a foreign language, that allowed Beckett to express himself with such unusual candor.

2. Esslin's translation is far closer to the original's tone—and, in many places, its terms—than Westbrook's. Esslin's version does, however, have a drawback: it gives the translation a greater fluency than the original (see Beckett 1984, 171–173). Westbrook's translation aims to rectify this, as well as to correct a few liberties Esslin took in the translation of individual epithets. The result, however, is mixed, as Westbrook's version fails to convey more than a faint echo of the bizarre exuberance of Beckett's German (which Esslin's translation captures so well). What is more, Westbrook's translation unfortunately takes a number of liberties out of keeping with what is largely a literal translation. For instance, Esslin renders what Beckett calls Ringelnatz's *"Verswut"* as the evocative "rhyming fury," toned down by Westbrook to the somewhat misleading "verse-obsession" (LSB 1.512; Beckett 1984, 171; LSB 1.517; a more literal translation would be "rabid versifying," as Beckett's pun is on the German word for rabies). On the other side of the scale, Westbrook returns capitalized substantives (like "Nothingness" and "All") to their proper, or at least a prudent, elevation (in German all substantives are capitalized; Esslin chooses to selectively capitalize certain of these; LSB 1.518, 519; Beckett 1984, 171, 172).

3. Gauging this is made exceptionally difficult by the fact that the letter has survived only as a draft given by Beckett to a friend (and critic) sometime between 1960 and 1966 to which extensive corrections have been made by Beckett (either at the time of composition or later) and might even include changes made in collaboration with this critic.

4. Tophoven 2005, 122. Noted in the so-called German Diaries—six notebooks discovered in a trunk in the cellar of Beckett's Paris apartment after his death by his nephew, and covering some five hundred closely written pages.

5. For a careful treatment of Beckett's trips to Germany between 1928 and 1932, as well as this later one, see Knowlson 1996. For an extensive examination of what Beckett once called his "German fever," and, more generally, his interests in and engagements with Germany, its language, and its art, see Fischer-Seidel and Fries-Dieckmann 2005 and Nixon 2011. For a treatment of Beckett's time in Germany with special focus on the weeks spent in Berlin, see Völker 1986, Tophoven 2005, and Beckett 2006b. For special focus on the role of studying the visual arts in Berlin, see Veit 2006.

6. Entry for March 18, 1937. See Pilling 1997, 153, 253n13; and Tophoven 2005, 8.

7. The eight-line poem is called *Die Briefmarke* and finds "life's tragic side [*die Tragik des Lebens*]" exemplified in the male postage stamp's inability to return the princess's kiss.

8. Ringelnatz was the pseudonym of Hans Bötticher (1883-1934). At the time of Beckett's writing he was banned as a "degenerate artist" by the Nazi Party, and had been since 1933.

9. Beckett's recording of the term *Tintenkuli* can be found at Tophoven 2005, 122.

10. Beckett's emphasis. Goethe's statement is from his *Elective Affinities*.

11. Beckett speaks somewhat dismissively of the *"Geheimrat"* (Goethe held the official position of privy counselor) in his German letter to Kaun, and very dismissively of him in other letters from the period. Writing to McGreevy a year earlier, he notes, "I have been reading wildly all over the place, Goethe's *Iphigenia* & then Racine to remove the taste" (LSB 1.324). On a still harsher note, upon reading Goethe's *Tasso* he finds that "anything more disgusting would be hard to devise" (LSB 1.319). In yet another letter, Beckett speaks of *Faust* in less scathing but far from positive terms, writing of part 1 of the poem, "It leaves me with the impression of something very fragmentary, often irrelevant & too concrete," as well as noting that "all the *on & up* is so tiresome also, the determined optimism à la Beethoven, the unconscionable time a-coming" (LSB 1.368; Beckett's emphasis).

12. *Dégueuler* can mean "vomit" in French, though *dégueulade* does not simply mean "throwing up," as the editors of Beckett's letters indicate (LSB 1.xciii). Its primary meaning in Beckett's day was a *rant*, which is what Beckett is asking forgiveness for when he writes, for instance, "God love thee & forgive the dégueulade" to McGreevy in one of the more important letters from the period (LSB 1.223).

13. A kindred sense and sensitivity to the one Beckett finds in Joyce is expressed by another of Joyce's friends, Ezra Pound, during these same years, as where Pound denounces "the crust of dead English" that the creative writer must remove (Pound 1954, 193). With customary caution Eliot, in turn, noted in 1920 that "few persons realize that the Greek language and the Latin language, and *therefore,* we say, the English language are within our lifetime passing through a critical period" (T. S. Eliot 2001, 118; Eliot's emphasis).

14. F. R. Leavis responded to Beckett's essay by rejecting this argument, taking the position that in Joyce's case it was "on the contrary, plain that the whole phenomenon is one of sophistication," although Leavis's conception of sophistication is so far from Beckett's as to be essentially incompatible, with the result that the two men disagree far less than Leavis thinks (Leavis 1933, 198).

15. These were French poems which Beckett was to publish only after the war (cf., especially, Clément 1994, 238n1).

16. Beckett deemed this passage important enough that he published it separately, in *Disjecta* (cf. Beckett 1984, 47ff.).

17. See also, from another early German letter, Beckett's remark: "No sooner do I take up my pen to compose something in English than I feel I've been mispersonified [*verpersonifiziert*], if I might be permitted such a grand expression" (LSB 1.202; translation modified).

18. Letter to Sighle Kennedy from June 14, 1967, first published in Kennedy 1971, 300, and reprinted in Beckett 1984, 113. See also Gluck 1979, 9ff.

19. This is wrong on at least one count, for Beckett was *far* more uneasy about the influence of Joyce on his work than about that of Proust, just as the influence of Joyce is far more visible in Beckett's English than the influence of Proust ever is in Beckett's French—or English.

20. Cf. LSB 1.565. In a conversation from 1984 Gussow asked Beckett whether he ever "changed anything" in the text he was helping Joyce put to paper. The reply was "No" with what Gussow described as "a hint of a smile" (Gussow 1996, 47).

21. Eliot's letter is dated May 21, 1921, and is cited in Ellmann 1982, 528.

22. Ricks finds fault with this point as "these observations by the enthusiastic young Beckett failed to allow for the uses of adversity, of anti-onomatopoeia, by which for English-speakers their word for doubt may help to steel them against its temptations" (Ricks 1993, 51). This is a sensitive and interesting idea in its own right, but it is beside Beckett's point, as the latter is quite clearly speaking of a different phenomenon which neither excludes it nor would be incompatible with it.

23. For a playfully uncertain sense of the importance of this overarching idea, see Joyce's letter to his patron, Harriet Shaw Weaver, where he writes, "I do not know if Vico has been translated. I would not pay overmuch attention to these theories, beyond using them for all they are worth, but they have gradually forced themselves on me through circumstances of my own life" (Joyce 1975, 314).

24. More than twenty-five years later Beckett will still have this phrase in mind, writing, in his own variation on it, that he is "in toothless twyminds" about whether to go to New York or not (he does not move) (LSB 2.561).

25. For the passage in question in the finished work, see Joyce 1966, 468. Beckett cites the passage from the work then still in progress at GC 4.503–504.

26. In Beckett's initial version of the essay, published in *transition,* this line read: "He is not writing about something: he is writing something."

27. The poet is Skaay. Cf. Bringhurst 2011, 85.

28. Joyce 1986, 15.338–339.

29. The line is drawn from the sonnet *"A se stesso"* ("To Oneself") from 1833. Beckett also borrows lines from it for his *Dream of Fair to Middling Women* (see *Dream,* 61–62; *"Or posa per sempre," "stanco mio cor," "Assai palpitasti,"* etc.). Given the importance this poem had for the young Beckett (who returned to it on many occasions and in many works), it bears noting that elsewhere in it Leopardi invokes the "radical deception" which is life and that its last lines denounce "the infinite vanity of everything [*l'infinita vanità del tutto*]." In his second untimely meditation Nietzsche cites this same pessimist credo to express "the endless excess of all that has happened [*unendlichen Ueberflusse des Geschehenden*]" (Nietzsche 1999, 1.256). Beckett's use of it as epigraph is interesting not only for its contrast with the flowing and branching metaphors of Proust's writing, but also for his taking a line of rich Romantic verse and stripping it of everything but its global pessimism.

30. It is a curious fact of Beckett scholarship that although this remark is often cited by Beckett's critics, it is almost never cited directly. Many, such as Cavell, cite Esslin's citing of Gessner (see Esslin 1969, 62; Cavell 2002, 161). In a novel variation on the theme, a recent book on Beckett cites Cavell citing Esslin citing Gessner (Szafraniec 2007, 186). It bears noting that Cavell appears unaware that Gessner wrote anything at all and seems to believe that what Esslin reports is a conversation that Esslin recorded rather than what was, in fact, the first book ever published on Beckett's writings (see Cavell 2002, 160–161).

31. This curious term is rendered as "eliminate" by Esslin and as "dismiss" by Westbrook (Beckett 1984, 172; LSB 1.518). Its unambiguous meaning is, however, "to switch off."

32. Though Bataille would not have seen this letter, he uses a kindred image in his early essay on Beckett, writing of an intention he perceives in *Molloy* that "in the end literature makes of language a gaping wind-ravaged façade [*à la fin la littérature fasse du langage cette façade échevelée par le vent et trouée*]" (Bataille 1988, 12.88).

5. To Hell with All This Fucking Scenery

1. Cf. Bair 1990 and Ackerley 2010a (esp. 19ff.).
2. Beckett translated this passage into English with unusual literalism—using "passed" for *"se passèrent."* In his original French the focus is not on the physical passing of things or time, but, instead, with what happened.
3. Beckett's English version of the text replaces this line with another: "what words are there for that, none I know, period" (GC 4.240).
4. This has been an appealing term for readers, from Anne Carson's use of it as an epigraph (to her poem "Peril," where she shortens the notation simply to "vaguen") to Gontarski's critical studies. Cf. especially Gontarski's discussion of a progressive "vaguening" that he compares to the trajectory of incompletion seen in J. M. W. Turner's painting a century earlier (Gontarski 2010, 1). The effect he notes is one of "imagery vaguened," "imagery hazened," and of "crafted indistinction" (Gontarski 2010, 3).

6. No Symbols Where None Intended

1. These remarks were not published until after Beckett's death. Beckett himself took an interest in Derrida's writing and discussed him with a young friend, then a student of Derrida (and Deleuze), André Bernold (Bernold 1992, 85–86).

2. The paraphrased lines are also found in the original in Beckett's *Whoroscope* notebook ("*tristi fummo / nell'aere dolce che dal sol s'allegra, / portanto* [sic] *dentro accidioso fummo. Inf. VII 123*"). It is these muddy people who seem to semi-surface in *How It Is,* where Beckett removes the writhing affect and adds a re-purposed tool for suffering (a can opener).

3. Beckett spent a good part of the summer of 1932 in the reading room of the British Museum reading, as his letters indicate, Plato, Aristotle, and the Gnostics (LSB 1.111; cf. also Knowlson 1996, 157).

4. Beckett remarked of *Godot* that "silence is pouring into this play like water into a sinking ship" (Beckett 1994, 1.xiv).

5. Lest we conceive of Beckett's writing as a response to this line in Wittgenstein, it should be noted that Beckett, by his own account, did not read Wittgenstein until 1959 (at which time he wrote, as noted above, that he did not understand a word of it) (cf. LSB 3.262; cf. also Fletcher 1964, 58).

6. While each of Beckett's names has its own suggestive elements, Murphy is richer than the rest. There is indeed Murphy's law. And as Kenner suggested and Ackerley documented, there are distinctly Joycean elements in the game of Murphy's name—not only Stephen's remark to Bloom that "Shakespeares were as common as Murphies," but the "murphy come, murphy go" of *Finnegans Wake* (the latter from a passage written in 1928 and thus well before the writing of *Murphy*) (Ackerley 2010a, 28; 115). Kennedy hears echoes of the god of sleep, Morpheus, in the name; Rabaté finds that the Greek root *morphe* more generally moves it (Kennedy 1971, 62ff.; Rabaté 1984, 136).

7. The Psychopathology of Character Creation, or The Series

1. Beckett developed aphasia after having mysteriously fallen in 1988. Knowlson speculates that this was due to an atypical onset of Parkinson's disease, Cohn that Beckett had suffered a stroke (see Knowlson 1996, 702, and Cohn 2001, 382—for more on the incident see also Salisbury 2008).

2. Foucault 1994, 794. The passage Foucault quotes here in his "What Is an Author?" is from the third of Beckett's *Texts for Nothing* and can be found at GC 4.302 (cited at Foucault 1994, 789; 821).

3. Cf. Tiedemann 1994b, 90.

4. Cf. Avrin 1991, 224, and Greenblatt 2011, 40.

5. First described in 1923 by the French psychiatrist Joseph Capgras, the syndrome has been described by a host of subsequent psychologists, neurologists, and artists. For a clinical case study see Ramachandran and Blakeslee 1998, 158–173; for an artistic one, see Galchen 2008.

6. Beckett's English translation reads "twenty-nine thousand nine hundred and seventy years *after* having purged his offense" (my emphasis), which makes no sense, both because Hercules was recounted to have liberated Prometheus long before the end of his sentence, not long after, and, more importantly, because the original French text reads *avant* (before). No English edition has yet elected to correct this slip.

7. Beckett means *Niemand wandelt ungestraft.*

8. In a far from positive review of the trilogy ("I find it unreadable") from 1960, V. S. Pritchett called Beckett's novels "anti-novels" because of "their pretension to evoke the whole of life, i.e. life unfixed by art" (Pritchett 1979, 197). It says much about a shared sense of what art is that a novel which aspires to express nothing of life and one that aspires to express the whole of life might be mistaken for one another, as here.

Conclusion

1. This is a favorite phrase of George Steiner, always used with grace, and always misquoted (as "this craze for explication") (e.g., Steiner 2011, 38).

2. The Swiss Stanislaus Wawrinka's left forearm reads: "Ever tried. Ever failed. No matter. Try again. Fail again. Fail better." (The lines are to be found at GC 4.472.) Tennis fans may see a particular pathos here as Wawrinka has spent the near-entirety of his quite illustrious career in the shadow of his friend and doubles partner, the James Joyce of tennis, Roger Federer (genial, multilingual, improbably versatile, essentially invincible, abundantly good-natured, etc.).

3. Translation modified. This passage is translated in Beckett's *Letters* as "only the beauty of attempt and failure." This is not quite right, because what Beckett says is not quite right. It is thus impossible to tell whether Beckett meant "the lonely beauty of attempt and failure" or "only the beauty of attempt and failure" (or both). The (excellent) translator of Beckett's French letters, George Craig, notes in this regard that "The translator must hope to stretch English to a point where it will allow a glimpse of the sheer strangeness of Beckett's French" (LSB 2.xxxi).

4. This passage (from 1949) seems to echo Blanchot's declaration in *Faux pas* (from 1943) that "The writer finds himself in the increasingly ludicrous condition of having nothing to write, nothing with which to write and constrained by the utter necessity of always writing it." See Weller 2007, 25 on this point in particular. For a more general discussion of the affinity and interactions between Beckett and Blanchot, see Clément 1994.

5. Ackerley sees Beckett's expression as a conflation of the above fragment and a separate remark reported by Diogenes Laertius (cf. Ackerley 2010a, 197).

6. An English translation of the German rendering of the Greek would then run: "The nothing exists just as much as the *Ichts*," a made-up German word for a made-up Greek one and so might be made up in English as *ning* ("The nothing exists just as much as the ning").

7. In its standard translation it is rendered as "wherein you have no power, therein neither should you will"—a formulation which Ackerley qualifies, not without reason, as "clunky," and suggests, not without reason, misses the imperative (Geulincx 2006; Ackerley 2010a, 200).

8. Letter of December 21, 1817.

9. This is an—ancient—opposition Beckett knew well from a variety of sources. It is to be found in Seneca, for instance, as well as many later literary and philosophical commentators. It is, if anything, still more familiar from the visual arts, and it should be recalled that setting Democritus good humor alongside Heraclitus's black one was a frequent motif in the Renaissance art Beckett loved (see especially Wind 1968, 48–49).

10. Wahl 1957, 131. In his translation of these remarks Peter Fiefield silently corrects Wahl's memory at several points (Fiefield 2015, 146).

11. Cf. esp. Tiedemann 1994a, 22.

12. For a general account of the two men's interaction, from their tense initial encounter to their final warmth, see Knowlson 1996 (428ff.) for a focus on Beckett, and Tiedemann 1994a for a focus on Adorno. Beckett wrote to Barbara Bray in 1967 that he did not know why Adorno liked him nor why he liked Adorno, confirming, however, that both things were the case (Van Hulle 2010, 209). Beckett's final card to Adorno reads: "I can't make it. Forgive. Bless you. Sam. Beckett" (Tiedemann 1994a, 75n13).

13. Critchley writes of the "characteristic black *gusto*" of Adorno's writing on Beckett and is almost unreserved in his praise (Critchley 2004, 184). He finds Adorno's essay on *Endgame* "the philosophically most powerful and hermeneutically most nuanced piece of writing on Beckett," as well as, on a separate occasion, that "the philosophically most nuanced discussion of Beckett is Adorno's by several kilometers" (Critchley 2004, 187; Critchley 2008, 11). Critchley, however, levels a strange charge at Adorno: Adorno's "failure to evoke Beckett's idiom" (Critchley 2004, 184). This would be a fair assessment if reproducing Beckett's idiom, rather than developing or employing the critic's own, were Adorno's goal—or should be. Critchley, for instance, has a delightful idiom, but it does not more strongly evoke Beckett's idiom than Adorno's, and so the point must lie elsewhere.

14. Deleuze will have a similar notion. "Many authors are too polite," he observed in his study of Beckett, and are "content to proclaim" such matters as "the death of the self," rather than to dramatize them (Deleuze 1992, 62).

15. Van Hulle and Weller (2014) translate it as "blinding element" (161); Shierry Weber Nicholsen translates it as "veil of delusion" (Adorno 1992, 148).

Works Cited

Abbott, H. Porter. 1994. "Beginning Again: The Post-Narrative Art of *Texts for Nothing* and *How It Is*." In Pilling 1994b, 106–123.

Ackerley, C. J. 2010a. *Demented Particulars: The Annotated "Murphy."* Edinburgh: Edinburgh University Press.

———. 2010b. *Obscure Locks, Simple Keys: The Annotated "Watt."* Edinburgh: Edinburgh University Press.

Ackerley, C. J., and S. E. Gontarski. 2004. *The Grove Companion to Samuel Beckett.* New York: Grove.

Adorno, Theodor Wiesengrund. 1973–1986. *Gesammelte Schriften.* 20 vols. Herausgegeben von Rolf Tiedemann unter Mitwirkung von Gretel Adorno, Susan Buck-Morss und Klaus Schultz. Frankfurt am Main: Suhrkamp. [Internally as Adorno GS; citations from vol. 11 are given in the translation and with the pagination of *Notes to Literature,* edited by Rolf Tiedemann, translated by Shierry Weber Nicholsen (New York: Columbia University Press, 1991), and *Negative Dialectics,* trans. E. B. Ashton (London: Routledge, 1990).]

———. 1992. *Notes to Literature.* Vol. 1. Edited by Rolf Tiedemann. Translated by Shierry Weber Nicholsen. New York: Columbia University Press.

———. 1994. "Elf Nachträge zu den *Gesammelten Schriften.*" In Tiedemann 1994a, 135–147.

Adorno, Theodor Wiesengrund, Walter Boehlich, Martin Esslin, Hans-Geert Falkenberg, and Ernst Fischer. 1994. "'Optimistisch zu denken ist kriminell': Eine Fernsehdiskussion über Samuel Beckett." In Tiedemann 1994a, 78–122.

Albright, Daniel. 2003. *Beckett and Aesthetics.* Cambridge: Cambridge University Press.

Anzieu, Didier. 1998. *Beckett.* Paris: Gallimard.

Asmus, Walter. 2012. "Rehearsal Notes for the German Premiere of *That Time* and *Footfalls.*" In *On Beckett: Essays and Criticisms,* ed. S. E. Gontarski, rev. ed. London: Anthem Press.

Atik, Anne. 2001. *How It Was: A Memoir of Samuel Beckett.* London: Faber.

Augustine. 1998. *The City of God against the Pagans.* Translated by R. W. Dyson. Cambridge: Cambridge University Press.

Avrin, Leila. 1991. *Scribes, Script, and Books: The Book Arts from Antiquity to the Renaissance.* Chicago: American Library Association.

Bachmann, Ingeborg. 1983. *Wir müssen wahre Sätze finden: Gespräche und Interviews.* Edited by Chrstine Koschel and Inge von Wiedenbaum. Munich: Piper Verlag.

Badiou, Alain. 1995. *Beckett: L'increvable désir.* Paris: Hachette.

Bair, Deirdre. 1990. *Samuel Beckett: A Biography.* Rev. ed. New York: Simon and Schuster.

Banville, John. 2006. "In Beckett's Own Words . . ." In *Samuel Beckett: A Passion for Painting,* edited by Fionnuala Croke. Dublin: National Gallery of Ireland, 91–93.

Bataille, Georges. 1988. *Œuvres complètes.* 12 vols. Paris: Gallimard.

Baudelaire, Charles. 1975–1976. *Œuvres complètes.* Edited by Claude Pichois. 2 vols. Paris: Gallimard.

———. 1993. *The Flowers of Evil.* Translated and edited by James McGowan. With an introduction by Jonathan Culler. Oxford: Oxford University Press.

Beckett, Samuel. 1951a. *Malone meurt.* Paris: Minuit.

———. 1951b. *Molloy.* Paris: Minuit.

———. 1953. *L'Innomable.* Paris: Minuit.

———. 1955. *Nouvelles et Textes pour rien.* Paris: Minuit.

———. 1957a. *Fin de partie.* Paris: Minuit.

———. 1957b. *Tous ceux qui tombent.* Paris: Minuit.

———. 1959. *La dernière bande.* Paris: Minuit.

———. 1961. *Comment c'est.* Paris: Minuit.

———. 1963. *Oh les beaux jours!* Paris: Minuit.

———. 1970a. *Le Dépeupler.* Paris: Minuit.

———. 1970b. *Mercier et Camier.* Paris: Minuit.

———. 1970c. *Premier amour.* Paris: Minuit.

———. 1980. *Compagnie.* Paris: Minuit.

———. 1981. *Mal vu mal dit.* Paris: Minuit.

———. 1982. *Catastrophe.* Paris: Minuit.

———. 1984. *Disjecta: Miscellaneous Writings and a Dramatic Fragment.* Edited by Ruby Cohn. New York: Grove.

———. 1988. *L'Image.* Paris: Minuit.

———. 1993. *Dream of Fair to Middling Women.* Edited by Eoin O'Brien and Edith Fournier. New York: Arcade.

———. 1994. *The Theatrical Notebooks of Samuel Beckett.* Vol. 1, *Waiting for Godot.* Edited by Dougald McMillan and James Knowlson. New York: Grove.

——. 1995a. *Complete Short Prose: 1929–1989.* Edited by S. E. Gontarski. New York: Grove.

——. 1995b. *Eleutheria.* Paris: Minuit.

——. 2006a. *En attendant Godot / Waiting for Godot.* Bilingual edition. New York: Grove.

——. 2006b. *"Obergeschoss Still Closed": Samuel Beckett in Berlin 1936/1937.* Ausstellung Literaturhaus Berlin. Edited by Lutz Dittrich, Carola Veit, and Ernest Wichner. Berlin: Matthes & Seitz.

——. 2011. *Samuel Beckett's German Diaries.* Edited by Mark Nixon. London: Continuum.

——. 2014. *Echo's Bones.* Edited by Mark Nixon. New York: Grove.

Beer, Ann. 1994. "Beckett's Bilingualism." In Pilling 1994b, 209–221.

Benjamin, Walter. 1966. *Briefe.* Herausgegeben und mit Anmerkungen versehen von Gershom Scholem und Theodor W. Adorno. Frankfurt am Main: Suhrkamp.

——. 1974–1989. *Gesammelte Schriften.* 7 vols. Edited by Rolf Tiedemann and Herman Schweppenhäuser. Frankfurt am Main: Suhrkamp.

——. 1996–2003. *Selected Writings.* Edited by Marcus Bullock, Howard Eiland, Michael W. Jennings, and Gary Smith. 4 vols. Cambridge, MA: Harvard University Press.

Bernold, André. 1992. *L'amitié de Beckett.* Paris: Hermann.

Blackman, Jackie. 2009. "Beckett's Theatre 'After Auschwitz.'" In *Samuel Beckett: History, Memory, Archive,* edited by Sean Kennedy and Katherine Weiss. New York: Palgrave Macmillan, 71–88.

Blanchot, Maurice. 1959. *Le livre à venir.* Paris: Gallimard.

——. 1990. "Oh tout finir." *Critique* 519–520 (August–September): 636.

Blau, Herbert. 1960. "Meanwhile, Follow the Bright Angels." *Tulane Drama Review* 5 (September): 90–91.

Blin, Roger. 1957. Extended cover blurb for *Fin de partie.* Paris: Minuit.

Bloom, Harold. 1985. "Editor's Note." In *Samuel Beckett: Modern Critical Views,* edited by Harold Bloom. New York: Chelsea House, i–ii.

Boccaccio, Giovanni. 2014. *Decameron.* Edited by A. Quondam, M. Fiorilla, and G. Alfano. Milan: Rizzoli.

Booth, Wayne. 1974. *A Rhetoric of Irony.* Chicago: University of Chicago Press.

Bowles, Patrick. 1994. "How to Fail: Notes on Talks with Samuel Beckett." *PN Review* 96 (20, no. 4, March/April): 24–38.

Boyd, Brian. 1990. *Vladimir Nabokov: The Russian Years.* Princeton, NJ: Princeton University Press.

Bringhurst, Robert. 2011. *A Story as Sharp as a Knife: The Classical Haida Mythtellers and Their World.* 2nd ed. Madeira Park, British Columbia: Douglas and McIntyre.

Bryden, Mary. 2009. "Beckett's Reception in Great Britain." In *The International Reception of Samuel Beckett,* edited by Mark Nixon and Matthew Feldman. London: Continuum.

Calder, John. 2012. *The Theology of Samuel Beckett*. London: John Calder.

Calvino, Italo. 1995. *Saggi 1945–1985*. Vol. 1. Milan: Mondadori.

Caselli, Daniela. 2005. *Beckett's Dantes: Intertextuality in the Fiction and Criticism*. Manchester, UK: Manchester University Press.

——. 2009. "Thinking of a Rhyme for 'Euganean': Beckett in Italy." In *The International Reception of Samuel Beckett,* edited by Mark Nixon and Matthew Feldman. London: Continuum, 209–233.

——. 2013. "Italian Literature." In *Samuel Beckett in Context,* edited by Anthony Uhlmann. Cambridge: Cambridge University Press, 241–254.

Cavell, Stanley. 2002. *Must We Mean What We Say? A Book of Essays*. Updated ed. Cambridge: Cambridge University Press.

Chesterton, G. K. 1965. *Charles Dickens*. New York: Schocken.

Cioran, E. M. 1976. "Quelques Rencontres." In *Samuel Beckett: Cahier de l'Herne,* edited by Tom Bishop and Raymond Federman. Paris: L'Herne, 45–54.

——. 1979. "Encounters with Beckett." Translated by Raymond Federman and Jean M. Sonnermeyer. In Graver and Federman 1979, 334–339.

Clément, Bruno. 1994. *L'œuvre sans qualités: Rhétorique de Samuel Beckett*. Preface by Michel Deguy. Paris: Editions du Seuil.

Coe, Richard. 1969. *Samuel Beckett*. New York: Grove.

Coetzee, J. M. 2006. Introduction to vol. 4 of *The Grove Centenary Edition of the Works of Samuel Beckett,* edited by Paul Auster. New York: Grove, ix–xiv.

——. 2009. "The Making of Samuel Beckett." *New York Review of Books* 56, no. 7 (April 30): 5–8.

Cohn, Ruby. 2001. *A Beckett Canon*. Ann Arbor: University of Michigan Press.

Coleridge, S. T. 1983. *Biographia Literaria or Biographical Sketches of My Literary Life and Opinions*. Edited by W. J. Bate and J. Engell. 2 vols. Princeton NJ: Princeton University Press.

Critchley, Simon. 2004. *Very Little—Almost Nothing: Death, Philosophy and Literature*. London: Routledge.

——. 2008. "Beckett, Adorno, Blanchot, Comedy, Death, and So On . . ." Interview with Tom McCarthy. December 9. http://voidmanufacturing.wordpress.com/2008/12/09/tom-mccarthy-and-simon-critchley-in-conversation-beckett-adorno-blanchot-comedy-death-and-so-on/.

Cronin, Anthony. 1997. *Samuel Beckett: The Last Modernist*. New York: Da Capo Press.

Dante Alighieri. 1973. *The Divine Comedy*. Translated and with a commentary by Charles S. Singleton. Princeton, NJ: Princeton University Press.

Danto, Arthur. 2003. *The Abuse of Beauty: Aesthetics and the Concept of Art*. Chicago: Open Court.

D'Aubarède, Gabriel. 1961. Column in *Nouvelles littéraires,* February 16, 1, 7. English translation by Christopher Waters in Graver and Federman 1979, 215–217.

Deleuze, Gilles. 1992. "L'épuisé." In *Quad et autre pièces pour la télévision*. Paris: Editions de Minuit, 57–106.

De Man, Paul. 1979. *Allegories of Reading: Figural Language in Rousseau, Nietzsche, Rilke, and Proust*. New Haven, CT: Yale University Press.

Derrida, Jacques. 1989/1992. "This Strange Institution Called Literature: An Interview with Jacques Derrida." Interview with Derek Attridge (1989) in Jacques Derrida, *Acts of Literature,* edited and translated by Derek Attridge. New York: Routledge.

Diels, Hermann and Walther Kranz, eds. 1935. *Die Fragmente der Vorsokratiker II.* Berlin: Wiedmannsche Buchhandlung.

Driver, Tom. 1961. "Beckett by the Madeleine." *Columbia University Forum* 4, no. 3 (Summer): 23.

Duthuit, Georges. 1993. *"Bram Van Velde ou Aux colonnes d'Hercule."* In *Bram Van Velde: Lithographies originales.* Paris: Maeght Editeur.

Eagleton, Terry. 1996. Preface to Pascale Casanova's *Samuel Beckett: Anatomy of a Literary Revolution.* London: Verso.

Eco, Umberto. 1994. *Le poetiche di Joyce.* Milan: Bompiani.

———. 2008. "Recitare Dante." In Roberto Benigni, *Il mio Dante.* Turin: Einaudi, 5–11.

Eliot, George. 1985. *Middlemarch.* Edited by W. J. Harvey. New York: Penguin.

Eliot, T. S. 2001. *"The Waste Land" and Other Writings.* New York: Modern Library.

Ellmann, Richard. 1982. *James Joyce.* New York: Oxford University Press.

Esslin, Martin. 1969. *The Theatre of the Absurd.* New York: Anchor.

Fiefeld, Peter. 2015. "Samuel Beckett with, in, and around Philosophy." In *The New Cambridge Companion to Samuel Beckett,* edited by Dirk Van Hulle. Cambridge: Cambridge University Press, 145–157.

Fischer-Seidel, Therese, and Marion Fries-Dieckmann, eds. 2005. *Der unbekannte Beckett: Samuel Beckett und die deutsche Kultur.* Frankfurt am Main: Suhrkamp.

Fletcher, John. 1964. *The Novels of Samuel Beckett.* London: Chatto and Windus.

Foucault, Michel. 1994. *Dits et écrits 1954–1969.* Paris: Gallimard, 789–821.

Frye, Northrop. 1960. "The Nightmare Life in Death." *Hudson Review* 13 (Autumn): 442–449.

Furlani, Andre. 2012. "Beckett after Wittgenstein: The Literature of Exhausted Justification." *PMLA* 127, no. 1 (January): 38–57.

Galchen, Rivka. 2008. *Atmospheric Disturbances.* New York: Farrar, Straus and Giroux.

Gessner, Niklaus. 1957. *Die Unzulänglichkeit der Sprache: Eine Untersuchung über Formzerfall und Beziehungslosigkeit bei Samuel Beckett.* Zurich: Juris Verlag.

Geulincx, Arnold. 2006. *Arnold Geulincx' "Ethics": With Samuel Beckett's Notes.* Translated by Martin Wilson. Edited by Han van Ruler, Anthony Uhlmann, and Martin Wilson. Leiden: Brill.

Gluck, Barbara Reich. 1979. *Beckett and Joyce: Friendship and Fiction.* Lewisburg, PA: Bucknell University Press.

Goethe, Johann Wolfgang von. 1972. *Wahlverwandtschaften.* Edited by Hans-H. Weitz. Frankfurt am Main: Insel.

Gontarski, S. E. 1977. *Beckett's Happy Days: A Manuscript Study.* Columbus: Ohio State University Libraries.

———. 1985. *The Intent of Undoing in Samuel Beckett's Dramatic Texts.* Bloomington: Indiana University Press.

——. 2010. Preface to C. J. Ackerley, *Obscure Locks, Simple Keys: The Annotated "Watt."* Edinburgh: Edinburgh University Press.

——, ed. 2012. *On Beckett: Essays and Criticisms.* Rev. ed. London: Anthem Press.

Graver, Lawrence, and Raymond Federman, eds. 1979. *Samuel Beckett: The Critical Heritage.* London: Routledge and Kegan Paul.

Greenblatt, Stephen. 2011. *Swerve: How the World Became Modern.* New York: Norton.

Gussow, Mel. 1996. *Conversations with and about Beckett.* New York: Grove.

Harmon, Maurice, ed. 1998. *No Author Better Served: The Correspondence of Samuel Beckett and Alan Schneider.* Cambridge, MA: Harvard University Press.

Harvey, Lawrence. 1970. *Samuel Beckett: Poet and Critic.* Princeton, NJ: Princeton University Press.

Hemingway, Ernest. 2006. *The Sun Also Rises.* New York: Scribner.

Hoefer, Jacqueline. 1959. *"Watt." Perspective* 11: 166–182.

Iser, Wolfgang. 1979. *Die Artistik des Mißlingens. Ersticktes Lachen im Theater Becketts.* Heidelberg: Carl Winter Universitätsverlag.

James, William. 2000. *Pragmatism and Other Writings.* New York: Penguin.

Jelinek, Elfriede, Jutta Heinrich, and Adolf-Ernst Meyer. 1995. *Sturm und Zwang: Schreiben als Geschlechterkampf.* Hamburg: Klei.

Joyce, James. 1966. *Finnegans Wake.* New York: Viking.

——. 1968. *A Portrait of the Artist as a Young Man.* Edited by Richard Ellmann. London: Jonathan Cape.

——. 1975. *Selected Letters of James Joyce.* Edited by Richard Ellmann. London: Faber and Faber.

——. 1986. *Ulysses.* New York: Vintage.

Kawin, Bruce. 1984. "On Not Having the Last Word: Beckett, Wittgenstein and the Limits of Language." In *Ineffability: Naming the Unnamable from Dante to Beckett, ed.* Peter Hawkins and Anne Schotter. New York: AMS Press, 189–202.

Keats, John. 1977. *The Complete Poems.* 2nd ed. Edited by John Barnard. New York: Penguin.

Kennedy, Sighle. 1971. *Murphy's Bed: A Study of Real Sources and Surreal Associations in Samuel Beckett's First Novel.* Lewisburg, PA: Bucknell University Press.

Kenner, Hugh. 1961. *Samuel Beckett: A Critical Study.* New York: Grove.

——. 1971. *The Pound Era.* Berkeley: University of California Press.

——. 1973. *A Reader's Guide to Samuel Beckett.* New York: Farrar, Straus and Giroux.

——. 1979. *"How It Is."* In Graver and Federman 1979, 236–251.

Knowlson, James. 1996. *Damned to Fame: The Life of Samuel Beckett.* London: Bloomsbury.

——. 2006. "Beckett's First Encounters with Modern German (and Irish) Art." In *Samuel Beckett: A Passion for Painting,* edited by Fionnuala Croke. Dublin: National Gallery of Ireland, 60–75.

Kraus, Karl. 1965. *Werke.* Vol. 3: *Beim wort genommen.* Edited by Heinrich Fischer. Munich: Kösel.

Lamartine, Alphonse de. 1963. *Œuvres poétiques complètes*. Edited by Marius-François Guyard. Paris: Gallimard.

Leavis, F. R. 1933. "Joyce and 'The Revolution of the Word.'" *Scrutiny*, September: 193–201.

Leventhal, A. J. 1965. "The Beckettian Hero." In Esslin 1969, 37–51.

Lukács, György. 1979. *The Meaning of Contemporary Realism*. Translated by John and Necke Mander. London: Merlin.

Mercier, Vivian. 1977. *Beckett / Beckett*. New York: Oxford University Press.

Murphy, Peter John. 2009. *Beckett's Dedalus: Dialogical Engagements with Joyce in Beckett's Fiction*. Toronto: University of Toronto Press.

Nabokov, Vladimir. 1981. *Lectures on Literature*. New York: HBJ, 1981.

———. 1990. *Strong Opinions*. New York: Vintage, 1990.

Nehamas, Alexander. 2007. *Only a Promise of Happiness: The Place of Beauty in a World of Art*. Princeton, NJ: Princeton University Press.

Nietzsche, Friedrich. 1999. *Kritische Studienausgabe*. Herausgegeben von Giorgio Colli und Mazzino Montinari. Berlin: Walter de Gruyter Verlag.

Nixon, Mark. 2011. *Samuel Beckett's German Diaries, 1936–1937*. London: Continuum.

Nussbaum, Martha. 1990. *Love's Knowledge: Essays on Philosophy and Literature*. Oxford: Oxford University Press.

Oppenheim, Lois. 2000. *The Painted Word: Samuel Beckett's Dialogue with Art*. Ann Arbor: University of Michigan Press.

Perloff, Marjorie. 1996. *Wittgenstein's Ladder: Poetic Language and the Strangeness of the Ordinary*. Chicago: University of Chicago Press.

Pilling, John. 1994a. "Beckett's English Fiction." In Pilling 1994b, 17–42.

———, ed. 1994b. *The Cambridge Companion to Beckett*. Cambridge: Cambridge University Press.

———. 1997. *Beckett before Godot*. Cambridge: Cambridge University Press.

Pound, Ezra. 1954. *Literary Essays of Ezra Pound*. Edited with an introduction by T. S. Eliot. London: Faber and Faber.

Pritchett, V. S. 1979. "The Trilogy." In Graver and Federman 1979, 194–198.

Proust, Marcel. 1971. *Contre Sainte-Beuve*. Bibliothèque de la Pléiade. Paris: Gallimard.

Queneau, Raymond. 1950. *Bâtons, chiffres et lettres*. Paris: Gallimard.

Ramachandran, V. S., and Sandra Blakeslee. 1998. *Phantoms in the Brain: Probing Mysteries of the Human Mind*. Foreword by Oliver Sacks. New York: William Morrow.

Ricks, Christopher. 1993. *Beckett's Dying Words*. Oxford: Clarendon Press.

Rimbaud, Arthur. 1972. *Œuvres complètes*. Édition établie, présentée et annotée par Antoine Adam. Paris: Gallimard.

Sacchetti, Franco. 1979. *Il Trecentonovelle*. Edizione critica a cura di E. Faccioli. Turin: Einaudi.

Salisbury, Laura. 2008. "'What Is the Word': Beckett's Aphasic Modernism." *Beckett Studies Journal* 17: 78–126.

Schneider, Alan. 1986. "Working with Beckett." In *On Beckett: Essays and Criticism,* edited and with an introduction by S. E. Gontarski. New York: Grove, 236–254.

Schopenhauer, Arthur. 1986. *Sämtliche Werke.* 5 vols. Textkritisch bearbeitet und herausgegeben von Wolfgang Frhr. Von Löhneysen. Frankfurt am Main: Suhrkamp.

Seward, William. 1797. *Supplement to the Anecdotes of Some Distinguished Persons.* London: Cadell and Davies.

Shenker, Israel. 1956/1979. "Interview with Samuel Beckett." *New York Times,* May 5, 3. In Graver and Federman 1979, 146–149.

Smith, Frederik. 2002. *Beckett's Eighteenth Century.* New York: Palgrave.

Stein, Gertrude. 2008. *Selections.* Edited by Joan Retallack. Berkeley: University of California Press.

Steiner, George. 2009. *George Steiner at the New Yorker.* Edited and with an introduction by Robert Boyers. New York: New Directions.

———. 2011. *The Poetry of Thought: From Hellenism to Celan.* New York: New Directions.

Stevens, Wallace. 1997. *Collected Poetry and Prose.* New York: Library of America.

Stoppard, Tom. 1978. *If You're Glad I'll Be Frank.* New York: Samuel French.

Szafraniec, Asja. 2007. *Beckett, Derrida, and the Event of Language.* Stanford, CA: Stanford University Press.

Thirlwell, Adam. 2008. *The Delighted States.* New York: Farrar, Straus and Giroux.

Tiedemann, Rolf. 1994a. *Frankfurter Adorno Blätter III.* Herausgegeben vom Theodor W. Adorno Archiv. Munich: Edition text+kritik.

———. 1994b. "'*Gegen den Trug der Frage nach dem Sinn': Eine Dokumentation zu Adornos Beckett-Lektüre.*" In Tiedemann 1994a, 18–77. [Partial translation in "Notes on Beckett," translated by Dirk Van Hulle and Shane Weller. *Journal of Beckett Studies* 19, no. 2 (2010): 157–178.]

Tóibín, Colm. 2006. Introduction to vol. 1 of *The Grove Centenary Edition of the Works of Samuel Beckett.* Edited by Paul Auster. New York: Grove, ix–xvi.

Tophoven, Erika. 2005. *Becketts Berlin.* Berlin: Nicolai Verlag.

Updike, John. 1979. "*How It Is.*" In Graver and Federman 1979, 254–258.

Van Hulle, Dirk. 2009. Review of *The Metaphysical Vision,* by Ulrich Pothast. *Journal of Beckett Studies* 17: 225–229.

———. 2010. "Adorno's Notes on *Endgame.*" *Journal of Beckett Studies* 19, no. 2: 196–217.

Van Hulle, Dirk, and Shane Weller, eds. 2014. *The Making of Samuel Beckett's "L'Innommable" / "The Unnamable."* Beckett Digital Manuscript Project, vol. 2. London: Bloomsbury.

Vasari, Giorgio. 1906. *Le vite de' più eccellenti pittori scultori ed architettori.* Edited by Gaetano Milanesi. Firenze: Sansoni.

Veit, Carola. 2006. "'Lovely Crucifixion': Beckett in den Berliner Museen 1936/1937." In Beckett 2006b, 26–82.

Völker, Klaus, ed. 1986. *Beckett in Berlin. Zum 80. Geburtstag.* Berlin: Edition Hentrich.

Wahl, Jean. 1957. "Cloture du colloque phenomenologique." In *Husserl. Cahiers de Royaumont*. Paris: Editions de Minuit, 428–432.

Warburg, Aby. 2010. *Werke*. Frankfurt am Main: Suhrkamp.

Weller, Shane. 2005. *A Taste for the Negative: Beckett and Nihilism*. London: Legenda.

———. 2007. "Beckett/Blanchot: Debts, Legacies, Affinities." In *Beckett's Literary Legacies*, edited by Matthew Feldman and Mark Nixon. Newcastle, UK: Cambridge Scholars, 22–39.

Wind, Edgar. 1968. *Pagan Mysteries of the Renaissance*. Rev. and enl. ed. New York: Norton.

Wittgenstein, Ludwig. 2009. *Philosophische Untersuchungen / Philosophical Investigations*. Bilingual edition. Translated by G. E. M. Anscombe, P. M. S. Hacker, and Joachim Schulte. Rev. 4th ed. by P. M. S. Hacker and Joachim Schulte. Malden, MA: Wiley-Blackwell.

Wood, Michael. 1999. *Children of Silence: On Contemporary Fiction*. New York: Columbia University Press.

———. 2010. "Vestiges of Ireland in Beckett's Late Fiction." In *Beckett and Ireland*, edited by Seàn Kennedy. Cambridge: Cambridge University Press, 171–178.

Zeifman, Hersh. 2008. "Staging Sam: Beckett as Dramatic Character." In *Beckett at 100: Revolving It All*, edited by Linda Ben-Zvi and Angela Moorjani. Oxford: Oxford University Press, 311–318.

Acknowledgments

I thank my students and colleagues in the departments of English and Comparative Literature at Harvard University and at the Claremont Colleges.

This book is deeply indebted to many critics, in many domains, but none more than the late Daniel Albright.

I thank The American Academy in Berlin, its former director, Gary Smith, his kind staff, and my fellow fellows.

I thank my editor, John Kulka, of Harvard University Press, without whom this project would not have gone far, for which he bears, of course, no blame. I thank John Donohue and Barbara Goodhouse for their copyediting, and all those at the Press who made this book possible.

I thank Chris Ackerley and Michael Wood for their readings of this book (in a still more imperfect form) and for their many insights.

I thank Katharina de la Durantaye, Jonathan Culler, Gordon Teskey, Nicole Carney, Jason Shure, Jonathan Laurence, Michael Vazquez, Doug Lavin, Fabio Benincasa, Tif Sigfrids, and August von Hardenberg for essential assistance.

Index